Commemorative Landscape Painting in China

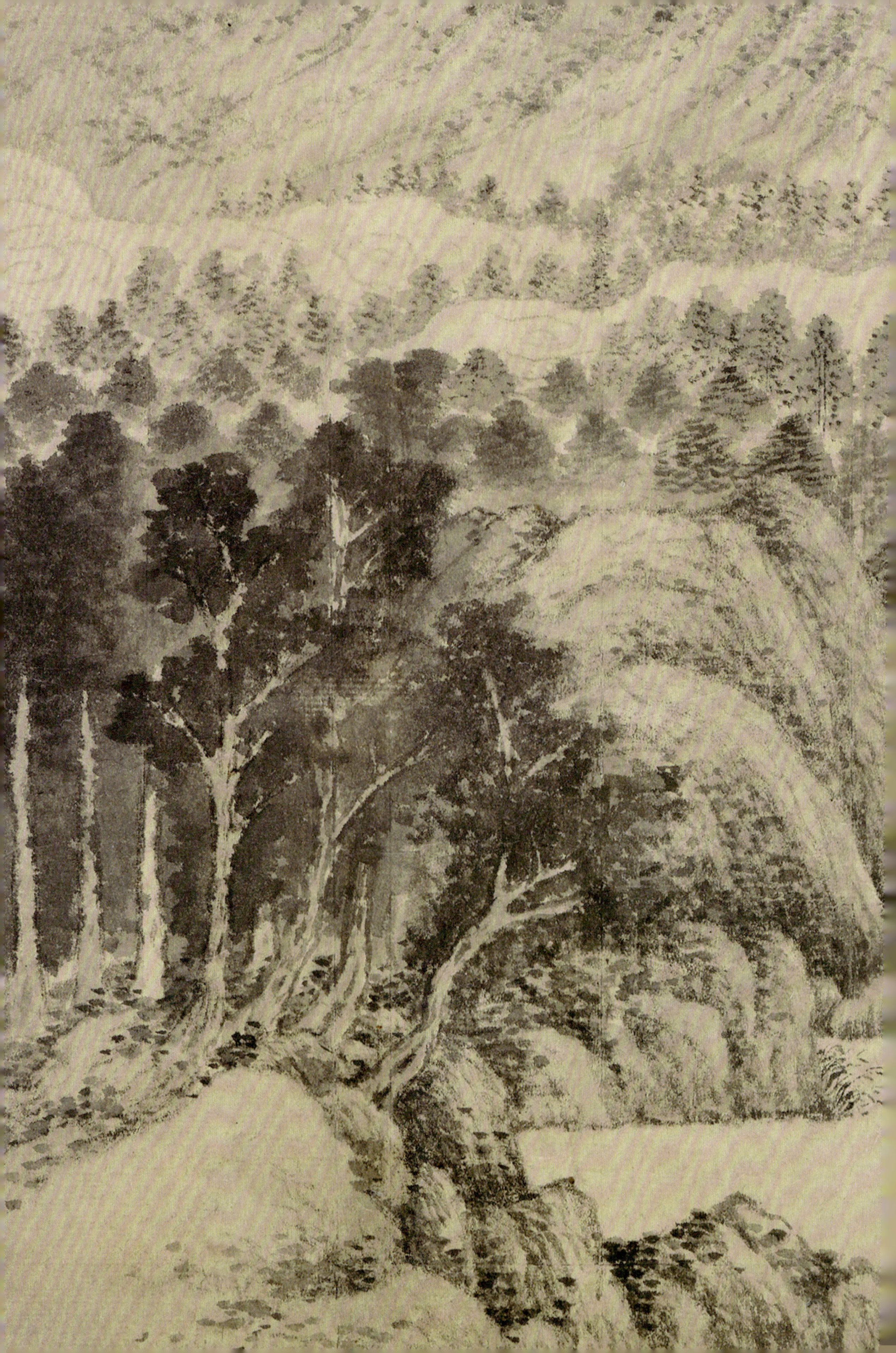

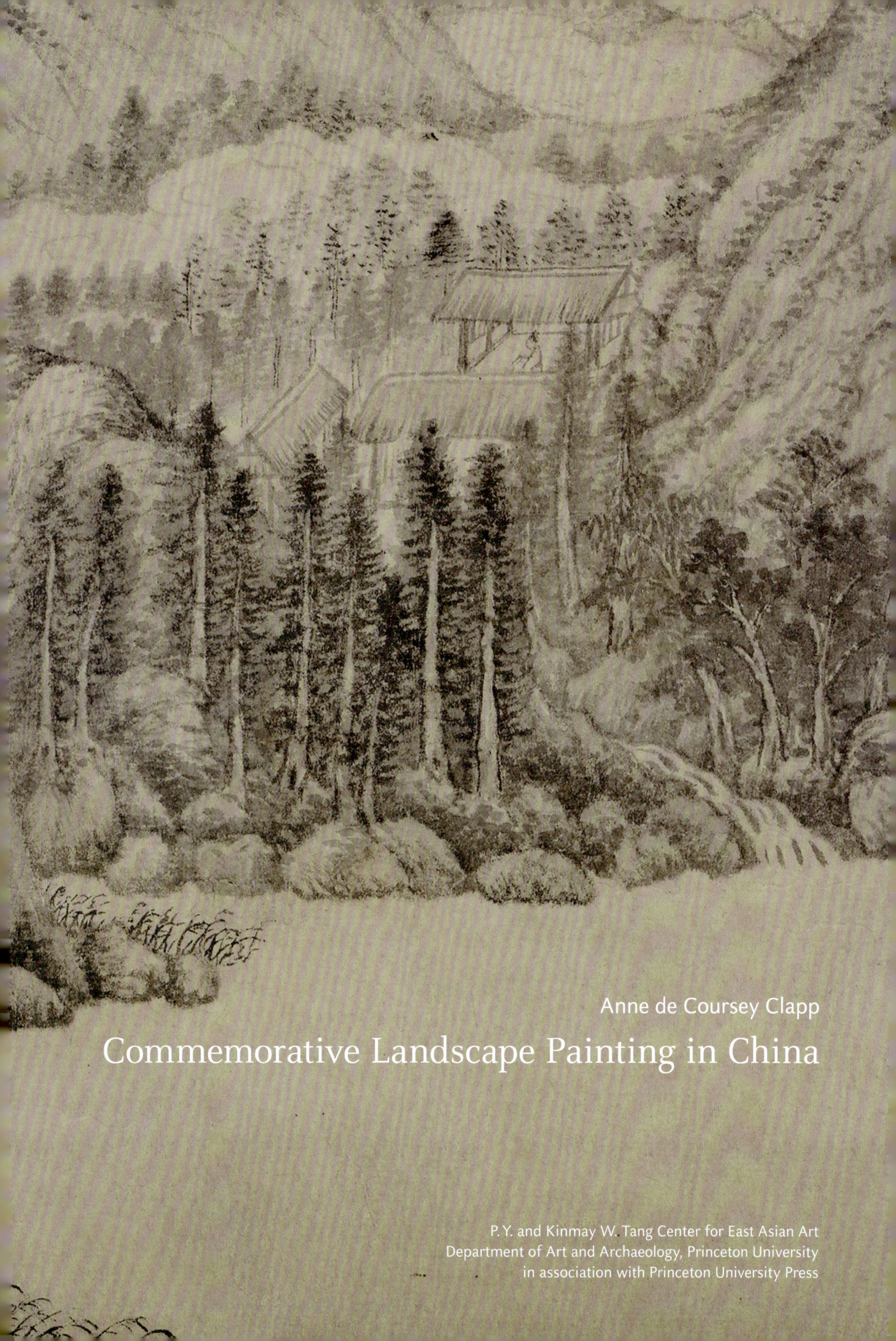

Anne de Coursey Clapp

Commemorative Landscape Painting in China

P. Y. and Kinmay W. Tang Center for East Asian Art
Department of Art and Archaeology, Princeton University
in association with Princeton University Press

Titles in the Tang Center Lecture Series are listed at the end of this volume.

Published by the
P. Y. and Kinmay W. Tang Center
for East Asian Art
Department of Art and Archaeology
Princeton University
Princeton, New Jersey 08544-1018
princeton.edu/tang
in association with
Princeton University Press

Distributed by
Princeton University Press
41 William Street
Princeton, New Jersey 08540-5237
press.princeton.edu

Library of Congress Control Number:
2011940116

ISBN: 978-0-691-15476-3

British Library Cataloging-in-Publication Data is available

Cover illustration: Lu Zhi (1496–1576). *The Jade Field* (*Yutian*), 1549. Detail of fig. 42

Frontispiece: Wang Meng (ca. 1308–1385). *Small Retreat of Master Cloudy Woods* (*Yunlin xiaoyin tu*). Detail of fig. 37

Photograph sources, in addition to those listed in captions: fig. 8: Reproduced by permission of the President and Fellows of Harvard College, photo: Antonio Quattrone; figs. 9, 10, 13: © The Metropolitan Museum of Art / Art Resource, NY; figs. 30–32: © The Art Institute of Chicago; figs. 35, 40: photo: John Lamberton; figs. 36, 37, 46, 47: photo: Bruce M. White

Managing Editor
Dora C. Y. Ching

Copy Editors
Naomi Noble Richard
Christopher Moss

Proofreader
Richard Slovak

Indexer
Susan Stone

Design and production
Binocular, New York

Separations and printing
Nissha Printing, Co., Ltd., Kyoto

This book was typeset in Celeste and Celeste Sans by Binocular, and printed on 127.9 gsm NPI Matt paper.

10 9 8 7 6 5 4 3 2 1

PRINTED IN JAPAN

Contents

Foreword

The Tang Center lecture series at Princeton was inaugurated in 2004 with the aim of inviting scholars in the field of East Asian art history to deal extensively with a well-defined problem, to treat a public audience to the benefit of their deep, rigorous thinking and clearly manifest methodology, and eventually to expand the listening audience to the readership of a fully developed, thoroughly illustrated publication.

In spring 2007, Anne de Coursey Clapp presented the second in this series of lectures. The author of two scholarly standards in the Chinese art field, on the Ming period painters Wen Zhengming and Tang Yin, Professor Clapp took this opportunity to develop and expand upon a phenomenon she had previously set forth in two chapters of her book *The Painting of T'ang Yin*—a practice she refers to as "commemorative painting." The commemorative painting celebrates an individual. Generated under the guidance of a patron and produced through the collaboration of calligraphers and painters, the commemorative painting was both a disguised portrait (typically a landscape or a figure in a landscape) and a literary explication (in prefaces and colophons) that eulogized their subject, who became the recipient of the completed scroll. Occasionally, in a subgroup of this genre, the painting devised a visual pun on the studio name (the *hao* or *biehao*) of the recipient. In later times, without an alert reading of the attached texts, the meaning of these images could easily be lost. In her lectures and in this volume, Professor Clapp expands her earlier introduction to this subject and traces its origins back to the Song and Yuan dynasties.

It is perhaps no accident that the author of this volume about such careful and clever settings earned a master's degree in stage design at the Yale School of Drama before completing her PhD in Chinese art at Harvard University. Professor Clapp spent her entire teaching career at Wellesley College, where she was a popular and much honored professor and is now professor emerita.

The Tang Center is honored to bring forth this book, and there are many to thank for making its publication possible. Our special thanks go to Naomi N. Richard and Christopher Moss for editing the manuscript, Richard Slovak for his impeccable proofreading, and Susan Stone for indexing the book. Princeton graduate students in East Asian art and archaeology have often participated in Tang Center projects, and this one was no exception. Zoe S. Kwok undertook the task of obtaining photographs and permissions, Jun Hu performed valuable research assistance, and Kim Sum Li typed the characters of the numerous Chinese texts.

We wish to express our deep appreciation to Joseph Cho and Stefanie Lew of Binocular Design. Through their inventiveness and creativity, they have made a design that not only unifies all of the publications in the Tang Center Lecture Series but also preserves the individual character of each book. We thank them also for their untiring attention to detail throughout the entire production process.

Finally, our gratitude goes to the James P. Geiss Foundation, a private, nonprofit operating foundation that sponsors research on China's Ming dynasty (1368–1644), for a grant that subsidized in part the lavish color illustrations in this volume.

Jerome Silbergeld
Dora C. Y. Ching

Preface and Acknowledgments

I first encountered commemorative landscape paintings as a discrete and distinctive genre of Chinese painting in a study of the Ming master Tang Yin. A majority of his oeuvre consists of works made to honor a particular person whose character, history, and ambitions shaped the theme and style of the painting made for him. Further study revealed that the genre was already widespread in Ming dynasty Suzhou and that it was a fully developed social institution with its own rules of usage. I searched for its origins in the Yuan dynasty and found again that it was already mature and centered in Suzhou, but the gist of it was simpler and the favored theme was the house, studio, or estate of the owner. Traces of its origins emerged only in the Song dynasty, when six surviving examples of memorial landscapes appeared, all evincing only a few varied traits of the full-fledged form. But these few examples, differing markedly from one another, gave witness to a desire among the Song literati for a pictorial monument, other than the formal portrait, devoted to the private person and within the gift of their caste.

This book examines the early history of the genre, from the eleventh to the sixteenth century. The works that illustrate it were chosen to reveal its range of subject matter, the occasions on which it was requested or awarded, the ideals most frequently celebrated by the scholar class, and the styles that recipient and artist, separately or together, found most apt to their purpose.

I am obliged to many people who have helped to realize this book, notably the Tang Center for East Asian Art of Princeton University, which supported first the lectures on which the book is based and later its publication. In this undertaking Professor Jerome Silbergeld, director of the Tang Center, and Dora Ching, the associate director, have provided direction and assistance. Several colleagues have contributed advice and help in locating sources and photographs: Liu Heping, my successor in the Art Department at Wellesley College, corrected and refined several translations;

Julia Murray of the University of Wisconsin first realized that *Welcoming the Imperial Carriage* is an early instance of the family memorial. Joseph Chang's astute observations led to the identification of *Yuan An Sleeping during the Great Snow* as a commemorative work. To Celia Reilly and Wu Di, the distinguished calligrapher, I am beholden for arranging a rewarding visit to the Wuxi City Museum. Richard Barnhart read the manuscript and offered many useful suggestions that persuaded me to expand my first plan and strengthened the argument as a whole. I offer him my warmest thanks.

I also wish to acknowledge scholars and graduate students who have assisted me in translating the prefaces, records, and poems, that are an essential part of this study. Professor Andrew Plaks of Princeton University helped in solving the Daoist conundrum presented by Shiming's preface on the practice of tea. Jeff Moser and Alan Yeung, then doctoral candidates at Harvard University, examined and disciplined the translations. Phillip Bloom generously gave me new information from his recent study of Wuxing history in the late Yuan.

My debt to the staffs of Harvard-Yenching Library and of the Fine Arts Library at Harvard began forty years ago and continues unabated. I offer them again my gratitude. Our editor, Naomi Noble Richard, applied candid criticism and much patience to the manuscript, greatly improving it. Its remaining flaws are my doing. Last, I am obliged to my daughter, Katie Clapp, for repeatedly quelling my upstart computer.

Anne de Coursey Clapp
Cambridge, Mass.
May 2010

List of Illustrations

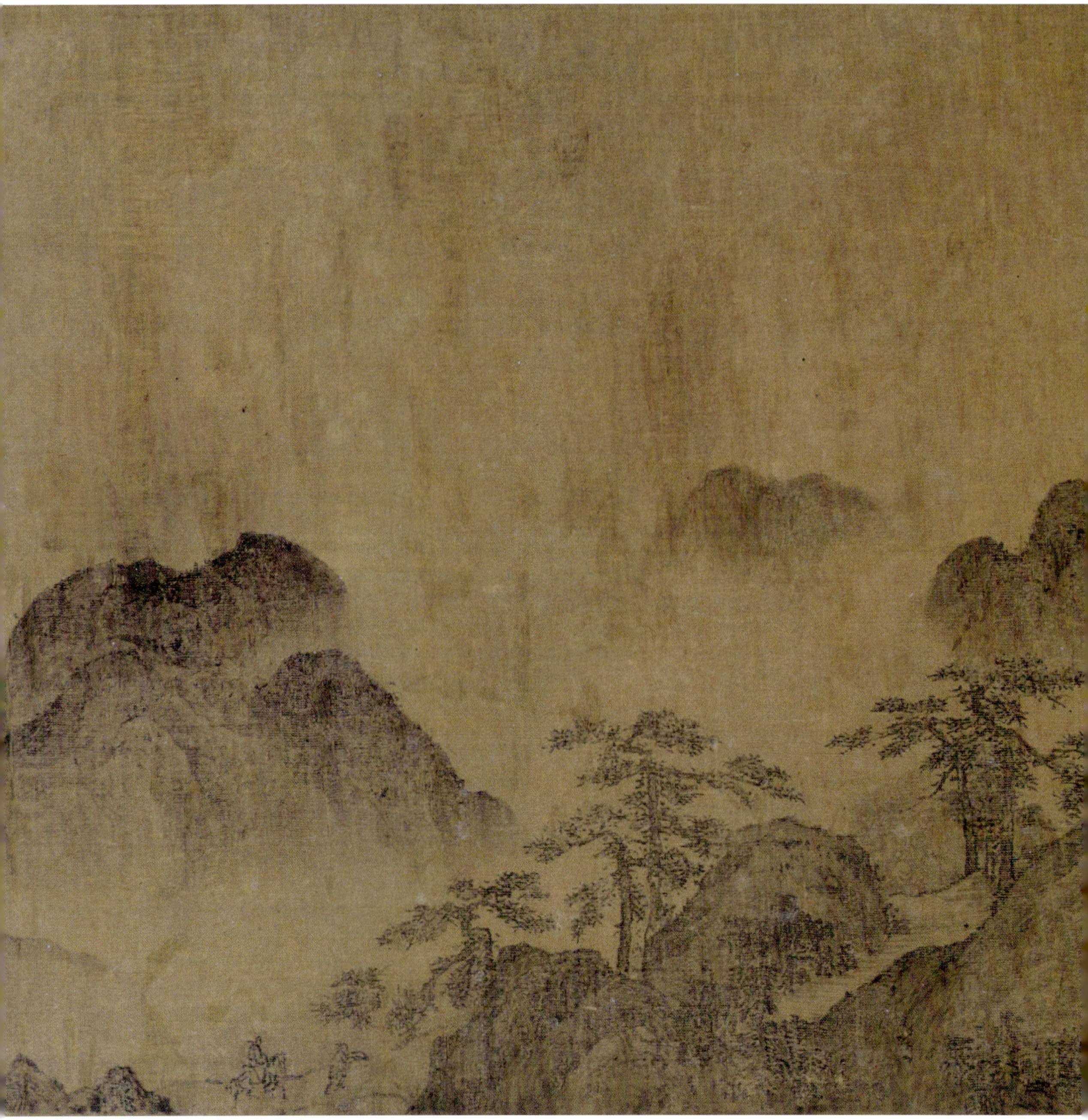

1 Hu Shunchen (active early 12th century). *Farewell to He Xuanming, Envoy to Qin* (*Song He Xuanming shi Qin tu*), 1122. Detail of figure 5

Chapter One
Early Commemorative Landscape in the Song Dynasty

This study concerns a genre of Chinese painting that takes landscape as its apparent subject but dedicates its discourse on landscape to the commemoration of an historical person. These paintings had a social function comparable to the portrait in the West because their purpose was to distinguish a named individual and grant him attention and honor among his fellows. Sometimes such paintings search out striking qualities and unusual achievements thought to reflect credit on the subject, while others may celebrate a specific rite of passage in his career. Like Western portraiture, they reveal the man adapting himself to the expectations of his society, within which he seeks to present himself in the most acceptable and prestigious light while at the same time asking to be recognized as unique in his talents and accomplishments—unmistakably himself.

In the early phase of this memorial art in the Song dynasty (960–1279), the claim to individuality and fame is made chiefly in the colophons attached to the scroll, which approximately follow the pattern of contemporary honorific writing. For the most part, the style of painting adheres to the idealized naturalism practiced at the Song courts. In this chapter, I try to uncover the roots of this genre and to identify the origin of ideas which came to full fruition only later, in the Yuan (1271–1368) and Ming (1368–1644) dynasties.

These paintings constitute an idiosyncratic genre peculiar to China and to the literati who invented it. Especially striking is the admittance of the written word almost to parity with the visual image. The word has gained so much weight that the real function of the picture often cannot be recognized without taking it into account. This does not mean that the literary quality of the colophons is equal to the artistic level of some of the paintings, but rather that the content of the colophons is essential to an understanding of the real function of the images. Not all commemorative paintings are freighted with inscriptions, but the typical example is, and the literary burden continued to grow with the passage of time, as

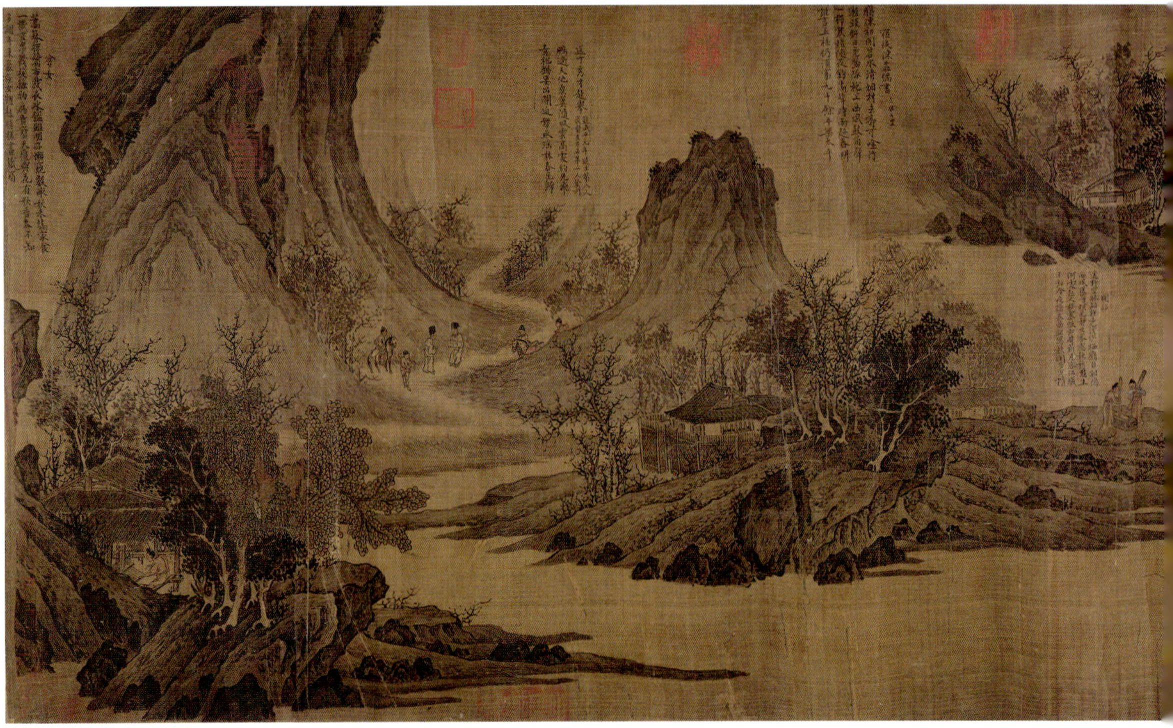

honorific poems, essays, and prefaces accumulated in explanation of the subject, and colophons were added, even centuries later, enlarging on the exegesis. They tell us who the subject is or was, extol his attainments, and eulogize his character. The entire scroll—painting and colophons together—is dedicated to the subject and recipient, but the contemporary colophons consist almost exclusively of biographical material already known to him. Thus the scroll was clearly directed to a larger audience—one that did not know him, certainly not as he would like to be known. As a composite whole, the scroll is like a portrait, personal but not private. It expects an audience, and this audience was composed of the subject's social peers, literati like himself, who knew how to read it and how the claims made for his distinction were to be valued.

It is apparent from surviving paintings that in the Song dynasty there were as yet few precedents for either the style or the iconography of this pictorial genre, which at this nascent moment in its history seems extraordinarily vague, inconsistent, and changeful, as if in the process of invention. Indeed, I cannot claim that the Song examples deserve recognition as an independent genre: some of them did not start life as unmistakable memorial works but were transformed to fit that new purpose by the addition of inscriptions that have the effect of altering their function.

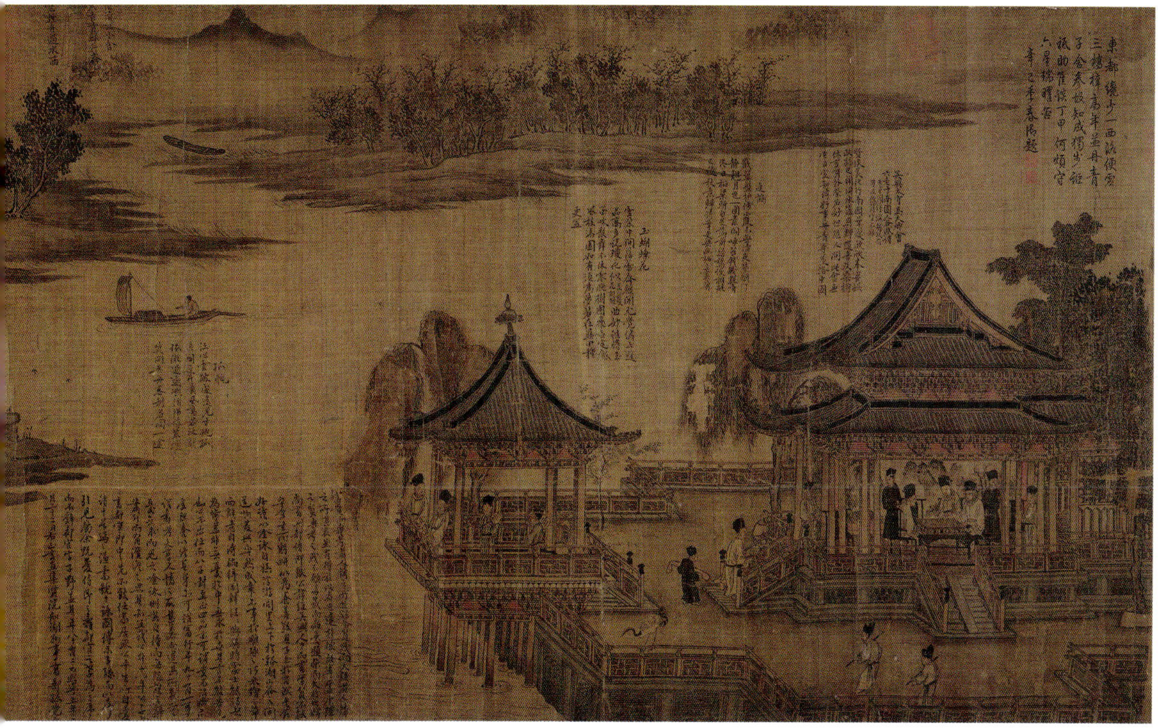

The painters sometimes follow contemporary styles or revive old styles that seem to better fit their purpose, sometimes set up new aims, each working alone toward the creation of an unprecedented kind of memorial art. The relationship between figures and setting usually follows the Song norm, in which the figure's diminished scale expresses man's deference to nature. In only one handscroll among six, *Fisherman's Lodge at Mount Xisai,* is the landscape itself actually interpreted to reflect the character and hopes of the recipient, anticipating the direction honorific landscape will take in the Yuan dynasty (see fig. 9). The temper of the painting is usually serene and contemplative, in keeping with the admired ideal of the Confucian gentleman and his dedication to scholarly pursuits. The subject is always cast in this role, whether it fits him or not, and this mood becomes typical of the genre from the Song dynasty into the Ming.

The memorial paintings of the Yuan and Ming dynasties are more easily recognizable: they are more consistent in iconography, expression, and psychological function, and they employ a limited range of styles. The genre is now recognized as such and has developed standards of its own. The same cannot be said of the small number of Song landscapes that can be identified as memorials. The correspondence between the image and its inscriptions and colophons is relatively loose,

2 Zhang Xian (990–1078). *Illustrations to Ten Poems* (*Shi yong tu*), ca. 1064. Handscroll; ink and red color on silk, 52 × 178.7 cm. Palace Museum, Beijing. See also figures 3 and 12

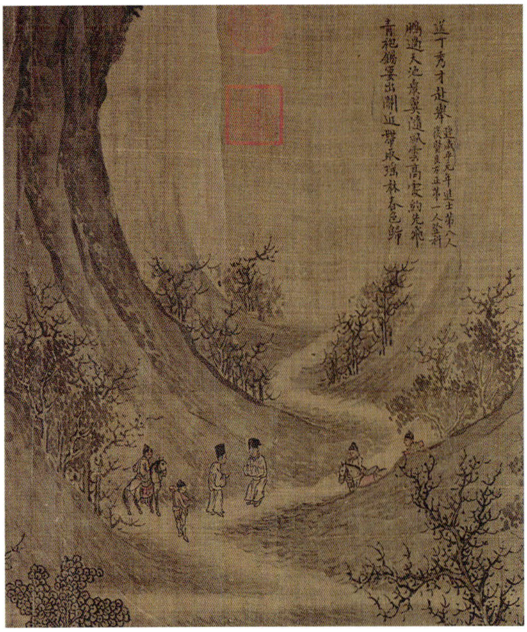

Departure of the *xiucai* Ding

although this slight dissonance does not make the paintings less interesting. In many, the inscriptions are far more direct and clear than the image in explaining the purpose of the scroll. At first glance, some scrolls could most plausibly be taken for history paintings, others for impersonal landscapes depicted qua landscapes. In these works I hoped that I had come across a genre in an early, simplistic stage of formation, when writing an inscription on a painting was still the chief and most explicit means of establishing its social function.

Already in the Song dynasty there were various categories of the commemorative landscape, one of the oldest of which showed the honorand about to depart on a journey. This occasion called for a ceremony marked by honorific poems and farewell feasting, often held at the first stage on the traveler's road. Stephen Owen, in introducing the literary type of the farewell poem in his *Anthology of Chinese Literature*, remarks that this celebration originated with a religious ritual of sacrifice to the god of the road.[1] In later centuries, the ritual character dissipated, and the literary aspect expanded into an act of commemoration in which poems were collected, introduced by a preface written by one of the guests, and formally presented to the traveler. The most famous instance of such an occasion, and the poem composed for it, was Wang Wei's (701–761; alt. 699–759) "Song of the Yang Pass,"[2] later set to music and sung by the guests as a last salute to the departing traveler.

The earliest known painted image of a departure scene is one of the vignette pictures in the *Illustrations to Ten Poems* (*Shi yong tu*), executed shortly after 1064, the detail titled "Departure of the *xiucai* Ding" (fig. 3). This unusual but important handscroll (fig. 2) is explained and its contribution to memorial painting discussed at the length it deserves later in this chapter. Above the scene of two gentlemen bowing to each other, a poem identifies one of them as the *xiucai* Ding leaving his home in Wuxing to sit for the civil service examination.

"Departure," *Ten Poems*

The phoenix has soared from Tianchi and the flock
    flies after him.
In the highest reaches of heaven wind and clouds
    join him in flight.[3]
Honored with the blue gown and the banquet,
    you will return from the pass
Bearing homeward the spring colors gathered
    at Qionglin.[4]

3 Zhang Xian (990–1078). *Illustrations to Ten Poems* (*Shi yong tu*), ca. 1064. Detail of figure 2

鵬過天池眾翼隨，風雲高處約先飛。
青袍錫宴出關近，帶取瑤林春色歸。

The figures of speech are all compliments to the candidate: "phoenix" is a figure for a scholar who wins early success; the "blue gown" was the official dress of the scholar; and Qionglin an imperial garden in Kaifeng where successful examination candidates were entertained. All assume that the candidate will conquer the examination with ease and will soon be launched on a promising career.

The painter is not concerned with the personalities present on the occasion of departure and so does not distinguish which figure is Ding nor tell us how many guests attended. The image of departure is summarized by two figures, representing a traveler leaving and a guest remaining behind, bowing formally to each other while their servants attend to the horses. The only other information is offered by two precipitous cliffs that place the departure at the entrance to a mountain pass hidden in mist. This pass must be significant, for it, too, is mentioned in the poem. Master Ding lived in Wuxing, whose local topography is notably flat and undramatic, so the setting may have been a conventional motif descended from Wang Wei's "Song of the Yang Pass," the poetic precursor of the departure scene as a literary type. That parting took place outside Wei City, not at the actual Yang Pass (many miles away in Central Asia), but the idea of bidding farewell to a friend remained connected with the entrance to a mountain pass. Thus, in the mid-eleventh century, an old and highly conventionalized theme like departure is reduced to the simplest unmistakable heraldic formula. We still occasionally find vestiges of its origin in literature clinging to the subgenre.

Master Ding's departure on land has a close cousin in a painting of departure by sea, published by Miyeko Murase and datable to/or before 1196.[5] *A Priest from the Eastern Sea Returning Home* (*Song hai dong shangren guiguo tu*) (fig. 4) is also a farewell scene and has the same distinguishing conventions as the *Ten Poems* vignette, except

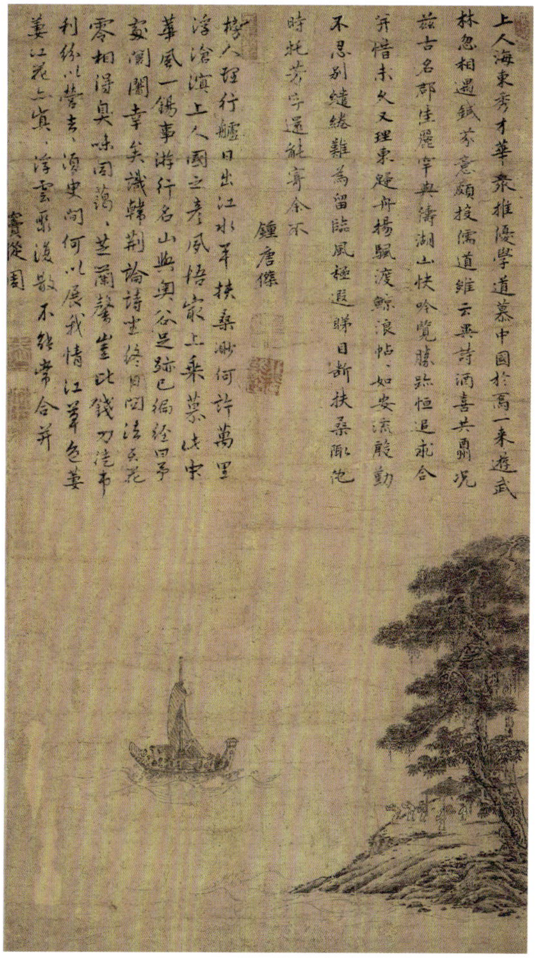

4 Anonymous. *A Priest from the Eastern Sea Returning Home* (*Song hai dong shangren guiguo tu*), 1196 or before. Hanging scroll; ink on silk, 63.6 × 36.3 cm. Tokiwayama Bunko Foundation, Tokyo

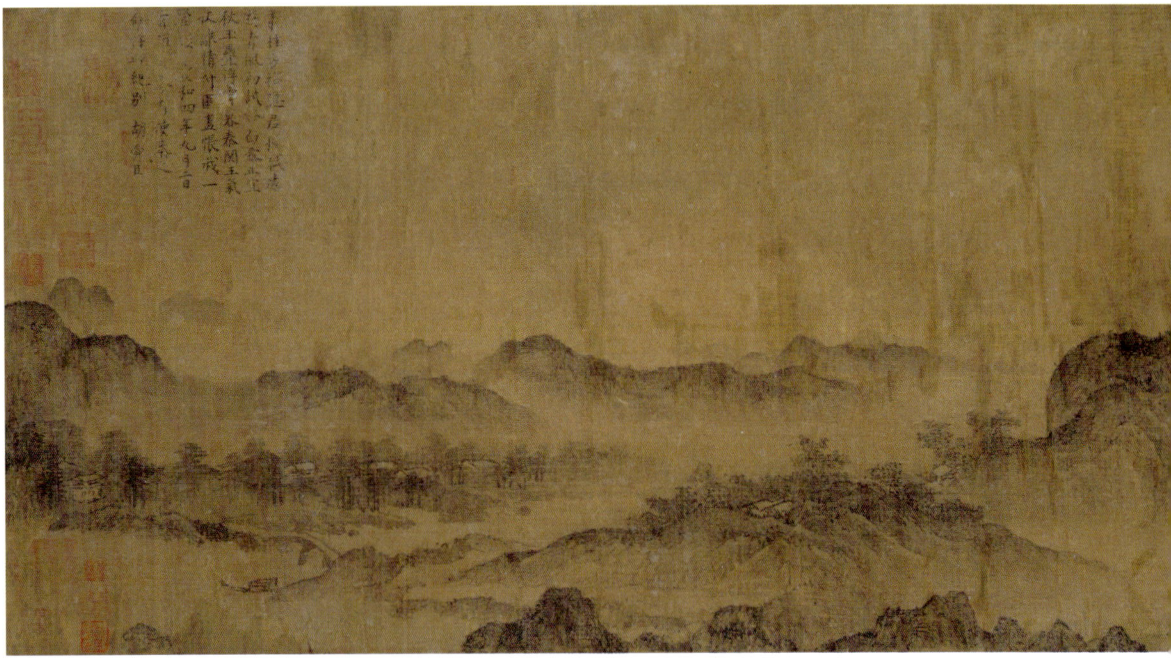

that the journey takes place by sea instead of by land and the mountain pass is replaced by a boat casting off from the shore. The painting was commissioned by two Chinese scholars to honor a Japanese Buddhist monk on his return to Japan. The monk, whom they address as *xiucai,* meaning he was a student who had achieved his first degree, had been studying the Confucian doctrine in China for some years, and, on his departure, his Chinese friends presented him with both written and painted testimonials of their esteem. Their colophons appear above the picture, preempting most of the space and implying that the literary component was as important as the picture. This probably increased its value to the monk, because the tone of the colophons is warmly personal, recalling the excursions the new friends made to famous sites in Wuxing, their drinking parties, and their discussions of literature. One of the writers was a distinguished student of Neo-Confucianism whose death in 1196 gives a terminus ante quem for the painting. Miyeko Murase concludes that the monk was Eisai (1141–1215), who was returning to Japan to introduce the teachings of the Rinzai Zen school.[6] Thus the scroll emerged from the educated circles of the Chinese and Japanese elites, where it played a quasi-ceremonial part in their social and cultural relations. The unknown artisan painter illustrated the departure directly and ingenuously, showing land, sea, and boat, but nothing of the actual port of Ningbo, where the sailing probably took place. As in the departure in the *Ten Poems,* the narrative purpose is foremost, the style frankly literal, the visible forms sharply

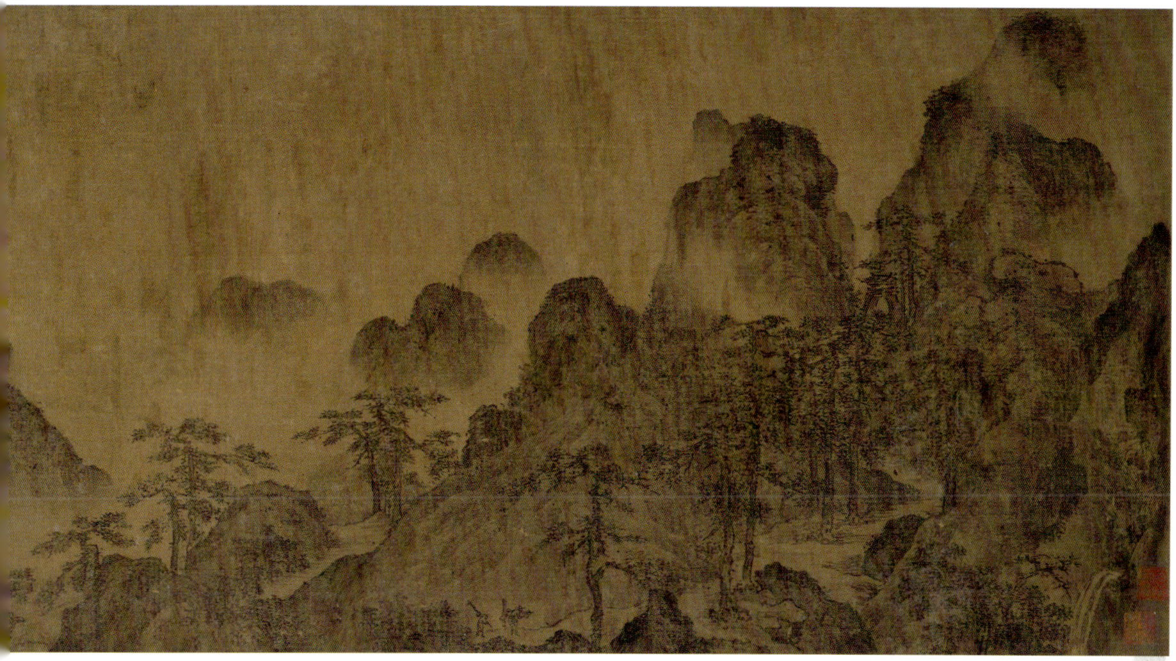

abbreviated, and the action limited to the moment of saluting the departing traveler. These two iconographical schemes for farewell scenes, by land and by sea, were repeated for centuries by both literati and Zhe school painters as a set of symbols that everyone recognized and cherished for its antiquity. Shih Shou-chien has traced its history into the Yuan and Ming dynasties, when, in 1507, Wen Zhengming abandoned the visual formulas we see here and reinterpreted the theme as a more personal message understandable only to the friends who shared it.[7]

The academic style of the two Northern Song (960–1127) departure paintings may not, however, represent the earliest style of the theme. If there was a preceding style, we do not yet know what it was, nor when or where it was introduced. The style shown in these two paintings is somewhat old-fashioned for the twelfth century and, though both paintings retain much of Song charm, the treatment of the motifs is well rehearsed and perfunctory.

Song literary sources indicate that the scholar-painter Li Gonglin (ca. 1041–1106) made paintings to commemorate the departure of friends. Li's colleague Zhang Shunmin (1034?–ca. 1100) wrote, "When the ancients were seeing off a traveler, they presented him with words. When Master Li gives a parting gift, he also gives a painting."[8] In the years before it disappeared, Li Gonglin's painting of the Yang Pass attracted repeated comment and admiration, and it clearly played an important part in the history of the departure theme. In particular, the commentaries confirm that not only

5 Hu Shunchen (active early 12th century). *Farewell to He Xuanming, Envoy to Qin* (*Song He Xuanming shi Qin tu*), 1122. Handscroll; ink on silk, h. 29.5 cm. Osaka Municipal Art Museum. See also figures 1 and 6

professionals but also literati painters dealt with this theme and probably introduced it. The theme occurs earlier in the history of literature than in the history of painting, and literature was in fact its first and proper art.

Almost contemporary with *A Priest Returning Home* is a handscroll that, according to its colophons, is equally a farewell scene and is dated to 1122, just preceding the fall of the Northern Song. This much-admired scroll, *Farewell to He Xuanming, Envoy to Qin* (*Song He Xuanming shi Qin tu*) (fig. 5), has long been considered a history painting made by an academy landscapist at the court of Emperor Huizong (1082–1135; r. 1100–1126) as a record of one of several embassies dispatched to Qin.[9] The minute figure astride a galloping horse is the emissary He Xuanming (active early twelfth century) riding into the northern mountains (see fig. 1). The painter of the scroll, Hu Shunchen (active early twelfth century), inscribed a poem on the scroll dedicating it to He Xuanming "to commemorate our parting." A second poem by Huizong's prime minister, Cai Jing (1046–1126), is appended as a colophon that repeats the farewell

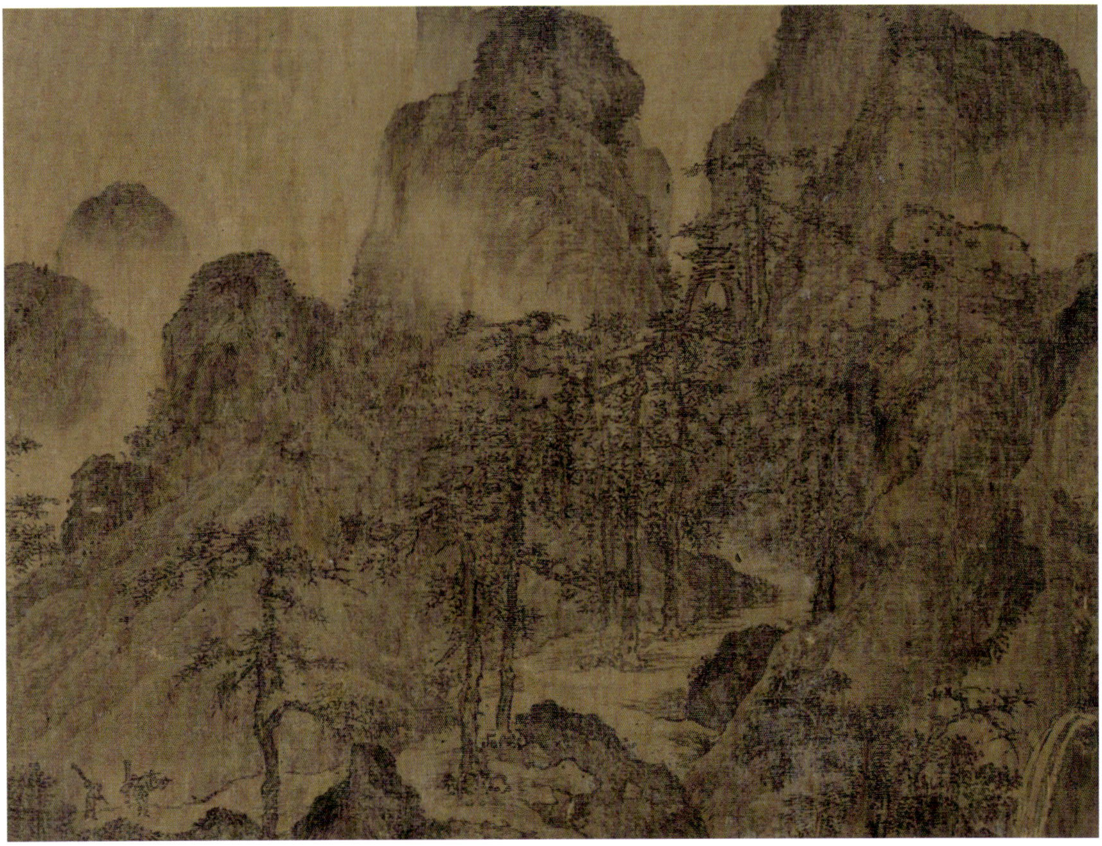

6 Hu Shunchen (active early 12th century). *Farewell to He Xuanming, Envoy to Qin* (*Song He Xuanming shi Qin tu*), 1122. Detail of figure 5

theme. The poetic forms here are the same ones used in writing a purely literary memorial, but the scene and temper of the picture are very different. The documentation reveals a personal communication from two friends to a third who was setting out on a journey. If the scroll was in fact made by the artist and Cai Jing on their own initiative to honor He Xuanming, we must be surprised that it pictures a grandly impersonal landscape and that the protagonist of the story can scarcely be distinguished among the figures. Hu Shunchen, a member of Emperor Huizong's academy and a recognized follower of the famous artist Guo Xi (active ca. 1000–ca. 1090), moved south with the court academy after 1127.[10] Working at the Northern Song court in 1122, Hu Shunchen must have been aware of an established iconography for the farewell theme of the kind discussed above. It is possible that he knew the simple formula devised for northern journeys, exemplified in the *Shi yong tu* handscroll of circa 1064, but thought it too slight to do credit to He Xuanming's diplomatic mission. He may well have felt that he could lend more weight to the enterprise by adopting the forms of monumental landscape (fig. 6) that had been introduced into the imperial academy by such classical masters as Guo Xi and Yan Wengui (active ca. 970–1030). This academy tradition paid homage to nature, not man, and here the sheer magnitude of the landscape overwhelms the historical event and its protagonist, effectively concealing the memorial purpose of the painting. Hu's rivers and mountains are so grand and stirring that no one could now regret his choice, but they were not called on again for the farewell theme.

A fine narrative scroll in the Shanghai Museum, dated to 1142, has been accepted for some time as an expository painting illustrating either a historical event or an "old tale" (*gushi*) (fig. 7). Julia Murray has published a fascinating explanation of its tangled history. The painting lost its original documents and title, and, with them, its history; thereafter, it circulated alone and unidentified before coming to rest in the Shanghai Museum. There it was recognized as a Song work of real stature, and several possible titles for it were put forward, but none seemed to fit until Xu Bangda suggested *Welcoming the Imperial Carriage*. Murray then discovered in the Ogata collection in Kyoto a document, still unpublished, which stated that Emperor Gaozong had presented a painting with this title to Cao Xun (1098–1174) for his services to the crown.[11] Thus the discovery of the lost colophons finally made it clear that the scroll was a commemorative work made in honor of Cao Xun.

Welcoming the Imperial Carriage, however, is also a history painting, crowded with historical persons and concrete details that are more in keeping with the illustration of an actual event than with a personal memorial. In fact, it represents the return of Emperor Gaozong's mother, the empress dowager, to the Southern Song (1127–1279) court. She brought with her for burial in their homeland the remains of Huizong and two empresses, who had died in captivity at the Jin court, where they had been held since the fall of the Northern Song. In the painting, the Jin emissary leads the entourage entering on the left, and an emissary of Gaozong receives it on the right. The empress dowager is conveyed in a sedan chair, followed by the coffins of Huizong and the two empresses. Their return was one of the few concessions Gaozong had been able to wring from the Jin. Their detention in enemy

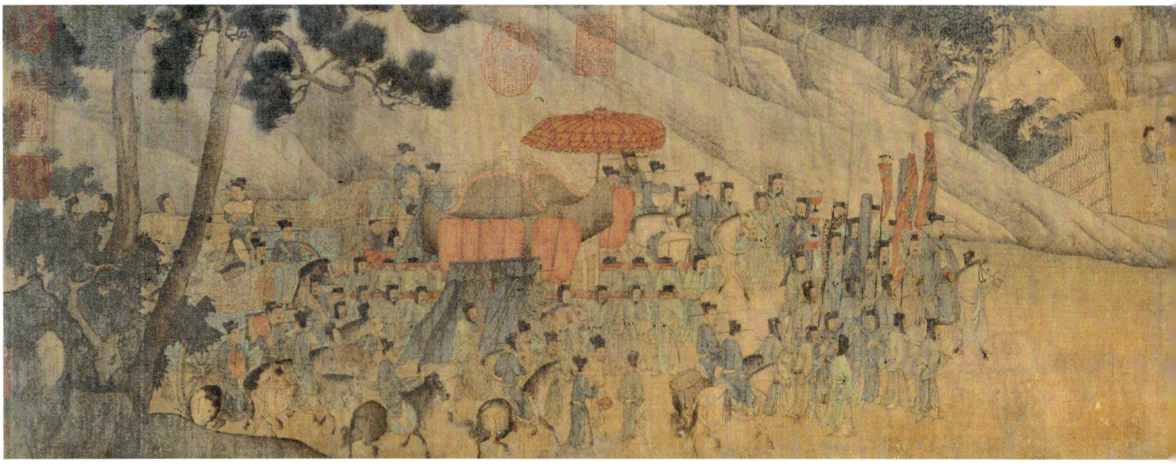

hands was an unflattering reflection on the emperor's filial piety, and their return a relief to him. The court and country viewed it as a diplomatic success and concrete evidence of heaven's approval of the Southern Song mandate.

The hero who had wrought this welcome outcome was a court official, Cao Xun, who had traveled to Jin at Gaozong's command and successfully negotiated the release of the prisoners. Shortly after the return of the empress dowager, Gaozong commissioned the painting from a still unknown but accomplished figure painter of the Song academy for presentation to Cao Xun. As far as is known, Cao Xun is not himself shown in the scroll. If the incident had occurred a few centuries earlier, the emperor would have awarded him a real portrait to be hung in the imperial memorial hall. But in 1142, a distinguished official is commemorated by representing the major political achievement of his career in an elaborate and formal figural composition. It is not the man himself who is pictured in a portrait, but the feat he accomplished, and even that is made clear only in the colophons. There is no reason to doubt that the emperor himself specified the subject and the episode. It is not unfair to think that he was as much concerned with the painting as a legitimating document of his reign as he was with its function as a personal memorial. Cao Xun, seeing it in a different light, took steps to ensure that the scroll would make his family name known far into the future. He inscribed on its colophon papers seven poems and a preface explaining its origin as an imperial honor. He adjured his family to hand it down as an heirloom, and his family kept it faithfully for five hundred years.

Again, it appears that among the visual arts there was no familiar and convenient iconographical formula that could be used to embody the honor Gaozong wished to bestow. Among the literary arts, however, there was the eulogy—a form of impressive age especially created to convey the praise and renown of an individual to posterity. Gaozong wrote one in his

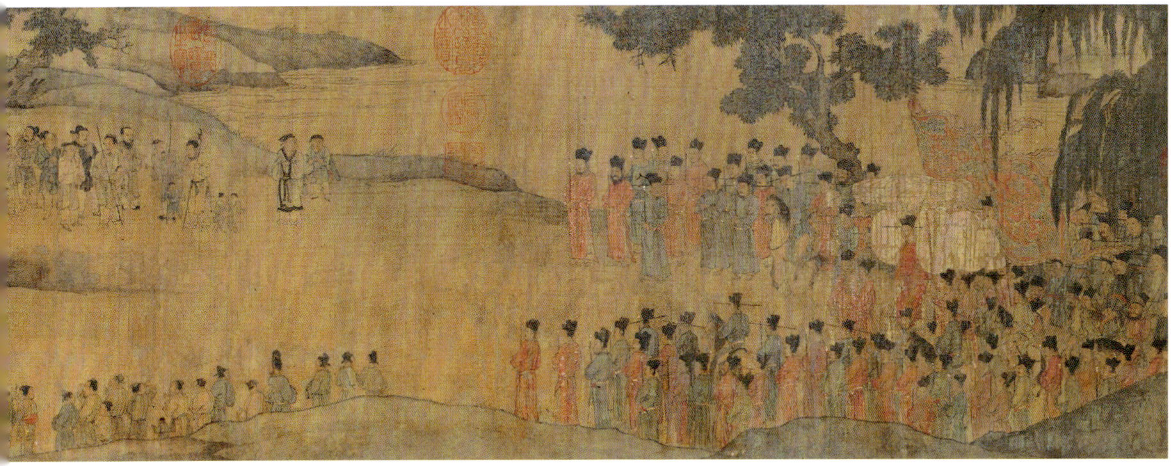

own hand and sent it to Cao Xun's family a few days after his death.[12]

The most important iconographic event in Song painting was a revival of the theme depicting estates, property, houses, or studios that had first been introduced in the Tang dynasty by artists like Wang Wei and Lu Hong (active ca. 713–742). This theme has already received much scholarly attention under different titles, for it was by far the most popular and long-lived of all the categories of memorial painting. For reasons that are unclear and, I believe, may prove to have been only an accident of survival, this theme appears to have all but lapsed after the eighth century. In the late eleventh century, Li Gonglin restored it to life as an autobiographical memorial. Li's *Mountain Villa* (*Shanzhuang tu*) represents an entire estate at Longmian and the aesthetic activities that took place there as a reflection of the owner's memory (fig. 8).[13] He painted it between 1086 and 1093, when he was in office in Kaifeng, ostensibly as a topographical record of his country place but more fundamentally as an assertion of his own tastes and personality. He then invited Su Shi (1037–1101) to write a prose record of the Longmian estate and Su's brother, Su Che (1039–1112), to compose twenty poems to introduce the scenes. Thus Li re-created an old generic model—a self-portrait of the artist in the setting of his dwelling—which had fallen into abeyance after the Tang dynasty (618–907). The artist in effect "commissioned" a landscape from himself to declare himself to others and either composed, or requested his colleagues to compose, the literary complement. Painters of later dynasties followed him in droves. Many commemorative scrolls, including some of the finest, were initiated by the subject himself, either as "commissioner" or as painter, endeavoring to meet a psychological need that his society did not yet acknowledge.

Li took his *hao* Longmian from his estate, identifying himself with the place and the kind of life he lived there. But there is no pun here, as in later paintings; man and site, both carrying

7 Anonymous court painter (active 12th century). *Welcoming the Imperial Carriage* (*Renwu gushi tu*), 1142. Handscroll; color on silk, 26.7 × 142.2 cm. Shanghai Museum

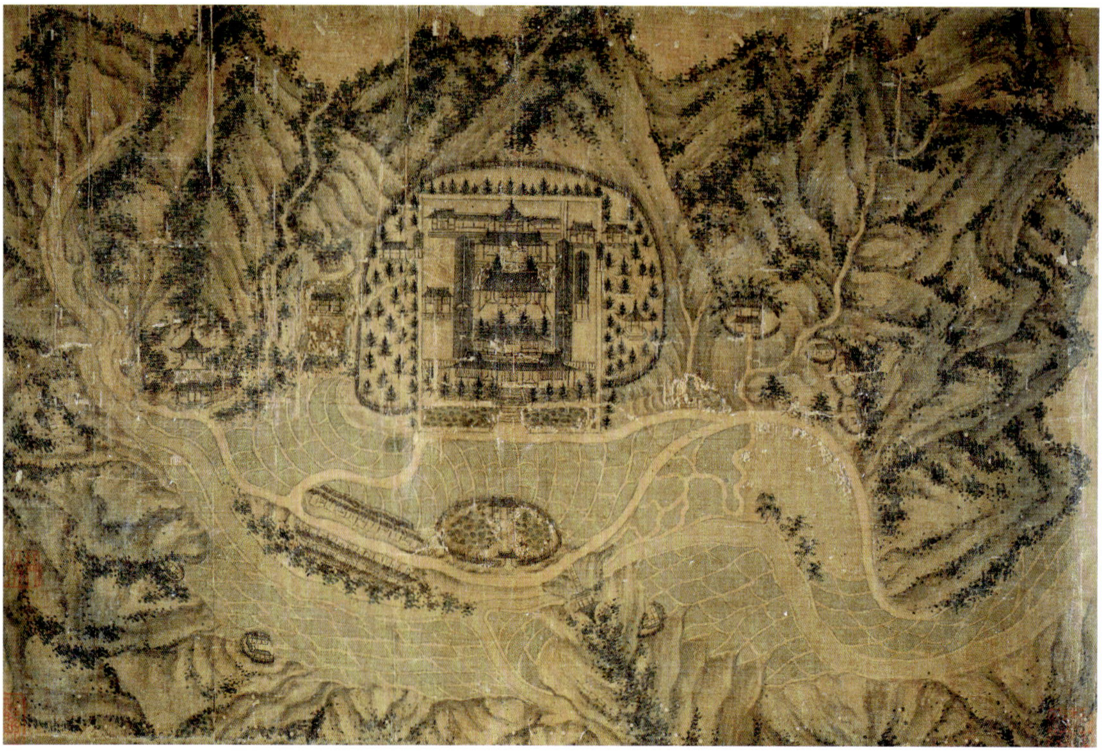

A. Lodge of Establishing Virtue

the same name, are illustrated together in the same image. Li had strongly antiquarian leanings and modeled his *Mountain Villa* on the famous *Wangchuan Villa* (*Wangchuan tu*) by Wang Wei. This accounts for the iconography—a series of landscape sites with occasional buildings—and an archaistic style even more mannered and self-conscious than the archaic simplicity of the surviving copies of the *Wangchuan tu*. The difference between the detached, pragmatic description of the surviving copies of the Tang painting and Li's tense, crowded interpretation of it show clearly that the *Mountain Villa* has undergone an intensive personal interpretation. The *Wangchuan tu* is a systematic account of Wang's estate, which was a working plantation producing several saleable commodities on which its owner depended for a living. In his design, Wang was intent on the layout and practical function of buildings and plantations. The figures in it are less significant. Moreover, the original painting which the later versions copied was a mural in a house occupied by Wang's mother that he transformed into a Buddhist shrine after her death. We do not know exactly what part that painting played in his family and his plans for the estate.

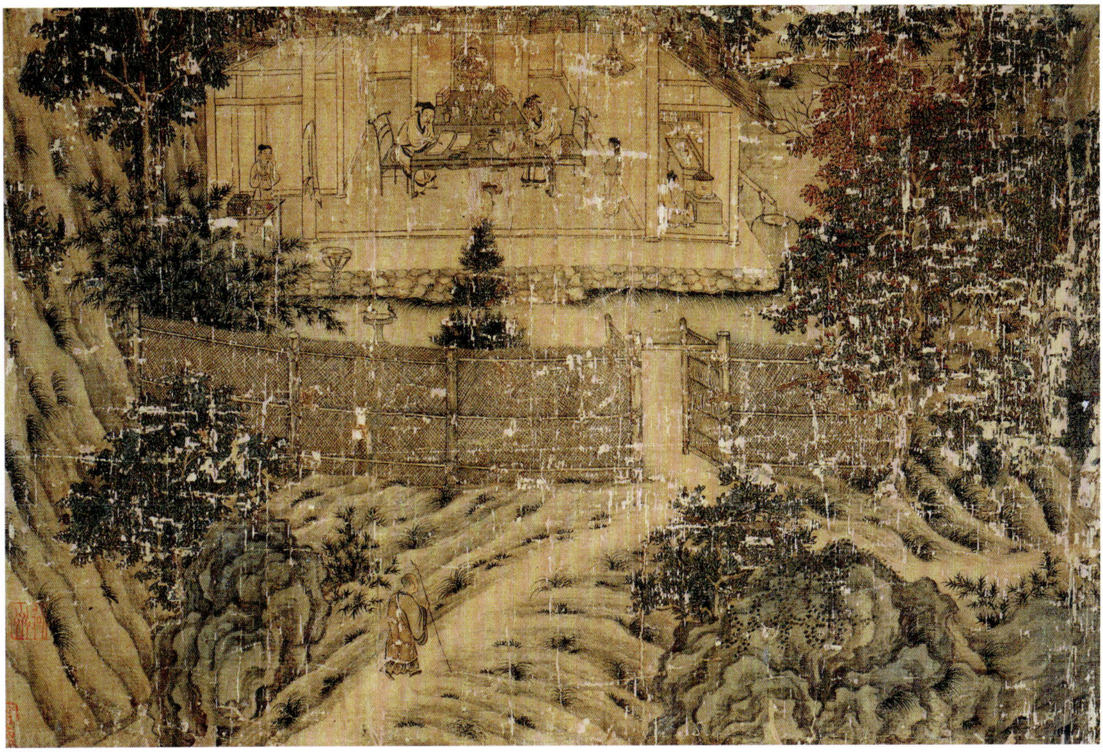

B. Hall of Meditating on Ink

Li Gonglin's *Mountain Villa* estate was also a working farm with economic value, but this function is acknowledged in only one scene of the main house facing extensive rice paddies (fig. 8a), and is completely ignored in ten others representing Li and his companions responding in the most subjective mood to the beauty of some striking view. The literary record and the poems by Su Shi and Su Che were conceived from the beginning as expressions of the deep personal feelings of the painter. Each scene in *Mountain Villa* has the same mood of intimacy and introversion, and scattered everywhere are the objects, both concrete and symbolic, of scholarly taste: pavilions, scrolls, figures composing poems, a visiting monk, wine, tea stove, antique bronzes, and even the curiously crabbed style of brushwork. Possibly in Li's view, the origin of this style (before it reached the manneristic stage) implied antiquarianism and so seemed a suitable vehicle to carry the subjective tone of the whole document.[14]

The next-to-last scene of the scroll is the Hall of Meditating on Ink (fig. 8b), the master's private study where Li and a friend are shown working with brush in hand. This was surely the heart

8 Copy after Li Gonglin (ca. 1041–1106). *Mountain Villa* (*Shanzhuang tu*). Handscroll; ink and color on silk, h. 27.8 cm. Harvard University Center for Italian Renaissance Studies, Villa I Tatti, Settignano. Florence, Berenson Collection

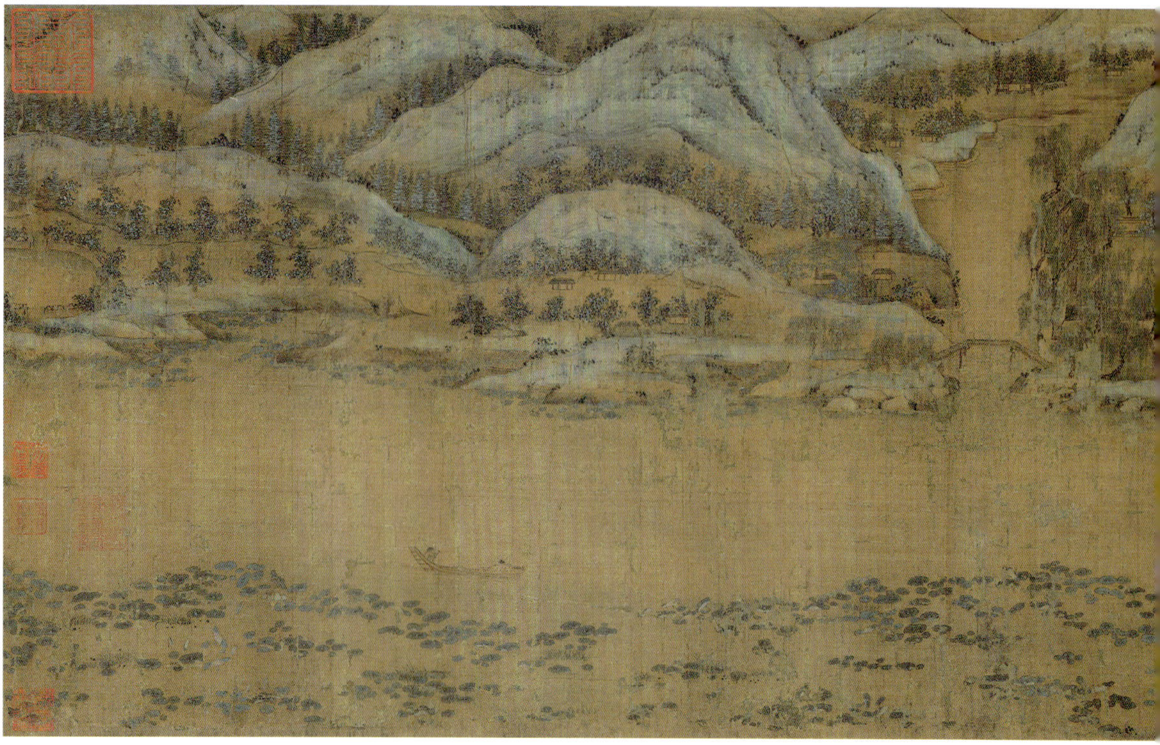

of *Mountain Villa* and of Li's life as an artist. It celebrated the practice and appreciation of art and asserted that they are the scholar's proper disciplines. This scene was one man's version of the popular "literary gathering," and the motif of his library-studio became riveted in the memories of his followers and was preserved in all later house or estate landscapes as a symbol of the scholarly ethos. It is interpreted here in a pedestrian spirit, with a literal description of furniture and architecture, for which I will blame the copyist. The followers would transform it into the simplest of thatched huts, thus removing it even further from real life than *Mountain Villa.* They would be most deeply indebted to Li for opening literati art to a new kind of discourse on the life of the mind and at the same time, as if it were a needed balance, strictly limiting the size of the audience to whom it was directed.

The contemporary literature tells us that the *Mountain Villa* was not unique in Li's oeuvre. He also painted a picture of his brother's estate in the country, which Su Shi celebrated in a poem, predictably comparing it to the *Wangchuan tu.*[15] Su Shi himself was susceptible to the attractions of the personal memorial painting. He wrote a poem on a painting by Guo Xi, saying that he ought to ask Guo to make a picture of a certain

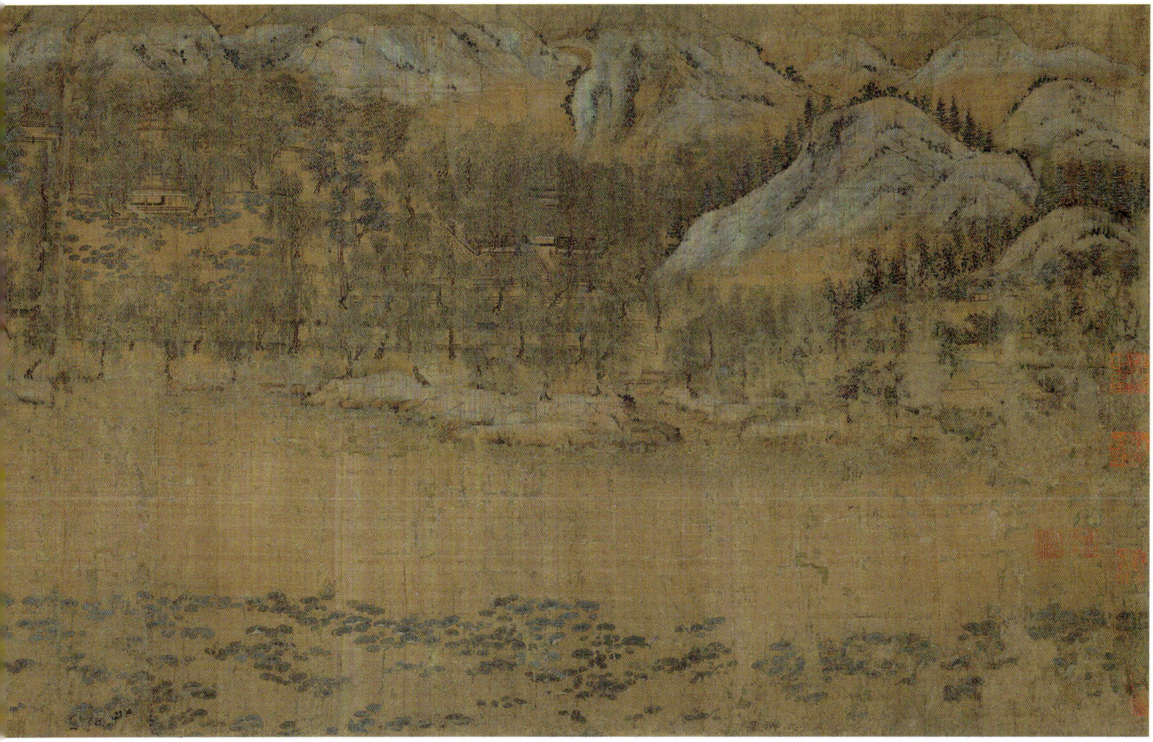

stream near Luoyang where Su Shi wanted to buy land and build a house. "Please paint me a picture of Longmen's Bajie stream / While I wait to buy a spring and rocks near Yi River."[16] He had chosen this particular site because the former prime minister Wen Yanbo (1006–1097) lived nearby, and he wished to spend his retirement with Wen. His plans, however, were frustrated by the troubles of his later career, and the house never materialized. But we may remark on the large number of Song literati who at this same time were thinking of having their estates, even nonexistent estates, memorialized in pictures. Did they perhaps feel in those politically uncertain times that a painting of the projected place of retirement would somehow lend substance to the dream?

Wangchuan tu and *Mountain Villa* set off a long train of estate paintings in the Yuan and Ming dynasties and were probably also the source of the idea of *Fisherman's Lodge at Mount Xisai,* dated about a hundred years later, to ca. 1170 (fig. 9).[17] This handscroll, now attributed to an amateur painter named Li Jie (ca. 1124–after 1191), is a lesson in the creation of a commemorative handscroll which the owner intended from the beginning as a personal memorial to be handed down in his family as a historical document. It also casts light on the value of the memorial work

9 Li Jie (ca. 1124–after 1191). *Fisherman's Lodge at Mount Xisai*, ca. 1170. Handscroll; ink and color on silk, 40.6 × 135.5 cm. The Metropolitan Museum of Art. Bequest of John M. Crawford, Jr., 1988 (1989.363.10a, b). See also figure 10

of art as a sign of social status and on the motive behind the owner's determination to acquire such a mark of prestige.

Li Jie was a civil official of the Southern Song who served the emperor over a long and ultimately successful career. When he came to planning his retirement about 1170, he made, or commissioned, a painting to represent land he had acquired at Mount Xisai in Wuxing with the intention of founding an estate. At the time, the land was overgrown and had no buildings, so he presumably was not in residence there, and the buildings we see in the painting are invented (fig. 10). The style of the *Xisai* handscroll is so unusual for the twelfth century that it finds few comparisons, perhaps only a Li Anzhong (active ca. 1117–1140) album leaf dated to 1117 (fig. 11). Li Anzhong served in the Northern and Southern Song painting academies in succession, excelling in an unusual landscape style remarkable for its commonplace air and seemingly careless execution. Aside from the brushwork, the *Xisai* painter is very like him: he constructs continuous horizontals, unpretentious and slow-moving, without focal point or stressed passages. He seems to have consciously avoided the appearance of composing—as if sitting in a boat on the river and recording what he saw directly, without trying to avoid repetition. He employed blue-green color lightly and transparently, evidently aiming at a simple naturalism. Thus the painting affords a surprising contrast to most blue-green landscapes of this period, where the pigment is usually heavily applied in conscious allusion to antiquity. These atypical traits suggest a gifted amateur with little academic training but a clear purpose and close attachment to the place represented.

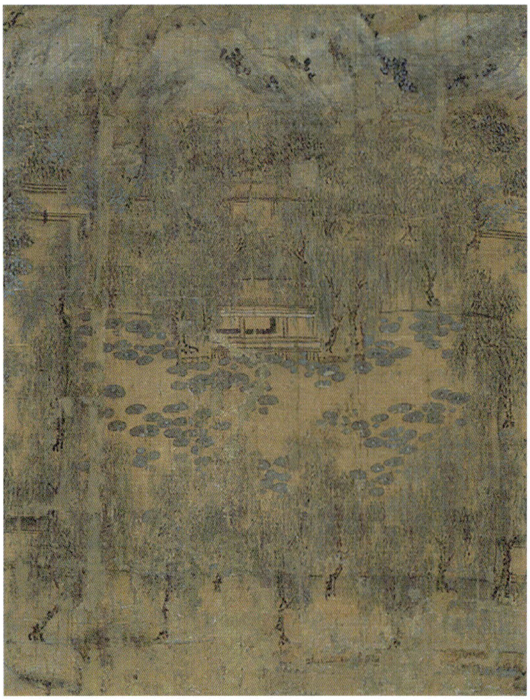

10 Li Jie (ca. 1124–after 1191). *Fisherman's Lodge at Mount Xisai*, ca. 1170. Detail of figure 9

Li Jie named the estate-to-be "Fisherman's Lodge," after a former owner of the Tang period, and immediately set about collecting colophons to give it a social license.[18] Like many Song officials, he had suffered sudden ups and downs in his career, and he was exacting in seeking only the most eminent persons to write for him. As he had fallen under a political cloud for a short period, he was turned down twice. But soon thereafter the cloud lifted, he built the house, and between 1185 and 1191 he successfully solicited seven colophons from major literati and government officials, including two who had rebuffed him earlier. The colophons are personal in tone and treat certain topoi which become standard in estate paintings in the Yuan and Ming dynasties. They commend

Li's official success, pass silently over his period in disfavor, acknowledge all his titles, and predict a brilliant future for him. Some writers discuss the history of the Xisai estate and his plans for building, others foresee visits there spent composing poems, drinking, and singing among the local fishermen and woodcutters. The motifs and the rhetoric are taken from the literary genres of poetry and social biography, which have been transferred unchanged to the colophon papers of the painting.

Evidently, Li Jie was an ambitious man who aspired to become a member of the landed gentry, and he knew how to go about achieving it. He needed the expected credentials, one of which was an honorific painting suitably witnessed with colophons by noteworthy figures. The history of this painting demonstrates what he was trying to accomplish: already in the twelfth century, the commemorative landscape could function as a socially legitimating document by which a man might represent himself to society in a preferred light.

Another subtype of memorial landscape—the metaphorical—relates to landscape generally rather than to a specific estate or place because it conveys human characteristics by means of simple substituted symbols. The symbols are derived from literature and transformed directly into familiar visual motifs which are easily compounded into a landscape that could pass for a view of nature with no imposed extraneous meaning. This metaphorical function of landscape became increasingly important during the Yuan dynasty and ubiquitous in the Ming.

Literary records describe two paintings, now lost, made for Wen Yanbo, the center and

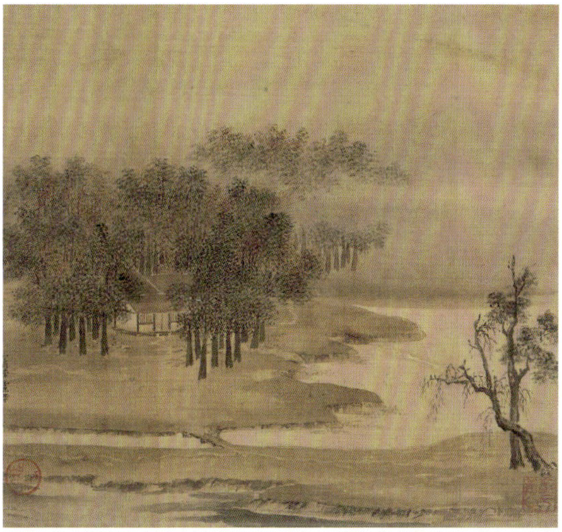

sometime host of a literary circle of thirteen gentlemen of Luoyang, whose gatherings were counted as one of the canonical literary gatherings of ancient China. The members were mainly retired government officials in their seventies, occasionally serving in government in Kaifeng and occasionally withdrawing to Luoyang, where they frowned at a distance upon their successors in the capital. One of these paintings was a mural executed by the academy master Chen Yongzhi (active ca. 1023–1032), on a ten-foot-high wall of Wen Yanbo's house, representing auspicious clouds spreading over the sky and giving the effect of rain falling at early dawn.[19] Auspicious clouds, meaning rain-bearing clouds, were a broad symbol of material benefits and, applied to a person, meant an upright and benevolent official who labored for the good of the people. Apparently Wen Yanbo himself was not represented in the painting, but every educated person knew the meaning of the clouds. This was certainly an

11 Li Anzhong (active ca. 1117–1140). *Cottages in a Misty Grove in Autumn*, dated to 1117. Album leaf; ink and color on silk, 24.2 × 27.2 cm. The Cleveland Museum of Art. Gift of Mr. and Mrs. Severance A. Millikin (1963.588)

honorific work, although who commissioned it is not known.

The other metaphorical picture was painted by Guo Xi and presented to Wen Yanbo on his sixtieth birthday to wish him many and successful sons.[20] Wen appeared in it carrying a staff and standing under a pine tree, alluding to vigorous old age. He gazed down into a valley filled with a forest of pine trees of various sizes—his large progeny. Guo's son commented, "There was never a composition like it before.... Duke (Wen) was greatly pleased." This was clearly a commissioned work presented by family or colleagues. The heavy dependence on symbols might strike us as labored, but in Chinese literature natural forms like pines, clouds, and bamboo had for centuries been used as metaphors of human virtues. Wen Tong (1018–1079) and Su Shi produced numerous bamboo and old tree pictures which they presented to friends, tacitly comparing the spirit of the recipient to the resilience and tenacity of the plants. The delight in signs, symbols, parallel meanings, and allusive and circuitous expression that rely on exchange between words and images is characteristic of writers and painters generally and of the Chinese literati in particular. It was a direct outgrowth of their training in the art and history of literature, and spilled over into the visual arts almost unconsciously. All these shifts are substitutes for simpler and more direct exposition, made in order to render the intrinsic meaning subtler to grasp, more stimulating to the intellect, and, not least, since the compliments implied were well worn, to lend it some air of freshness.

An unusual commemorative painting that came to light at a Beijing auction in 1995 must play an important part in any study of the type in the Song period. It is so thoroughly sui generis that it cannot be constrained within any particular subtype of the commemorative genre but appears to be a unique and unusually personal invention of the maker. It mourns a father's death but cannot be called an elegy because its mood is almost ebullient. It should probably be called a eulogy, for it vigorously and warmly acclaims the father's life and art and is more original in form than any memorial of the Song period. It was conceived and organized by a farmer's son to tell the story of his family's ascent from practicing agriculture as a living to an official career in government. Entitled *Illustrations to Ten Poems* (*Shi yong tu*), the handscroll, now darkened and abraded, represents a broad panorama of mountains and water overseen on the right by garden pavilions in which a literary reception is in progress (see fig. 2).[21] The guests in the small pavilion (fig. 12) are gazing intently at the landscape, where ten poems appear written on the sky like pictures hanging in an art gallery. Introducing the first poem, above the large pavilion, is a brief note explaining that the vignette below it represents a gathering of scholars: "The prefect of Wuxing, Ma Xun, invited six elderly gentlemen to the Southern Garden (in Nanjing), where they composed poetry. Hu Yuan of Anding, dated to 1046" (慶歷六年, 吳興太守馬尋, 宴六老於南園, 酒酣賦詩. 安定胡先生瑗, 教授州學, 為之序).[22] This was probably written by Zhang Xian (990–1078) when he copied out the poems as a substitute for the lost original preface by Hu Yuan. Hu was a much respected teacher of the classics who served at court as expositor to the emperor and had gathered around him a large following of disciples. The poems composed at the meeting were later introduced by Hu's original preface and engraved on stone. All were lost in later years, and the garden also disappeared.

The elderly gentlemen were invited to the Southern Garden to honor their skill in poetry. All were of advanced age, which suggests that, as a compliment to them, the prefect Ma Xun meant to emulate the literary gathering held on Mount Xiang in 817 by Bai Juyi (772–846).[23] All the gentlemen had degrees or were distinguished in some way except one, Zhang Wei (955–1046), a local farmer with a passion for poetry who had undertaken the civil service examination in his youth but was disappointed in his hopes and had returned to his life as a farmer. He did not repine but handed his ambitions on to his son, Zhang Xian, and carried on with his plow, chanting and composing poetry as before. By the time of the literary gathering in 1046, his achievements in poetry were sufficient for him to be included in a guest list of officeholders. He died later in the same year that he received that signal honor.

In time, Zhang Xian fully realized his father's ambitions, taking the *jinshi* degree in 1030 and prospering in government service. He won real distinction in poetry, which attracted the friendship of many literati, Su Shi among them. When he retired from government service and returned to Wuxing in 1064, he set about planning a memorial for his father. From the many poems his father had composed during his lifetime, Zhang Xian chose his father's ten favorites and wrote them out on silk under the title *Ten Poems*. He then commissioned (or himself painted?) a handscroll of ten vignettes, each illustrating one poem, in a landscape broad enough to encompass them all. The first three poems relate to the

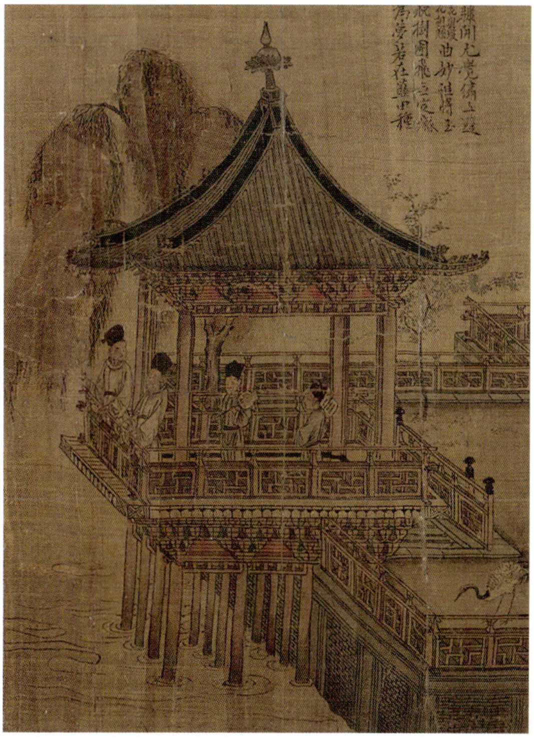

Literary Gathering

literary gathering; the remainder seem to have been composed for specific independent occasions. That they are gathered together, placed side by side in the same picture space, and each supplied with a brief illustration, suggests that Zhang Xian was consciously seeking some large unifying frame for his memorial. The first poem with the preface is a formal expression of Zhang Wei's gratitude to the prefect Ma Xun for his hospitality; from its elaborate illustration, it is patently the main episode. The next two verses are addressed to a crane strutting about on the terrace, a compliment to the great age of the guests, and to a butterfly fluttering around a blossoming tree, a

12 Zhang Xian (990–1078). *Illustrations to Ten Poems* (*Shi yong tu*), ca. 1064. Detail of figure 2

pun on the words for butterfly (蝶) and seventy or eighty years. The fourth is the high-spirited poem "A Single Sail," which seems to have touched a special chord in Zhang Wei's imagination.

"A Single Sail"
In the midst of the river where the clouds disperse,
Far away I spy a single sail disappearing.
In waves so vast it seems to climb the Milky Way;
In wind so high as if it sped over a lake.
Dimly seen it strikes out for a distant island,
Like a lost weed drifting in a wasteland.
Do not ask who sails that boat!
Not for him the path to fame and profit.[24]

孤帆
江心雲破處，遙見去帆孤。
浪闊疑升漢，風高若泛湖。
依微過遠嶼，彷彿落荒墟。
莫問乘舟客，利名同一途。

The remaining poems treat domestic subjects in the lives of the peasants,[25] except for the last, composed by Zhang Wei when he was ninety years old, evidently as a kind of valedictory. Zhang Xian gave this verse pride of place at the top of the scroll near the center:

"Ninety Years"
When the midwinter ice first breaks and the
  Tiao River clears,
I chant as I wander past misty villages, by distant
  towns.
On a sandbar the sun sets where wildfowl flock
  together,
From my pillow the west wind sounds like drums
  and horns.
A lone scull and a winter lantern follow me fishing
  through the night.
I seize the moment of timely rain to plow the
  spring fields.
Why say wealth is first among the five happinesses?
I have lived more than ninety years in perfect
  peace.[26]

臘凍初開苕水清，煙村去郭可吟行。
灘頭斜日鳧鷖隊，枕上西風鼓角聲。
一棹寒燈隨夜釣，滿犁時雨趁春耕。
誰言五福仍須富，九十餘年樂太平。

Eight years later, in 1072, Zhang Xian requested the then-prefect of Wuxing, Sun Jue (1028–1090), to write a preface for the *Ten Poems* scroll explaining their commemorative purpose and requesting his family to preserve the scroll for later generations. (Sun's preface is the large block at the bottom center of the scroll on a separate panel of silk, probably interpolated sometime later.)

Sun Jue's Preface
What man most desires are wealth, rank, and great age; and what he most laments are poverty, humble birth, and brief life. But he who wins some of these things may lack others. Therefore he would rather enjoy health, even in poverty, and old age, even in humble circumstances, than enjoy wealth afflicted by ills and sorrows or live a short life covered with honors.

The posthumous title of vice minister of the Justice Department was granted to Zhang Wei of Wuxing. In his early years he applied himself to his books, but he was poor and could not finish his studies. So he turned his hand to the plow to make a living. He educated his son well, which bore fruit.

All his life he loved to compose poetry and used to entertain himself with singing and chanting it, roaming about his native village and towns, up and down the valleys, mountains, and lakes. When he met with something that aroused his feelings he would compose a poem on it. He did not bother with mannered and extravagant figures of speech but conceived elegant ideas naturally. He wandered about free and unconstrained, consorting with private scholars skilled in poetry. If he had not been undisturbed within and free from anxiety without, his poetry would not have been what it was. He never served in office, but his son was awarded the fourth level of official rank, so we can say that Zhang Wei achieved high honor. He did not administer affairs, and yet he benefited from an official salary for his lifetime, so we can also say that he was wealthy. Moreover, he reached the age of ninety-one years, so we can add that he enjoyed great age. Receiving those things which men most desire and avoiding those which they most lament, he escaped disturbance and anxiety. As we read his poetry we feel the expression of ease and freedom from resentment, and thoughts solemn, profound, and tranquil—fitting indeed!

Zhang Wei died eighteen years ago, and now his son, the director of the Criminal Administration Bureau, has retired to his home [in Wuxing]. He has chosen ten of his father's favorite poems, has written them out on silk, and named them *The Ten Poems*. He did this so the poems and painting might be passed down to his sons and grandsons, and he entrusted me with writing the preface. Admiring both the vice minister's [Zhang Wei] longevity and the bureau director's [Zhang Xian] filial piety, I have willingly composed this preface for him [Zhang Xian]. His name [*zi*] is Ziye, and he is now eighty-two years of age.

1072, second month, twenty-second day. Sun Jue[27]

孫覺莘序：

富貴而壽考者，人情之所甚慕；貧賤而夭短者，人情之所甚哀。然有得於此者必遺於彼，故寧處康強之貧，壽考之賤，不願多藏而病憂，顯榮而夭折也。贈尚書刑部侍郎張公諱維，吳興人，少而學書，貧不能卒業，去而躬耕以為養。善教其子，至於有成。平居好詩，以吟詠自娛，浮遊閭里，上下於溪湖山谷之間，遇物發興，率然成章。不事雕琢之巧，采繪之華，而詞意自得。徜徉閒肆，往往與()時處士能詩者為輩，蓋非無憂於中，無求於世，其言不能若是也。公不出仕，而以子封至正四品，亦可謂貴；不治職而受祿養以終其身，亦可謂富，行年九十有一，可謂壽考。夫享人情之所甚慕而違其所哀，無憂無求，而見之吟詠，則其自得而無怨懟之辭，蕭然而有澄澹之思，其亦宜哉。公卒十八年，公子尚書都官郎中先亦致仕家居，取公平生所自愛詩十首，寫之縑素，號「十詠圖」，傳示子孫，而以序引見屬。余既愛侍郎之壽，都官之孝，為之序而不辭。都官字子野，蓋其年八十有二云。熙寧五年 [1072] 二月二十二日右正言真集賢院知湖州事高郵孫覺莘。

Sun presented the preface to Zhang Xian on his eighty-second birthday, complimenting him on his great age and filial devotion, adding the son's achievements to the father's, and, in effect, claiming for their family a place fairly won in the literati ranks of Wuxing.

The *Ten Poems* handscroll is distinguished among Song paintings for its historical interest: it speaks eloquently for the ambition and vitality of the Zhang family and lends greater depth to our understanding of the divide between the commoner and elite classes in the Song dynasty. It is the more disappointing, then, that it bears no signature or seal of the painter, and that he is not mentioned in all the accompanying literature except for the single comment "Zhang Xian made it," which can equally well be translated "Zhang

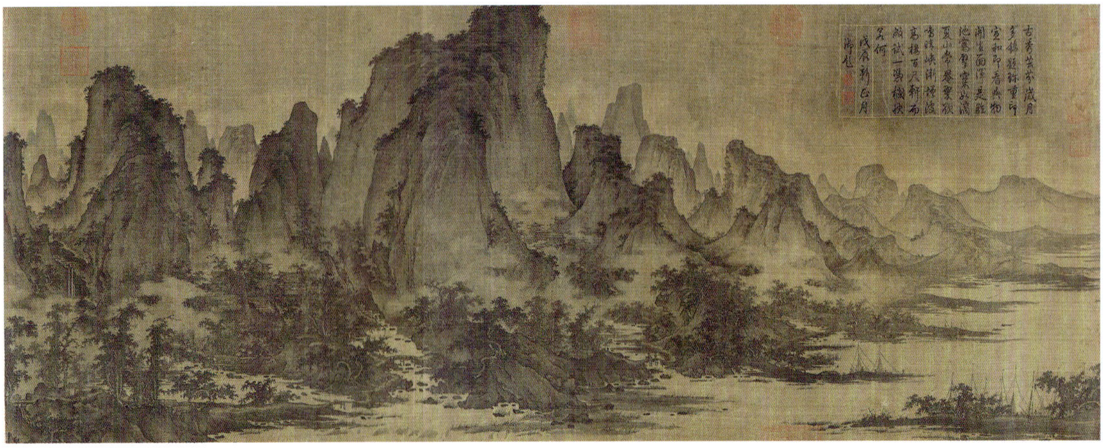

Xian had it made."[28] The records make no mention of Zhang as a painter but reiterate earnest praises of his poetry. A judgment on the attribution to him must rest on the style of the painting. This has all the earmarks of a professional painter trained under the somewhat tenuous influence of the imperial academy at Kaifeng. His style is plain and robust, but pedantic and laden with formulae. If we compare it to *Summer Mountains* (fig. 13), we can see that the artist was well acquainted with the forms of the heroic style of the great eleventh-century Song landscapists. He aimed at the grand cadences of their repeated spits of land and mountains rolling like breakers, but both the rhythm and the formal unity were beyond his reach.[29] The rendering of the architecture is sufficiently more elegant and disciplined that we should consider the possibility of two hands at work on the scroll—a specialist in *jiehua* (fine-lined architectural painting) and a somewhat pedestrian landscapist.

Early in the Northern Song, the tradition of portrait painting divided into two currents. In a study of the different iconographies of these two types of the portrait genre, Scarlett Jang distinguishes the "portrait sequence," originating in the Han dynasty (206 BCE–220 CE), from the "literary gathering," invented in the Song.[30] The oldest current, the portrait "pure and simple," derived from Han examples and continued through the Tang period, intensely scrutinized the human figure against a void ground, implying in the subject an authoritative force of character. The other, younger current made a direct and major contribution to the genre of commemorative painting. In response to the innovative landscape of the Song period, it surrounded the figures with a natural setting, gave them colleagues to talk to, and new poses and actions, suggesting the pleasures of society and the arts. This literary gathering draws on certain themes that would soon be declared the scholars' favorite pastimes: calligraphy, painting, music, and the *weiqi* board game, collectively "The Four Accomplishments." Alone or together, the accomplishments imply a broader concept of humanism and reinforce

13 Attributed to Qu Ding (active ca. 1023–ca. 1056). *Summer Mountains*. Handscroll; ink and pale color on silk, 45.3 × 115.2 cm. The Metropolitan Museum of Art, Ex. coll.: C. C. Wang Family, Gift of The Dillon Fund, 1973 (1973.120.1)

the literatus's claim to intellectual and aesthetic leadership.[31] In *Ten Poems*, the accomplishments are treated as familiar pleasures of social life but are weighted differently according to the tastes of the Zhang family. *Weiqi* is being played front and center, but it is eclipsed by an impressive landscape screen behind it, suggesting a fondness for landscape painting—possibly on the part of Zhang Xian, who had decided on a landscape setting for the entire scroll. A *qin* concert is planned but has not started. Responding to the Zhang family's delight in poetry, the sky and water are hung with verses, outshining the Four Accomplishments and declaring literature supreme among the arts. Song taste also introduced the elaborated setting and the differentiation of psychological types among the scholars (see fig. 12). All these modifications together have the effect of naturalizing the image as a whole, so that it is more plausible, more normal, closer to real experience. By contrast, in a portrait of the scholar Wang Huan, a single didactic figure, from the "portrait sequence" titled *Five Elders of Suiyang* (*Suiyang wulao tu*) (fig. 14), datable to around 1056, everything contributes to the impression of indomitable authority: the figure's stillness and solitude, the gravity of expression, the sense of thoughts turned inward.

The new Song type, the "literary gathering," presents subjects who take visible pleasure in society with greater ease. They assert their authority less forcefully, do not seek or desire political power, await impatiently the moment of retirement, and are by nature satisfied with contemplative pursuits. A gentleman of means wished to be remembered in this persona as a host consorting with and entertaining distinguished guests in his own study or in his garden, his other natural habitat. In the *Ten Poems*, the scholar meets his colleagues in a natural setting to converse, compose poetry, and practice and appreciate the fine arts. This modern type of Song scholar at play emanates an air of geniality quite alien to the remote magisterial chill of the "portrait sequence," although, I think, no less conscious and no less politically significant. Like the farewell theme, the literary gathering gained enormous popularity. With certain subsequent adaptations, it became a permanent part of the memorial genre, sometimes a component element, sometimes, as here, the main theme.

The literary meeting in the Southern Garden of 1046 was recorded by the noted critic Zhou Mi

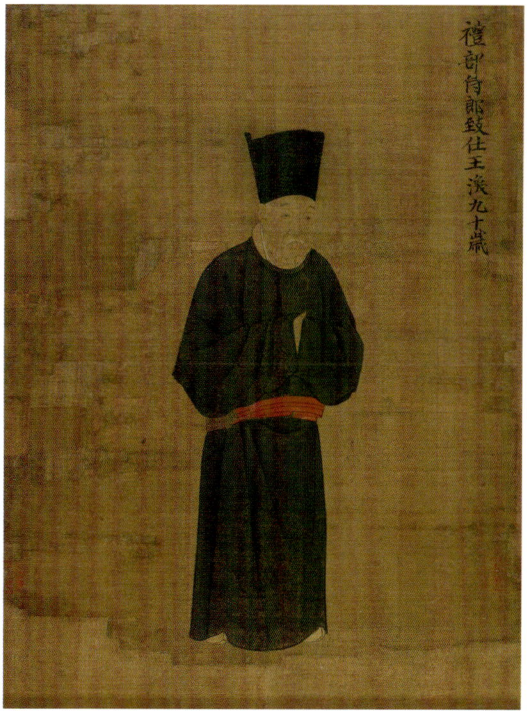

14 Anonymous (11th century). *Portrait of Wang Huan* (active ca. 1030). From the album *Five Elders of Suiyang* (*Suiyang wulao tu*), ca. 1056. Album leaf; ink and color on silk, 41.7 × 31.7 cm. Freer Gallery of Art, Smithsonian Institution, Washington, D.C. (F1948.10)

(1232–1299) in his *biji* (record).[32] Zhou investigated the theme of the scholarly gathering, which he recognized to be of peculiar and proprietary interest to the literati class. He defined it as a social occasion, acknowledging the artistic, philosophical, and intellectual excellence of the old and wise. Zhou also included a chronological list of the major literary meetings from the Tang dynasty to his own time, placing the event that took place in 1046 and was commemorated in 1064 in the *Ten Poems* together with the canonical examples of the type: The Nine Old Gentlemen of Xiangshan of 817, when Bai Juyi called together his closest friends; The Six Gentlemen of Wuxing of 1046; The Five Elders of Suiyang of 1056, in memory of a circle of Song scholars; and The Luoyang Septuagenarian Society, which congregated circa 1082, honoring members of the Yuanyou political party.[33] When Zhang Xian set out to commemorate his father, he made a place for him among the preeminent leaders of Song culture.

* * *

It is noteworthy that the names connected with Song commemorative painting reach across a spectrum of the educated elite from the emperor Gaozong to lesser officials like Li Jie, Li Gonglin, and Zhang Xian. Many of the distinguished gentlemen supposed to have met in the Western Garden are known to have engaged with this genre, most as patrons, commissioners of works, or recipients. We have seen at least three painters who were certainly literati: Hu Shunchen, Li Gonglin, and Li Jie. The painters of *Welcoming the Imperial Carriage*, the *Ten Poems*, and *A Priest from the Eastern Sea Returning Home* were professionals practicing the contemporary style of the imperial academy, the first probably at the center of Song art in Kaifeng, the last two more likely in the provinces. The professionals worked to commission and under the direction of educated men who exercised their own taste in the choice of style and theme, specifying quite exactly what they wanted. All six of the Song works were conceived by literati to serve themselves and, in most cases, to function long into the future as a record of family history.

I have also discussed Song examples of three iconographical subtypes of commemorative landscape painting known much earlier in Chinese literature and particularly favored in the Song. The occasion of departure on a journey was previously recognized with literary offerings alone. By 1064, this literary theme took visual form as a painting cast in a general symbolic form that, even in the absence of an inscription, was immediately understandable as a scene of leave-taking. This form had already become conventionalized by the *Ten Poems*.

The theme of the recipient's house (or estate or thatched hut) would become in short order the most sought after and cherished subject in Chinese art, standing for the owner in his personal surroundings. Its first appearance in the eighth century in the *Wangchuan tu* and *Ten Views from a Thatched Cottage* was followed by a long hiatus (possibly misleading) until Li Gonglin revived the type in the late eleventh century, after which it flourished in undiminished favor until the present.

The third subtype, equally important as a declaration of elite class distinctions and ideals, was the literary gathering. At least one of its roots could be traced as far back as the *Seven Sages of the Bamboo Grove* in the third century and the *Eighteen Scholars* assembled by Li Shimin (r. 626–649) in the early Tang dynasty.

The first Tang and Song examples of these types are all explicitly biographical or autobiographical, designed either by a commissioner or by the painter himself to celebrate some memorable place or event in the honorand's life. Cao Xun inscribed poems and preface on *Welcoming the Imperial Carriage* that effectively converted it from a memorial of imperial history to a memorial of the Cao family, a social role it filled for five centuries. Likewise, Li Jie, by his indefatigable search for colophons by distinguished writers, turned *Fisherman's Lodge at Mount Xisai* into a monument for his descendants. Zhang Xian, by a new and quite unprecedented alliance of word and image, proclaimed to the world that he, his father, and their family were members of the literati elite by right of merit. Li Gonglin discoursed in images on the most immaterial of all things, the taste and intellect of a private person in communion with his closest friends.

It is not a coincidence that themes of house and studio, departure, and literary gathering were adopted by the visual arts in the era of the Tang and Song. All three subjects require a landscape setting: the house and departure scenes require it by their nature, the literary gathering by long-standing tradition. From the time of the *Seven Sages of the Bamboo Grove*, scholars were represented composing, drinking, or whistling under trees—that is, in a garden or woods. Landscape painting reached its first maturity in this period, offering forms powerfully expressive but malleable enough to be adapted to a limiting, particularized function like the personal memorial. But even diminished in scale and becalmed in spirit, landscape continued to dominate the human figure throughout the Yuan and Ming periods. *Farewell to He Xuanming* (fig. 5) illustrates the dilemma faced by Hu Shunchen when he adopted the heroic landscape style as a setting for the journey of the envoy to Qin. The Song artist quickly learned how to work with fragments of nature and how to tone down the operatic pitch of the great Song landscapists. The painter of *Fisherman's Lodge at Mount Xisai* (fig. 9), whether he was the amateur Li Jie or an anonymous journeyman, caught just the right tone of ease and uneventfulness needed for the retirement theme.

The evidence outlined above gives reason to believe that private memorial painting was already under-way in the Song period, although it was not yet widespread and not all its makers were consciously searching for a style that would support the humanistic theme. They were aware that they had conceived a new content for art, and in *Ten Poems* we see Zhang Xian experimenting with an iconography that would allow him to discourse on the literary and the pictorial in the same work. This group of monuments is too limited to draw more precise conclusions, but it does suggest that the Song literati, and to a lesser degree their predecessors in the Tang dynasty, were the first to conceive the need for a kind of memorial painting separate and distinct from the traditional portrait.

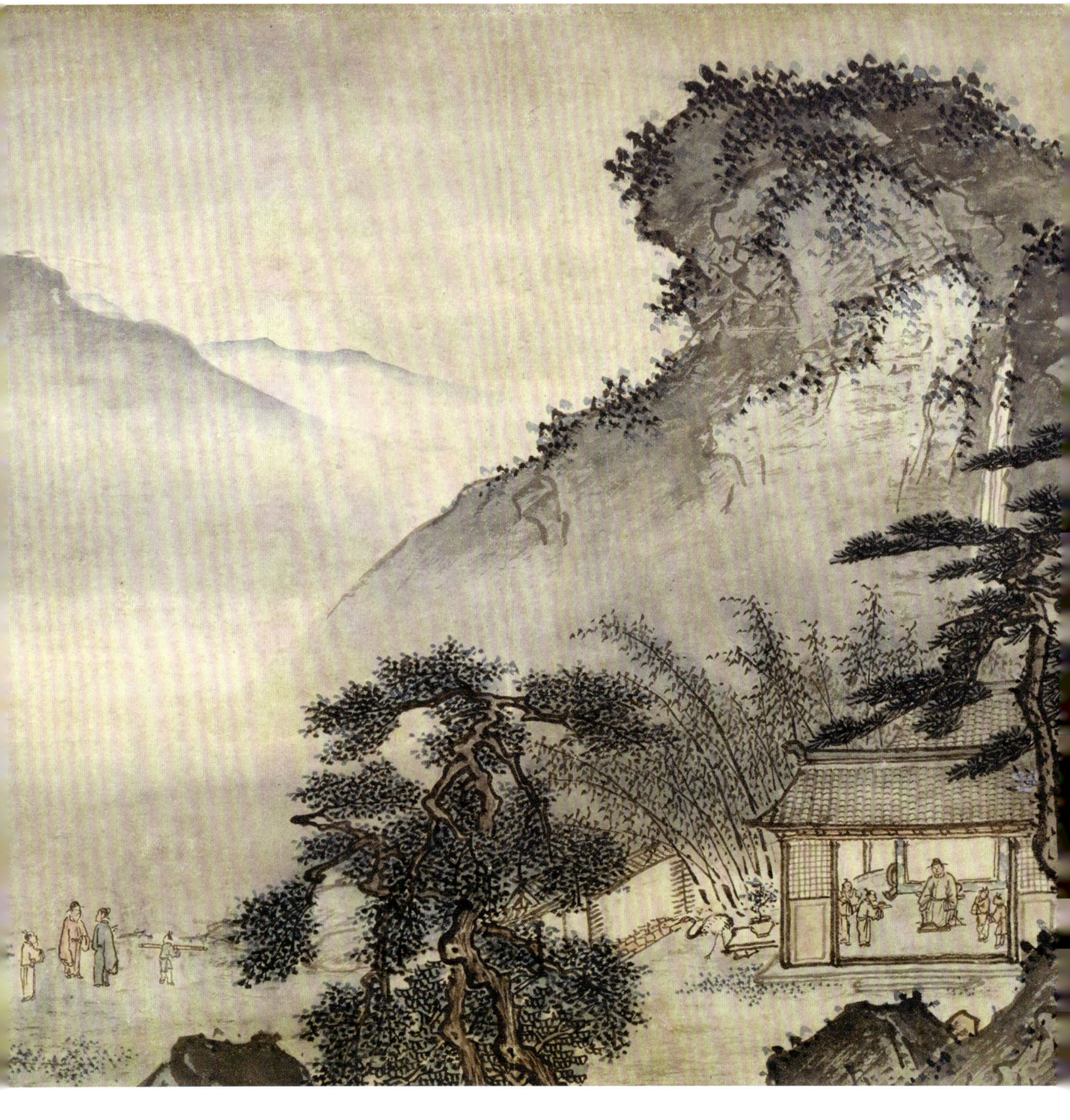

15 Dai Jin (ca. 1388–1462). *Congratulating Duan Muzhi on His Retirement* (*Gui tian zhu shou tu*), 1407. Detail of figure 21

Chapter Two
Conspicuous Seclusion

The genre of commemorative landscape painting came to full maturity in the Yuan dynasty and, over the seventy years of Mongol rule, clarified and confirmed its dedication to the individual honorand. Gradually, its styles withdrew from Song monumentality and from Song regard for naturalism. The paintings developed an increasingly subjective and introspective air, being only occasionally preoccupied with the artist's experience but always with that of the subject or recipient of the painting. Because the genre concentrated on a specific person, it was tied to a known time, event, or locale associated with him, and tended to ignore natural fact that was not relevant to him. Richard Vinograd has astutely observed that, as Yuan landscape concentrated more narrowly on its human subject and his works, its structural forms and brushwork grew steadily more abstract.[34] This apparent paradox resulted from a shift in the function of the setting from the representation of nature to the reflection of human sensibility. In his search for ways to do this, the painter never left the safe haven of landscape-as-ostensible-subject but showed himself increasingly willing to take liberties with natural form — to make daring omissions, to distort normal scale — if, by doing so, he could draw attention to his subject, elevate him above the setting, and grant him primacy and distinction.

The prefaces and colophons of works dated to the Yuan dynasty expanded vigorously in number and length as they were adapted to discursive purposes: they treat personal histories, declare private views and tastes, and offer to explain the honorand to the reader as a poet reveals himself in a poem. The memorial scroll won wide success in a short time because it came to life offering a private voice to Chinese scholars at a time when many of them were silenced and dispossessed by their Mongol overlords and faced a politically uncertain future. The circle of writers, painters, and patrons who supported the memorial scroll constituted its almost exclusive audience. They tended to ignore other classes — shopkeepers,

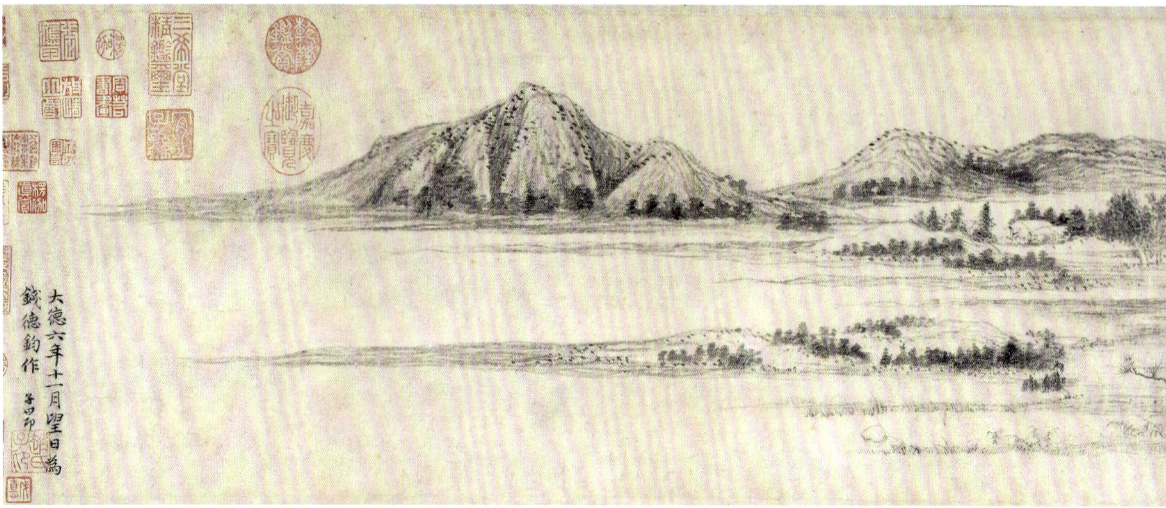

peasant farmers, aliens—but they occasionally lent their services to the larger community when unusual circumstances singled out an individual about to cross the bridge into their own class or a commoner showed himself a model of Confucian behavior. They especially appreciated the social value of specialists in the fine arts and recognized the rarity of real talent and its value to themselves and their community. These unusual persons they supported warmly, occasionally collaborating with them.

The appearance of a varied array of literary material on paintings occurred with a suddenness that is significant. In China, the history of literature was much older than the history of painting; literature had always been more highly esteemed; and biography was the oldest class of literature, reaching back to the Western Han (206 BCE–25 CE). By the Song dynasty, biography had been for centuries a genre of the literati.[35] In his essay on Chinese biography, David Nivison remarks that the "wealth of biographical literature is one of the striking things about traditional China."[36] This legacy was readily at hand and was familiar to writers of commemorative inscriptions on paintings, and it was an easy shift to adapt the literary component to the painting. This sort of biographical writing was originally drawn from the family biographies that played a part in the ancestral cult. The debt of memorial landscape painting to traditional biography is especially noticeable in the moralizing tone that clings to its colophons. But though this tone is almost always present, the obligation to treat it as such lay more lightly on memorial painting than it did on the writing of family records. That in turn meant that recipients and writers of memorial scrolls gained a new degree of freedom in addressing the private interests of the subject.

From the early Song to the middle Ming period, official biography (*ben zhuan*), compiled at court for the use of the bureaucracy, was

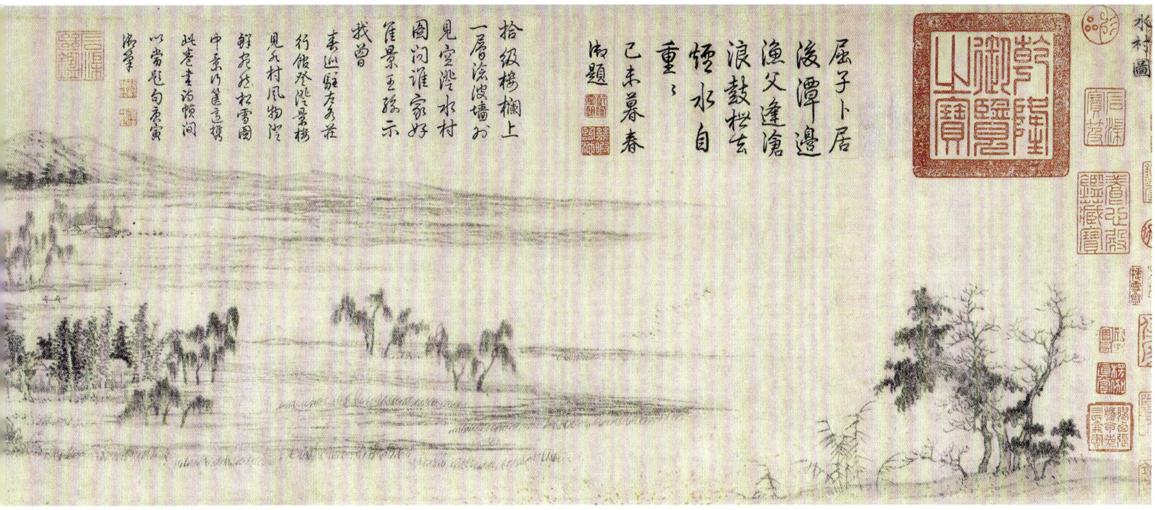

distinguished from private or family biography (*bie zhuan*), which was written for the family cult and preserved as clan records. These last, termed "social biographies" by Nivison,[37] contributed a number of literary forms to the memorial scroll. Most important was the record (*ji*) and the preface (*xu*), whose purpose was to explain the subject, to situate him in time and place, and to enlarge on an event or motive. The *bian* was another exegetical type, often used to discuss the origin of a *biehao* (literary name, sobriquet, assumed name). Funerary forms included the eulogy, epitaph, and elegy. These had the serious task of acknowledging the quality of a person's character and were marked by a tone both mournful and moralizing. Prose essays and poems could offer congratulations to the recipient in a celebratory mood or condole with him. Honorific prose required an experienced writer capable of nuanced levels of formality and adulation. The information necessary to compose these essays was supplied by the honorand's family in the form of a *xingzhuang* (similar to a curriculum vitae). This essential gathering of facts could be compiled by a family member or a disciple of the deceased but for great personages might be written by an official of the History Office. If these tasks were performed by someone other than a family member, he merited a reward, and as far back as the Tang dynasty many unappointed scholars made a living as writers of honorific pieces. This became an effective precedent for painters who sought to make the tradition that served writers also serve for painters.

Several of the occasions for composing a written congratulatory work carried over into memorial painting, especially when an eminent figure celebrated a rite of passage, of which the most important were success in the civil service examinations, appointment or promotion in the official hierarchy, and, finally, retirement from office. These turning points in an official career

16 Zhao Mengfu (1254–1322). *Water Village* (*Shui cun tu*), 1302. Handscroll; ink on paper, 24.9 × 120.5 cm. Palace Museum, Beijing. See also figure 17

were of the first consequence, duly reported to the ancestors and acknowledged by family and friends. But so also were lesser social occasions that might have meant almost as much to the recipient, such as literary meetings, departures and arrivals, excursions and travels, the celebration of festivals, and, far outstripping all others, the building of a new house or study pavilion.

Paintings and inscriptions were both ostensibly composed as private documents directed to a private person and to members of his family, including his descendants. It was understood that their audience also extended to men of his own education and standing, but, even then, only to those he invited to see them. Some of these forms showed up on the memorial scroll–cum–painting beginning roughly in the eleventh century, as was the case with the departure scene, and even earlier, as with the literary gathering and the theme of estate, house, or study.

The subject of estate, house, or study persisted with such tenacity because it arose from the fundamental instinctive devotion to home that in China was further conditioned by centuries of Confucian teaching on loyalty to the family. From early times it was believed that, on his death, a person's remains should be returned to the region of his birth for burial, and it was a filial obligation upon his sons to see that this duty was fulfilled. Even when it could not be, loyalty to and affection for the ancestral home bore inescapably on all descendants. We will examine three very different instances of such memorials in the fourteenth century: *Water Village*, made for a schoolmaster by Zhao Mengfu (1254–1322); the large set of paintings organized by Gu Dehui (1310–1369) for himself, now lost but recorded; and Xu Ben's (1335–1380) refuge away from home in the last fearful days of the Yuan dynasty, *Thatched Hut on Mount Shu*.

Water Village (*Shui cun tu*) (fig. 16), an extraordinarily beautiful painting, belongs to a genre that quite properly had an ancient ancestry and an extensive and important progeny.[38] It was the first estate or house painting to be cast in the tranquil, unpretentious style of Dong Yuan (active 930s–960s), a style ideally fitted to the personal and subjective mood of retirement. Its commonplace Jiangnan scenery and absence of tension match the prevailing idea of reclusion and escape from political and commercial burdens to a life given over to private interests. The great beauty of *Water Village* arises from an engaging simplicity and ease unmatched in any other Yuan painting. The slow drift of land spits and drawn-out horizontal lines convey a sense of serenity and uneventfulness. The terrain fades out at the margins, the fabric of the brushwork is intermittently transparent, and the whole image at times materializes out of the mist and at times vanishes back into it. Zhao Mengfu must have aimed quite consciously at this miragelike effect: its shadowy forms are suited to the portrait of a reticent man. Since the house had not yet been built in 1302, the picture was in every way a figment of the imagination. Painter and patron both knew the site but could only envision the house (fig. 17). Thus the painting was literally as well as figuratively a substitute for the real thing, and the owner, Qian Dejun (*zi*, courtesy name, Zhongding, late thirteenth century to after 1324), did not actually acquire a house and dwell in it until twelve years after he had received the painting. In the meantime, he contented himself with the picture, carried it about with him, and tirelessly collected colophons for it whenever he could prevail on some eminent friend or student to write for him. In 1314, he finally retired to the country and moved into the thatched house built for him on Fen Lake by his friend Lu Xingchi (1275–after 1349).

Many memorial scrolls, perhaps the majority, acquired their colophons gradually over a period of several years, as did *Water Village*. Relatively few were inscribed at literary meetings or on the spur of the moment because such meetings were difficult to arrange and, though the stamp of aesthetic spontaneity was aimed at in calligraphy and painting, it is actually hard to catch with an expectant crowd watching every brushstroke. Moreover, much information had to be gathered beforehand from the recipient and others and coordinated with the various contributors to the scroll. The inscriptions often appear surprisingly unified in subject and style, but that is because the writers were familiar with the themes and tone of the literary memorial as a social institution and knew whom they addressed and the traditional topoi to pursue. One of the earliest of these "compendium" scrolls, *Water Village* appeared at the very beginning of the fourteenth century and eventually accumulated some forty-eight colophons of Yuan date. A year after Zhao Mengfu had presented the scroll to him, Qian Dejun wrote

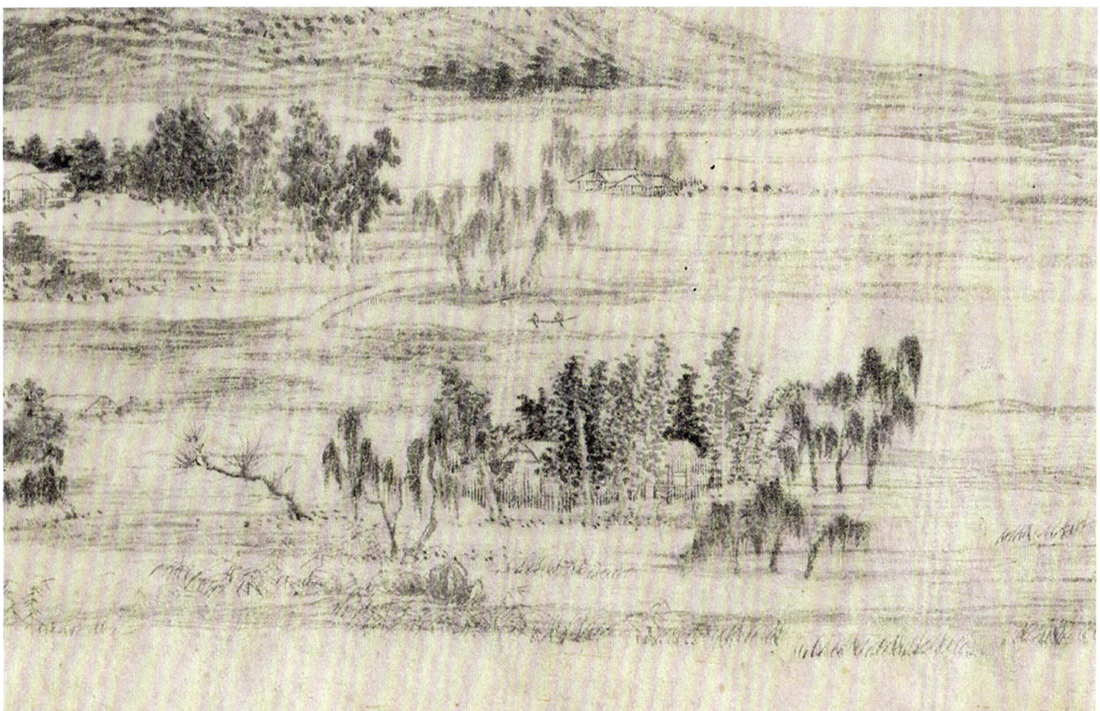

17 Zhao Mengfu (1254–1322). *Water Village* (*Shui cun tu*), 1302. Detail of figure 16

a *fu* poem on the picture celebrating the beauty of the site but, as there was still no house, did not yet invite anyone to contribute a preface or explanation.[39] A year after the house was finished, the need for a literary counterpart became clear, and in 1315 he composed two expository essays that were fairly detailed accounts of how the house came into existence and his great pleasure in it.[40]

Thus, in the early Yuan dynasty, the commemorative scroll began to gather in its wake a long train of literary complements. Almost immediately, these were regarded as a necessary adjunct to the memorial painting, in part for the additional information they supplied about the honorand and the occasion celebrated and in part because they gave witness to the collegial spirit in which the scroll was conceived.

It is peculiar to memorial painting that its contemporary colophons only remark in passing on the painter and are otherwise exclusively devoted to the owner of the work and his worldly, scholarly, and personal accomplishments. Questions of art history are scarcely mentioned, as they usually have no direct bearing on him. *Water Village* is exceptional in this respect because six of the colophon writers interrupt their compliments to Qian Dejun long enough to compare the painting to Wang Wei's *Wangchuan tu*. In the writing of modern art historians, these brief comparisons have been taken to mean that the *style* of the two paintings was similar. But we should remember that Western art historians of the twentieth century have been almost exclusively preoccupied with the history of style in Chinese painting to the neglect of its content. The repeated comparisons with the *Wangchuan tu* cannot be reasonably explained as a point of style—the two images have little, if any, stylistic likeness. However, the comparison becomes transparently clear if the *Wangchuan tu* is invoked as the earliest prototype known to the Yuan writers on the subject of a scholar's private estate. This is the overriding theme of *Water Village*, of its colophons, and of the very large number of commemorative landscapes that followed it. The main reason of the colophon writers for bringing up the *Wangchuan tu* is that the subject of estate, house, or study implying ownership of the land was newly attractive again in the early fourteenth century. In the prevailing political conditions, when the land was occupied by invaders, the comparison was possibly even more compelling than before. If the subject had been commonplace at that time, it would not have been mentioned at all.

Zhao Mengfu may well have been largely responsible for this decisive turn away from Song preoccupation with the natural world to a new concern with man and his social condition. In Zhao's oeuvre, there are no fewer than eleven paintings whose titles imply that they belonged to the house/study/estate category.[41] The most important comment on the history of *style* to be found in the inscriptions on *Water Village* is a single comparison to Dong Yuan, offered by the Suzhou native Qian Liangyou (1278–1344).[42] This does refer to its style and specifically to the detached impressionistic brushwork moving casually over the surface as if unplanned. The language of the Yuan and Ming writers is extremely succinct, especially in stating the subject of a discussion, and does not always indicate clearly whether the writer is speaking of iconography or of style. Their comments must be interpreted according to both the historical and pictorial contexts.

Water Village is a full-fledged memorial scroll with a full complement of literary ornaments, so close in style to later Yuan works of the kind that it may claim to be their origin or at least their inspiration. A great number of them ensued after 1302, setting off a flurry of pictures in this genre and, in one important case, a unified series of paintings and poems made to celebrate the life and estate of a single patron. As bad luck would have it, not one of these paintings has survived, but David Sensabaugh has written two accounts of their history, based on the literature, and of Gu Dehui, the patron who conceived the enterprise.[43] From these I have drawn the following account of the Yuan memorial landscape painting writ large by Gu Dehui, a man with the means and ambition to do it. Gu came from a wealthy landed family and in middle life built an estate in Kunshan, a market town in the eastern suburbs of Suzhou, where the social events he conducted became the chief business and record of his life. Quite deliberately, he followed the pattern laid down in the records of the most famous literary gatherings of the past, especially the "Orchid Pavilion" and the "Elegant Gathering in the Western Garden." Each of the twenty-eight major sites and buildings was recorded in poems and a painting executed by his guests, and the estate was celebrated at receptions to which Gu Dehui invited the literary lions who passed through Suzhou. Each painting was accompanied by a preface, a record, and a suite of poems, and was stored at the appropriate site. This series was gathered together under the title *Records of the Surpassing Scenery of Jade Mountain* (*Yushan mingsheng ji*), edited and published by Gu Dehui. Gu also arranged pictorial and literary records illustrating one of his receptions, held in 1348, which he titled *Picture of the Elegant Gathering at Jade Mountain*. He commissioned Zhang Wu (active ca. 1336–ca. 1364) to make the painting in the *baimiao* style of Li Gonglin, and Yang Weizhen (1296–1370) to write a preface, insistently modeled on the tradition of the "Elegant Gathering in the Western Garden." Still other literary records were edited or supported by Gu and were published so that scholarly circles in and beyond Suzhou might know of his accomplishments. He valued the integrity of the collections sufficiently so that in 1356, when some of the records and paintings were destroyed by marauding soldiers, he insisted that they be copied and replaced in their proper halls.

From this carefully recorded collection we know that Gu Dehui envisioned a comprehensive, systematic work combining art and literature and aimed at nothing less than a personal memorial that could be described as monumental. In defense of Gu's character, David Sensabaugh argues that he was only a host who arranged the occasions for painting and composing, rather than a patron who actually commissioned works. But Sensabaugh also allows that Gu was by habit always "choosing exemplars and playing a role."[44] He was certainly the most munificent and exacting recipient of the Yuan period. It is quite possible that he was also a patron in the full sense of the word.

Contemporary with the activity of this wealthy and determined collector, a small group of young scholars not appointed to government service congregated in Suzhou, calling themselves the "Ten Friends of the North Wall," after the district where most of them lived. They are of interest to art history because, though all belonged to the

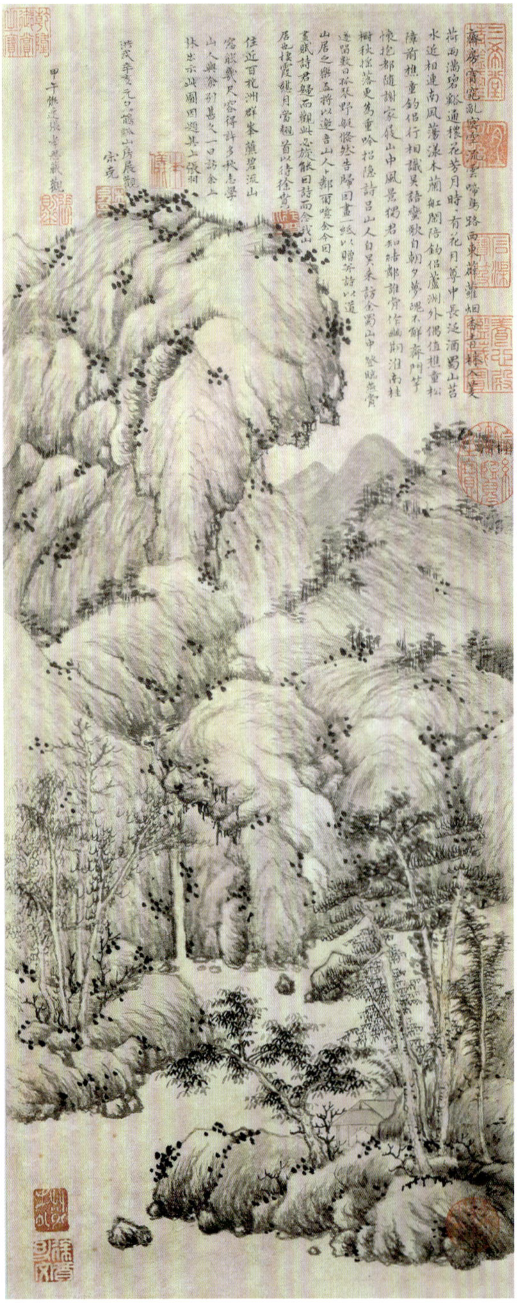

literati class and hoped for appointment to government office, five of them who were skilled in poetry and painting were once able to record their personal histories briefly on the same painting, *Thatched Hut on Mount Shu* (*Shu shan tu*) (fig. 18).[45] In *The Poet Kao Ch'i*, Frederick Mote gives an account of the Ten Friends and the precarious circumstances in which they lived.[46] Educated for government service and driven by political ambition, they were constantly obstructed by lack of opportunity and by the suspicions of both the legitimate Yuan government and the warlord Zhang Shicheng (1321–1367). The local political situation was further complicated by a third contender for the mandate, Zhu Yuanzhang (1328–1398), who would eventually prevail and become the founding emperor of the Ming dynasty. In the 1360s, Zhu was maneuvering in the hinterland with his eye on Suzhou, and the Ten Friends regarded him as an outright rebel.

About 1364, the circle of the Ten Friends of the North Wall began to break up, the members casting about for opportunity and, when that failed, taking refuge in reclusion. Two of the painters, Xu Ben (1335–1380) and Zhang Yu (1333–1385), decided on solitude as the better part of wisdom and withdrew to the Wuxing Mountains, where they built thatched huts on adjacent hills and settled down to study. At Xu Ben's request, Gao Qi (1336–1374), the leader of the Ten Friends, wrote a commemorative essay on the opening of Xu's mountain study:

My friend Mr. Xu is the owner of the study on Mount Shu; that is the place in which Youwen [Xu Ben's *zi*] pursues his studies. Youwen has written me a letter

18 Xu Ben (1335–1380). *Thatched Hut on Mount Shu* (*Shu shan tu*), before 1371. Hanging scroll; ink on paper, 66.3 × 27.3 cm. National Palace Museum, Taipei

from Wuxing saying: "Mount Shu is east of the city a few miles. My house on the mountain consists of a few rooms. The books in my room consist of a few volumes. The mountain, although small, is exceedingly beautiful. The house, although rustic, is roughly adequate. The books, although not numerous, are enough to provide me with reading. I shall complete my studies here. Would you do me the favor of writing a commemorative piece about this for me?…" Youwen possesses talents that could be employed. Yet he is not hasty in his pursuit of advancement and reward; rather he devotes himself to study in order to seek knowledge beyond that which he has yet encountered. Is this not a scholar of great purpose? And myself—beyond the northern wall I have some land. At home in the eastern village I have books. Both were left to me by my forebears. Encountering times of many troubles, I have left the land to fall to weeds and thorn, have left the books to deteriorate through dust and insects. Blindly I rush about doing unimportant things, not knowing [how] to return to reason. Such frantic, unworthy conduct shames me before Youwen. Who am I to write this commemorative essay for him? Nonetheless, not refusing him, I have written this because I did not want to deny his request, and also in order to spur myself on thereby.[47]

Gao Qi especially commends Xu for taking the high path to learning, the better to prepare himself for office in the future, but still wonders where to turn himself. Thereafter another one of the Ten Friends, Lü Min (later fourteenth century), paid a visit to Xu Ben on his hilltop and stayed for several days. Xu Ben seized the opportunity to persuade him to settle on the mountain, too. Reclusion was an admirable position to adopt, but its price was loneliness.

Xu Ben's Dedication
Lüshan ren [Lü Min] came from Wu [Suzhou] to visit me on Mount Shu. He climbed up to "Delight of Swallows Cliff" and lingered several days. We enjoyed ourselves with a single *qin* and a country skiff until he declared he had to go. I painted a picture for him and composed a poem recounting the pleasures of my mountain dwelling. [I hoped] to persuade this mountain man to build a house next door to me, but alas [he could not]. Now when he goes home and looks at the painting and poem he will return, for they will remind him of my mountain house. We will perch on a sunset cloud and wait for the moonlight. I await him eagerly.—Xu Ben[48]

呂山人自吳來訪余蜀山中，登臨燕賞。遂留數日。孤琴野艇，倏然告歸。因畫一紙以贈。并詩以道山居之樂，蓋將以邀吾山人卜鄰爾。噫。余今因畫賦詩。君歸而觀此。必旋能因詩而念我山居也。棲霞憩月。當翹首以待。徐賁

When Lü Min declined to join him in reclusion, Xu composed for him a painting of his house and a poem, pleading the beauty of the mountain and begging Lü to remember him when he looked at the picture. Lü carried the painting home, and, a little later, Zhang Yu, also a poet and painter, wrote a poem and inscription on it in the same lyrical spirit, explaining that Lü Min had called on him to show him the painting so that he too might make a contribution. In 1371, still another member of the Ten Friends, Song Ke (1327–1387), wrote a date and a short statement on the scroll when it was shown to him in the "Crane and Gourd Study."[49] The actual date of execution of *Thatched Hut on Mount Shu* must fall between 1364, when Xu Ben built his study there, and 1371, when Song Ke inscribed the scroll.

The poems written for *Thatched Hut on Mount Shu* describe it in glowing terms, extolling its serene and beautiful site and the splendor of the mountain views in autumn. But the painted image reveals massive hills looming over the little mountain house, which is so deeply buried in the landscape it can scarcely be seen. Indeed, the owner seems to be incorporated into his library, which now functions as his symbol and equivalent—a metonym for him. We must wonder at the sharp contrast between the serene temper of the poems and the oppressive painted image. The history recorded on Xu Ben's painting is like a literary gathering at which the guests failed to arrive, but later and severally contributed their thoughts in an effort to preserve some semblance of a coherent society. Owing to the disturbances of the late Yuan and early Ming period, only two of them actually met together on Mount Shu, but the painting survived as a record of friendship maintained in a time out-of-joint.

The appearance and growing popularity of commemorative landscape art among the Yuan literati was stimulated in part by the Mongol occupation, which left most of the Chinese literati without official appointments or means of income. Disturbed at the disorder around them, they took refuge in seclusion or formed groups that promised the company and support of their own kind. Poems and paintings were a solace against the Mongol presence, a reminder that they shared the same views and ambitions and might yet live to see them realized. With the founding of the Ming dynasty, some of the Ten Friends achieved a part of their ambitions, serving under the Hongwu emperor (r. 1368–1398); others, among them Xu Ben, Gao Qi, and Zhang Yu, fell victim to the terror that darkened his reign.

Of all the important occasions in a scholar's life that were felt to deserve recognition, success in the government examinations and promotion through the ranks of the civil service were foremost. Government office was, of all careers, the most taxing and the most unpredictable, but nothing else equaled it in rewards, influence, and prestige. Countless memorial scrolls record the struggles of candidates to win the prize. We shall consider three addressed to men at different stages in government service.

Near the bottom of the official ladder was the obligation to perform corvée service at government command in a great variety of tasks, from road building to secretarial service. A young man by the name of Zhou Zimei[50] was summoned for this duty in the heat of autumn. To mark the occasion, someone unknown today presented him with a painting by Ni Zan (1301–1374), one of China's greatest masters. The painter titled it *Lonely Stream and Winter Pines* (*Youjian hansong zhou*) (fig. 19)[51] and wrote its only colophon, dedicating it to Zhou Zimei. Ni tells us that he composed this frozen image of pines in winter for Master Zhou about to depart from his family home and friends. As the autumn weather was hot and the forthcoming journey could only be distasteful, Ni Zan began by commiserating with him:

The heat of autumn is so heavy and oppressive
The traveler shuns the road ahead.
The wind soughs amid pines and streams,
Cool shade blankets the courtyard door.

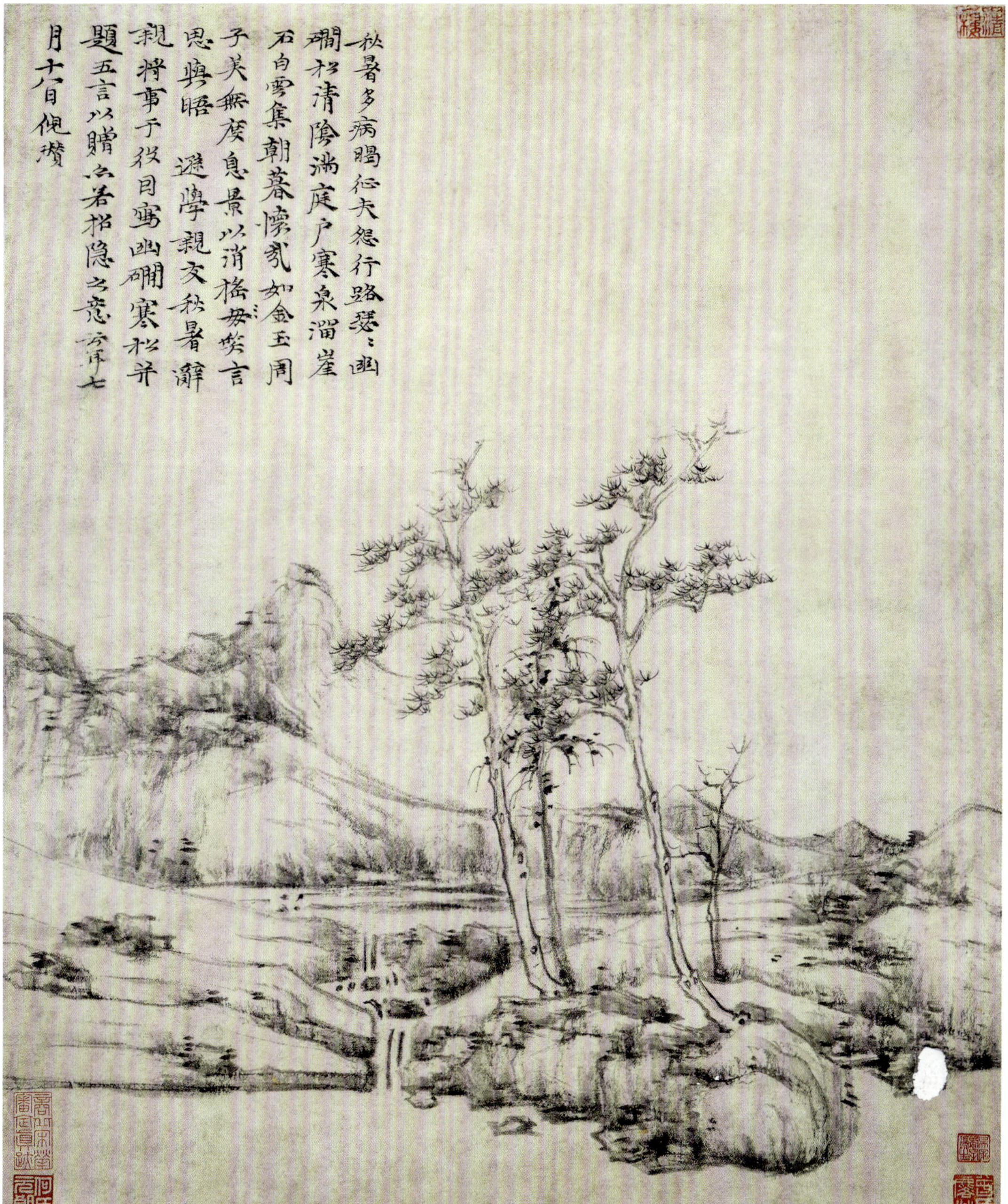

19 Ni Zan (1301–1374), *Lonely Stream and Winter Pines* (*Youjian hansong zhou*). Hanging scroll; ink on paper, 59.9 × 50.4 cm. Palace Museum, Beijing

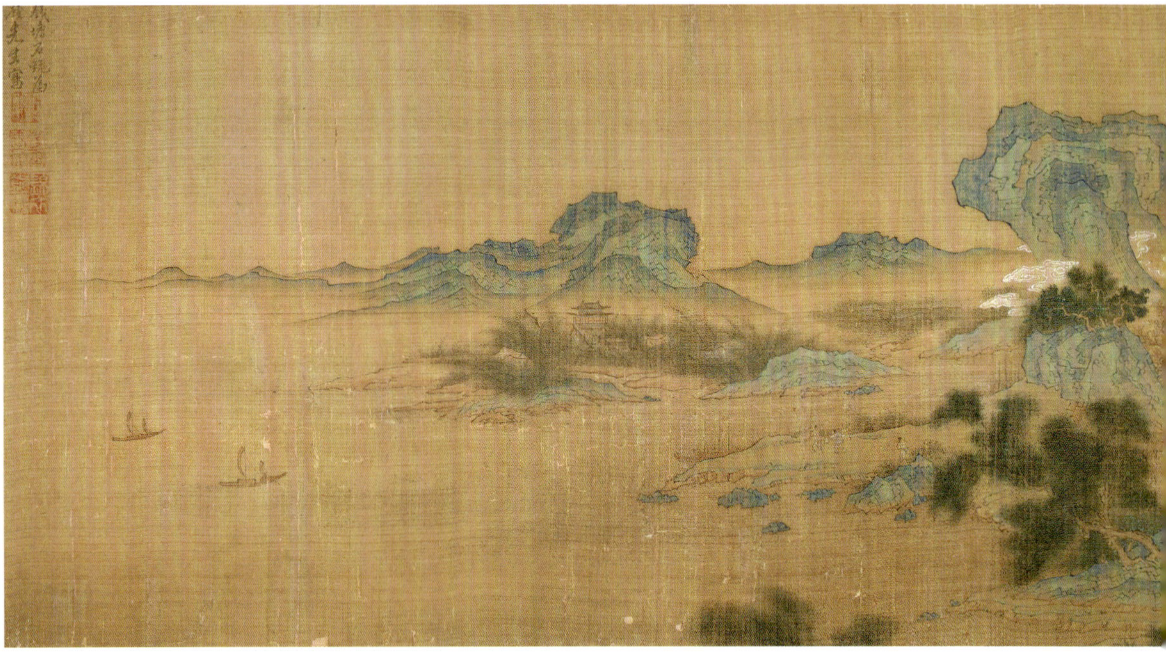

The icy stream flows over stony cliffs
Where white clouds gather morning and evening.
Ah, rare as gold and jade,
Zhou Zimei is incomparable.
Carefree he wanders back and forth,
And, laughing, utters whatever comes to mind.

Giving up his studies, Zhou Zimei leaves family and friends and in the autumn heat bids farewell to his parents. He goes to render corvée service. So I painted *Lonely Stream and Winter Pines* and added a five-character poem to send him—in the spirit of "Summoning the Hermit from Seclusion."[52]

秋暑多病暍，征夫怨行路，
瑟瑟幽澗松，清陰滿庭戶。
寒泉溜崖石，白雲集朝暮，
懷哉如金玉，周子美無度。
息景以消遙，笑言思與吾。

遜學親友，秋暑辭親，將事于役，因寫幽澗寒松并題五言以贈。亦若招隱之意云耳。七月十八日倪瓚

Ni Zan compares Zhou's appointment to the ancient poem "Summoning the Hermit from Seclusion," the title of one of the *Songs of Chu*. By the Yuan dynasty, the phrase "summons from seclusion" had become a euphemism for the reappointment in the civil service of a retired official, and it was used both seriously and sometimes sardonically in writing of the time. Ni Zan uses it in a kindly sense, comparing Zhou's modest rank and the task facing him to those of a senior official summoned by the emperor for some lofty responsibility.

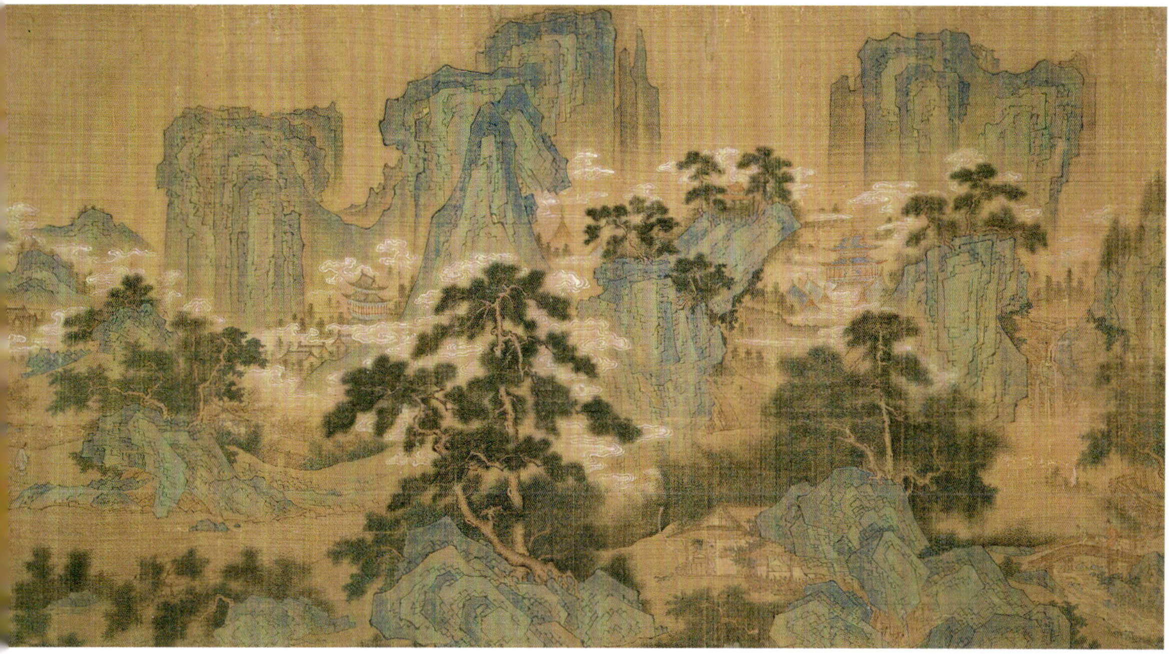

Ni Zan rarely adapted his very distinctive style to a specialized commemorative subject, though he painted a very large number of memorial works in his career. In his later years, after 1352, he had no settled domicile but lived an itinerant life. Most of his inheritance having been lost or plundered, he was forced to become an at least quasi-professional painter, which must have seemed a bitter fate to him, since he had grown up in easy circumstances. Nevertheless, patrons in search of memorial works were a boon to the professional master because they offered regular work even to a wandering painter. If we scan a list of the titles of Ni Zan's paintings, especially those made after 1350, we cannot escape noticing the large number dedicated to specific persons on special occasions and that, like the present painting, few of these have extensive colophons. This implies that Ni was no longer living in a settled, structured, social world, supported by friends who could supply literary complements, but was accepting requests for memorial paintings where he could find them and supplying the inscriptions as well as the pictures. Even in these sad late years his style remained steadily consistent, growing ever more spare and elegant with time. In this small quiet sketch of a landscape he has completely effaced the figure of the man honored, allotting the whole stage to the winter scene consoling Master Zhou for the hot weather he must shortly endure. As in his other commemorative works, Ni relied on the power of the word alone to convert the painting into a memorial and change its content from the study

20 Shi Rui (active ca. 1426). *Searching for Flowers* (*Tan hua*). Handscroll; ink and color on silk, 32.7 × 122 cm. Hashimoto Taotsu Collection, The Shoto Museum of Art

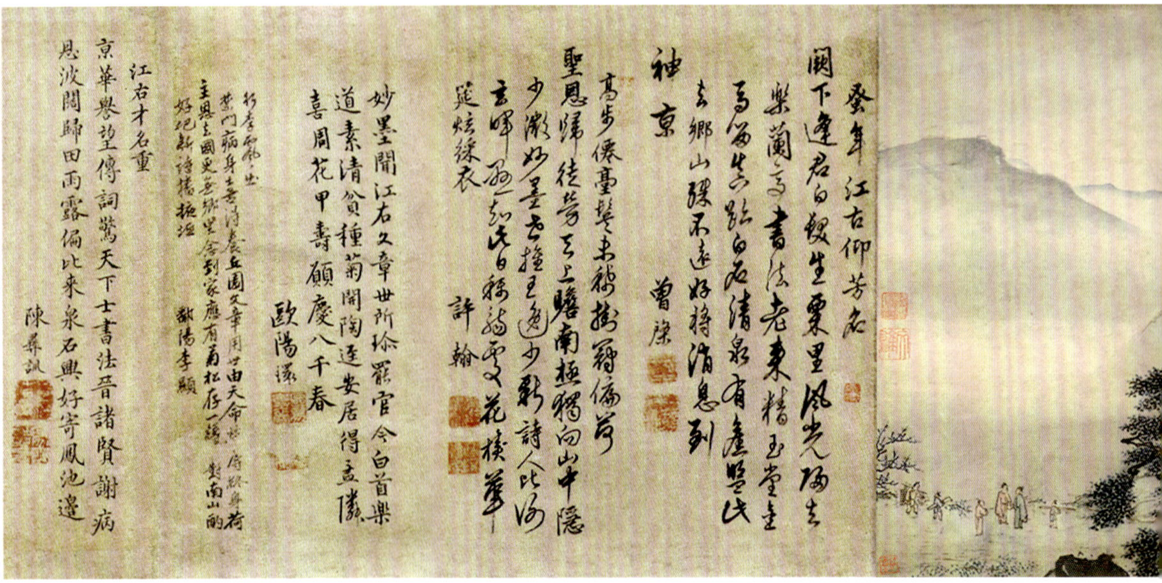

of nature to the concerns of a client. If by chance he had not written the dedication, we would not be able to deduce from the painting its original function.

At first sight, many honorific landscapes appear to be such simple unmediated studies of nature, without extraneous meaning imposed by the artist. Since these are not immediately recognizable as commemorative works, they are often taken to be landscapes pure and simple, unreservedly devoted to nature. I cannot help but wonder if some of these paintings were not, in fact, executed before the artist knew to whom they would eventually be dedicated and were only adapted to that purpose afterward by the inscription.

Another phase of the experience with government service is illustrated in Shi Rui's (active mid-fifteenth century) vivid handscroll in blue-green color titled *Searching for Flowers* (*Tan hua*) (fig. 20). *Tan hua* means seeking recognition for literary talent, "flowers" alluding specifically to distinguished writing. Shi Rui was a court painter when he executed this scroll in 1469 for a Master Gu who was setting out on a journey to sit for the civil service examination. Gu can be seen riding over the bridge in the lower right corner.[53] This is a rare example of the archaizing blue-green landscape style used for a memorial scroll. It was the imperial style par excellence, invented to represent Han and Tang palaces and hunting preserves and mythological Daoist themes. The style remained popular long after the Song dynasty, even into modern times, for the obvious reason of its visual appeal. The gaiety of the color, the lively rhythm of the hills, and the finely wrought brushwork attract attention and lend the picture a celebratory air in keeping with the message of good wishes to the candidate. The

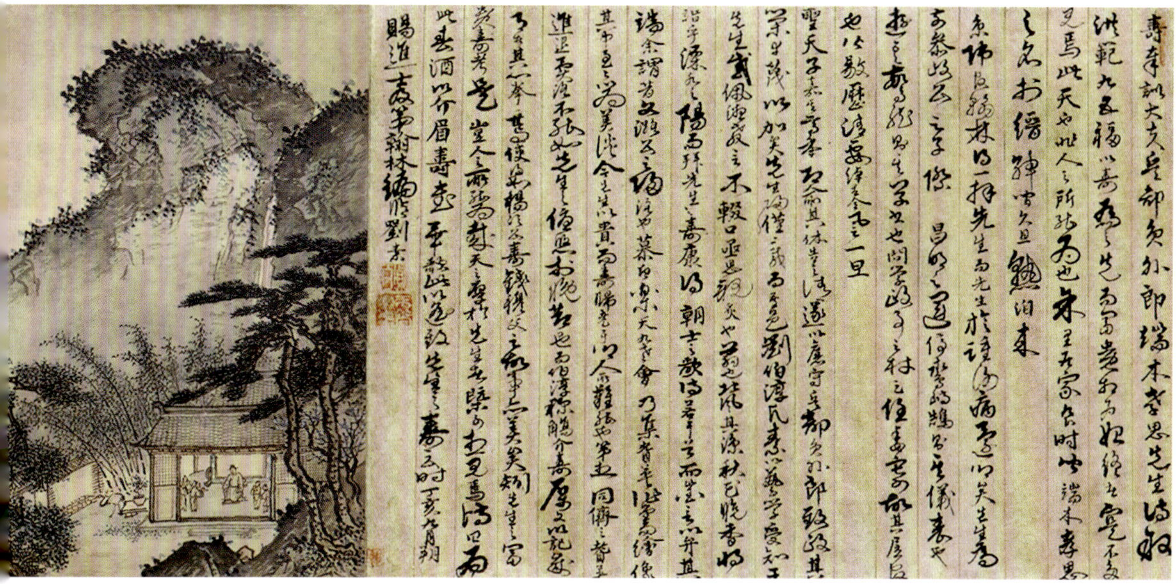

painter of the honorific scroll was not put off by the sporadic naturalism of the blue-green style because he was not in search of naturalism. What he sought was a triumphal mode that aroused the senses and the spirits.

Like other ancient styles adopted for the memorial scroll, the blue-green style developed a new content and was adapted to its unfamiliar task by the expedient of the literary metaphor, of which untold thousands had accumulated in the Chinese lexicon over the centuries. Shi Rui revives this style yet again, this time to wish success to a private person and to express hope that he will someday live like an immortal in paradise. Thus, by the adroit use of literary figures of speech in titles and inscriptions, the literati could turn painting styles once dedicated to Daoist institutions or for imperial use to the service of individual patrons.

An official's career in government service terminated, it was hoped, in a blaze of honors, gifts, and congratulations, which often included a memorial painting presented to him by his colleagues. Such was the successful conclusion of Duan Muzhi's (1347–after 1407) public service when he retired in 1407 on his sixtieth birthday and was presented with the handscroll *Congratulating Duan Muzhi on His Retirement* (*Gui tian zhu shou tu*) (fig. 21).[54] As a high official of the Hanlin Academy and the Board of War, Duan Muzhi merited a full-dress handscroll with painting and a whole panoply of literary ornaments that consisted of eight colophons offering good wishes and a preface explaining the occasion. The information offered is copious, highly creditable to Duan Muzhi, and is couched in flattering terms. All of it was, of course, well known to Master Duan and was addressed ultimately to the larger

21 Dai Jin (ca. 1388–1462). *Congratulating Duan Muzhi on His Retirement* (*Gui tian zhu shou tu*), 1407. Handscroll; ink and color on paper, 40 × 50.3 cm. Palace Museum, Beijing. See also figure 15

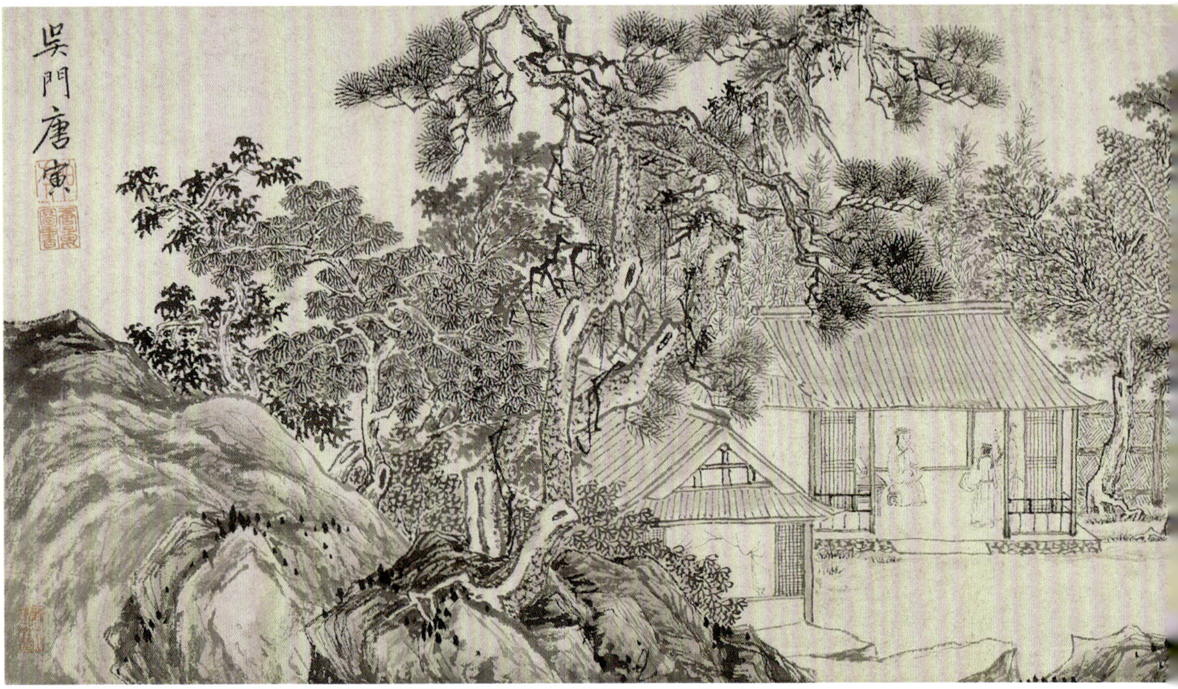

audience of his colleagues, not just to those who already knew him but especially to those to whom he would like to be known. He was a distinguished calligrapher, and, possibly because they knew he loved the visual arts, his associates elected to give him a painting and chose the painter Dai Jin (ca. 1388–1462) to execute it. At the time, Dai was only nineteen years old and at the threshold of his career, but so richly gifted that he would one day be accounted the founder of the Zhe school.[55] In a warm-spirited and attractive picture suited to the distinguished subject and the occasion of retirement–cum–anniversary, Duan Muzhi is presented as the official type most approved by society: a leader of men receiving the congratulations of Nanjing official circles as he retires from public service to a well-earned rest. He escapes the burden of government and withdraws to a convivial society and the private study of history and the fine arts. As Dai shows him, he is a near descendant of the literary gentlemen represented in the *Ten Poems* of ca. 1064 (pages 16–17), but the changes in the iconographical type of the "Song scholar" have been carried even further. The natural setting has expanded on all sides to enclose a simple thatched hut standing by itself deep in the country. The rusticity of the dwelling implies that Master Duan lived in "holy poverty," a verbal and pictorial cliché not to be taken at face value, for in the Yuan dynasty the thatched hut had become the conventional symbol of the abstemious life of the retired scholar. Conspicuous by

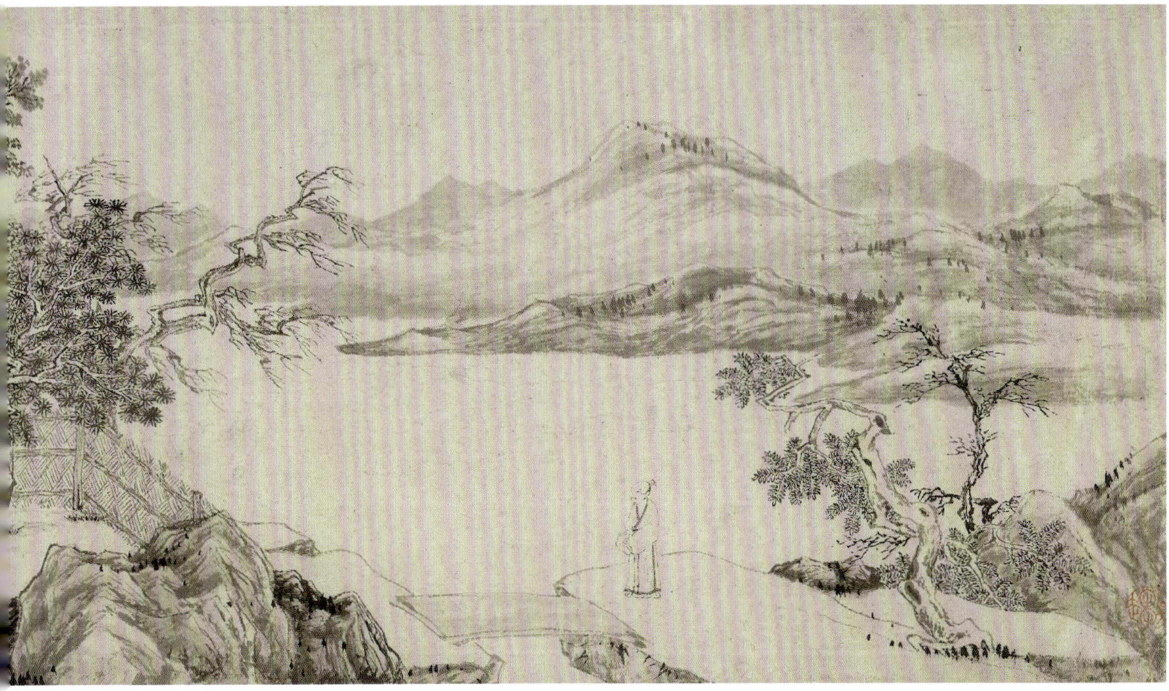

its absence is any sign of wealth, luxury, political power, or regret for his splendid past. In the rhetoric of the Yuan and Ming periods, the retired scholar is likened to a monk who lives without worldly luxuries and yet is utterly unaware of deprivation. Master Duan sits in an expansive pose, welcoming with genial warmth his guests, who arrive bringing a *qin* and scrolls that were probably calligraphies and possibly the honorific painting itself (see fig. 15). The last vestiges of the early Song style are the scale of Duan Muzhi's figure, just perceptibly larger than the guests, his central position, and the screen framing him.

This is an art of disguised portraiture in a staged setting—a portrait because the subject is a known historical personage, a monument because the colophons give witness to his merit. From the Yuan to the late Ming period, it was the preferred type of painted memorial, in which the subject secludes himself from notice while at the same time other men explain him to the world in written documents.

The category of commemorative scroll customarily called the *zhenshou tang* (hall of honorable old age) had a quasi-public character but was in use only at the village level. These scrolls were initiated and presented by local officials, often working with the local literati. The particular task of the literati was to compose poems to be inscribed on the scroll recording the occasion. This honor was offered in compliment to old women, often widows who had distinguished themselves

22 Tang Yin (1470–1524). *Zhenshou Tang*, 1486. Handscroll; ink on paper, 28.2 × 102 cm. Palace Museum, Beijing

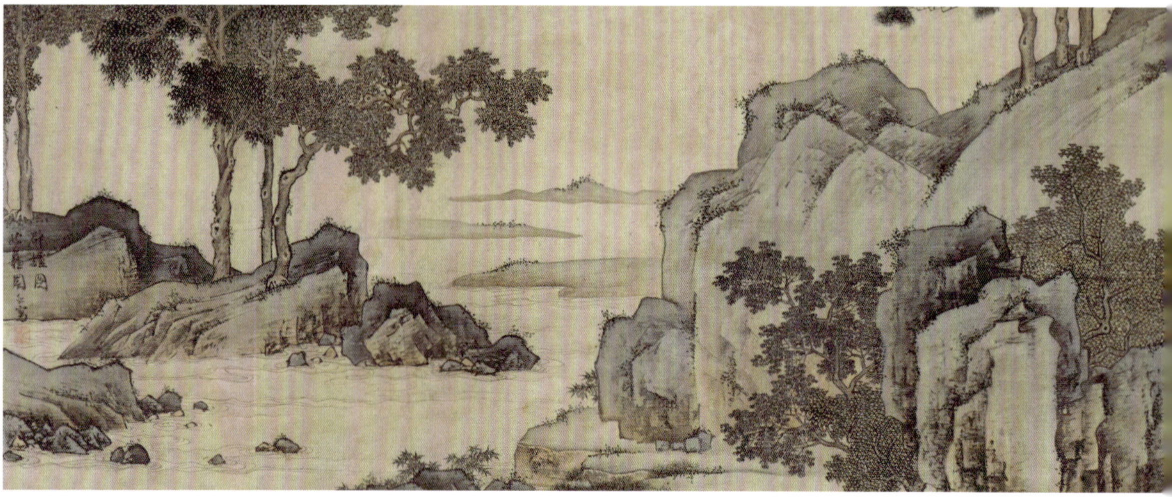

in service to their families, by the presentation of a plaque engraved with the characters *zhenshou tang* to be hung above the door of the house. The purpose of these collaborative events was to make a public display of the respect due to old age and to commoners who had shouldered more than their share of the social burden. The Suzhou literati organized such a scroll, named the *Zhenshou Tang* (fig. 22), for a Mme Zhou who was widowed early in marriage but had succeeded in bringing up and educating two sons by relying on her spinning. The honor was conferred on her when her older son passed the *juren* examination in 1486 and received an official appointment that enabled him to support the family. He, in turn, commissioned the painting for his mother to celebrate the end of their hardships, and the Suzhou community of scholars duly set brush to paper to seal the *zhenshou tang* with their approval.[56]

Mme Zhou is shown seated in her cottage, attended by her sons, with the all-important books that led to prosperity in evidence on the table.[57] She is in the same pose and setting conventionally used for scholar-gentlemen who have taken refuge in reclusion, and the cottage is surrounded by the customary idealized countryside, the piled-up rocks and tangled pines of the recluse's thatched hut. The city of Suzhou, where she lived, is nowhere to be seen but offers its homage in the figure of a lone scholar standing on the bridge benignly surveying the house of the selfless widow.

A committee of distinguished citizens arranged for seventeen colophons by leading poets and essayists of the local gentry to congratulate her; they included Shen Zhou (1427–1509), Wu Kuan (1436–1504), and the calligrapher Li Yingzhen (1431–1493), who wrote the preface explaining the occasion and may have stage-managed the whole enterprise. The senior members of society arranged such public demonstrations in part to encourage worthy persons as models for commoners and in part to engage in the search

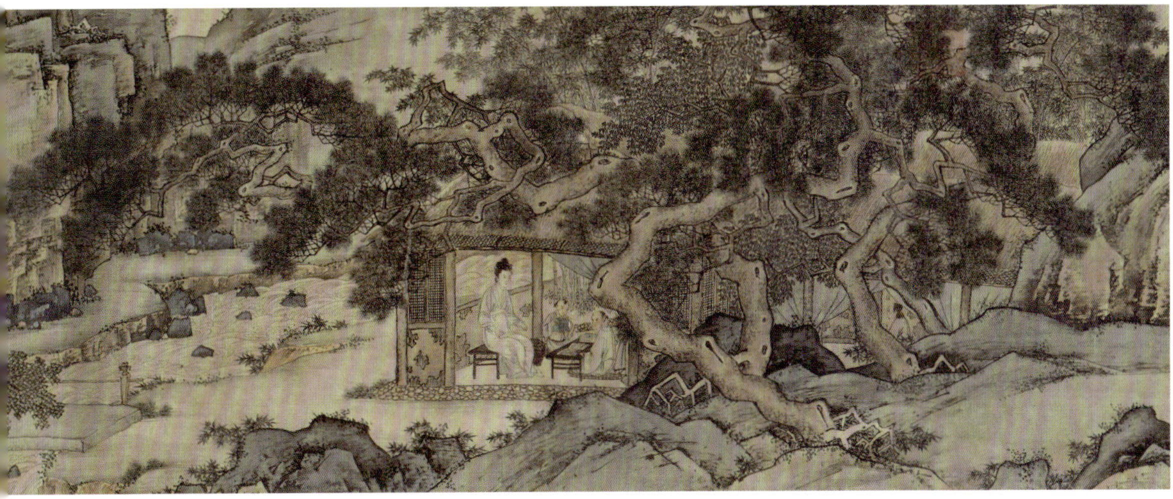

for talent, both of which they felt to be their civic duty.

When an honor of this sort was granted in Suzhou, where painting was valued almost as highly as writing, the memorial was sometimes expanded into a picture scroll and a local artist invited to execute the painting. Tang Yin (1470–1524) was sixteen years old in 1486 when he made this picture, which may well have been his first public performance. (We may note that Wen Zhengming [1470–1559], who was sixteen the same year, was invited to contribute an inscription that appears in sixteenth place on the colophon papers, in accordance with his junior status. Dai Jin received commissions for similar honorific works at the age of nineteen.)

The award of the *zhenshou tang* honor is not a common subject in commemorative painting: the only two examples I have come across are Tang Yin's handscroll, titled *Zhenshou Tang,* and a similar composition signed by his master, Zhou Chen (ca. 1455–ca. 1535), titled *Spinning Yarn* (*Pi lu*) (fig. 23). Shown here again is a specific domestic scene in which a woman appears to be listening to her sons recite a lesson while she continues a household task. She spins while they read, and she coaches them. A dense, luxuriant landscape crowds around a half-ruined cottage, alluding to their early poverty, whereas the woods opening out in a view over a river intimate an auspicious future. The compositional formula is an old one, offering a narrative stage on one side, where the story is told, and a landscape panorama on the other that serves as a sounding board. Tang Yin repeats the formula in reverse, but he is not yet capable of lending his picture the warmth and balance of his master. His method is distinctly eclectic, combining Zhou Chen's iconography and structure with Shen Zhou's brush technique and type forms: the foliage patterns, the stage-like platforms presenting the main actors, the stubby toylike figures. Tang Yin's *Zhenshou Tang*

23 Zhou Chen (ca. 1455–ca. 1535). *Spinning Yarn* (*Pi lu*). Handscroll; ink and color on silk, 31.5 × 159 cm. Tianjin City Art Museum

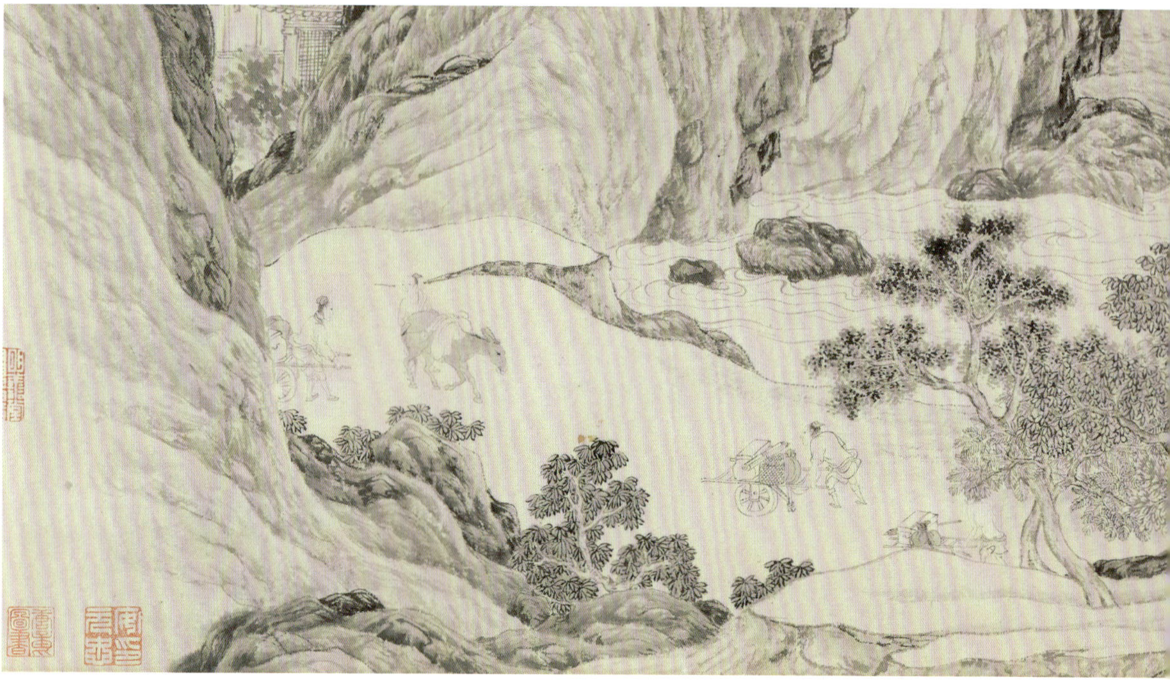

conclusively answers three long-standing questions about his early career: when did he begin painting, when did he become professional, and who was his first master? Evidently he had two, Shen Zhou and Zhou Chen, and their influence bore upon him at the same time, for in *Zhenshou Tang* he was already manipulating elements of both styles in response to a commemorative commission. He was probably at that time a formally accepted apprentice of Zhou Chen and a junior friend and protégé of Shen Zhou. Apparently he was also entertaining the possibility of two quite different careers, for in 1498 he suddenly abandoned the métier of painter, threw himself into preparation for the civil service examinations in Beijing, and astounded Suzhou and himself by taking first place in the *juren* exam. Almost at once he became entangled in a notorious examination scandal, lost the degree and the gamble for official appointment, and returned to Suzhou, grateful that he had begun to paint in his early youth and that his friends and advisors had already brought him forward in the role of painter.[58]

* * *

Among of the virtues of Wu school painting are the collegial spirit of its society and its readiness to disguise the sometimes prosaic and worldly function of commemorative art. The scholarly community was ready to assist gifted persons who could contribute to the local culture, of which they

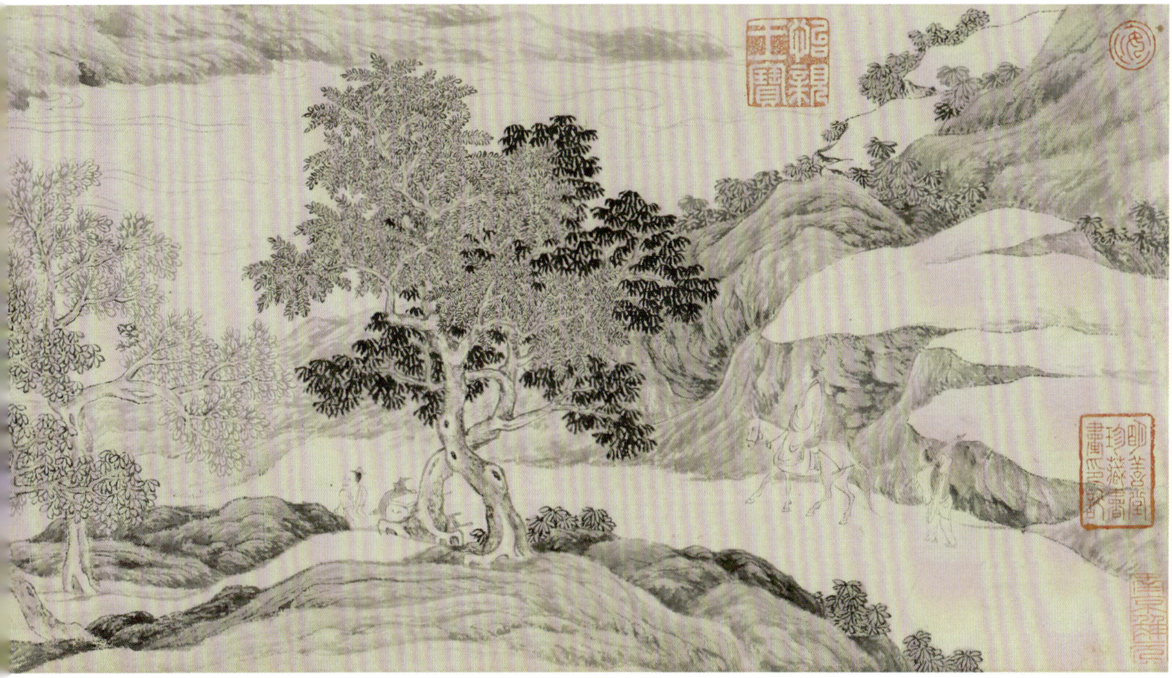

were deeply conscious and proud. In the early sixteenth century, Suzhou, then the wealthiest city in China and the city most deeply committed to the fine arts, also supported Yang Jijing (ca. 1477–1530), the scion of a family of professional musicians. The sheer number of paintings and writings dedicated to Master Yang implies a concerted effort by the donors to establish his reputation as a *qin* player and a historian of classical music and to introduce him to potential patrons. The families of Wen Zhengming and Tang Yin seem to have been the leaders in this undertaking: Tang painted what might be called a promotional handscroll for Yang, *The Southern Journey* (*Nan you tu*) (fig. 24),[59] on the occasion when he set out as a young man to look for a sponsor in Nanjing. Yang is presented to us as a gentleman, dressed in the scholar's robe and mounted on a donkey, while behind him a servant carries his instrument. The scroll was equipped with an explanatory preface and ten eulogies by famous Suzhou writers praising Yang's musical gifts, his graceful manners, his knowledge of Confucian studies. Assembled into a formal programmatic handscroll, the whole enterprise has something of the commendatory ring of a testimonial letter. The writers combine to support Yang Jijing as sponsors and to advertise him to the right musical circles: their aim is veiled in oblique and polished language, but it is clearly a letter of recommendation.

In this first portrait he made of Yang, Tang Yin shows him in rather literal terms, plodding along

24 Tang Yin (1470–1524). *The Southern Journey* (*Nan you tu*), 1505. Handscroll; ink on paper, 24.3 × 89.3 cm. Freer Gallery of Art, Smithsonian Institution, Washington, D.C. Purchase (F1953.78)

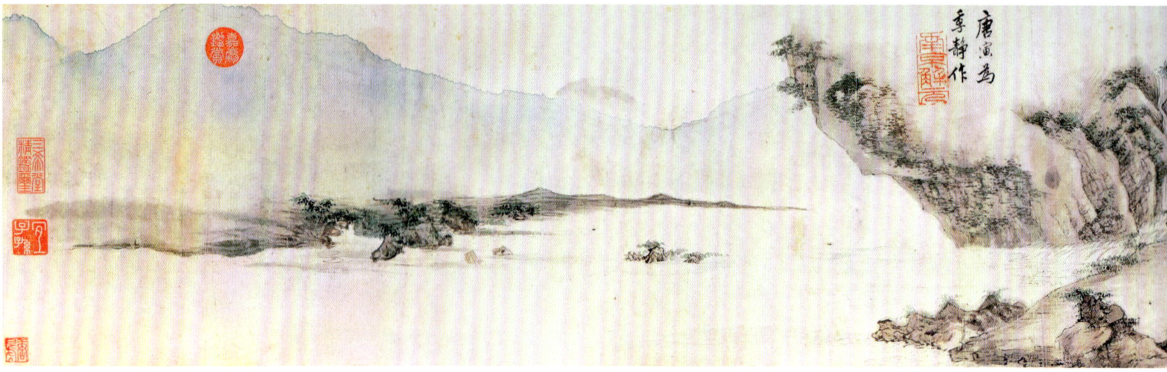

the road to Nanjing, passing farmers moving goods to and fro. The painting is nicely executed but has a commonplace air which does little to commend the young musician. It does not yet persuade us that he has exceptional gifts and could look forward to a brilliant future.

Fifteen years later, Tang Yin painted a second portrait of Yang Jijing, *The Lute Master* (*Hui qin tu*) (fig. 25), in which he interpreted the musician and his music in an entirely different light, calculated to convince the viewer he was in the presence of genius.[60] The date was 1520, when Yang Jijing had gained some success in his career and performed regularly at literati gatherings in Suzhou. This time he is noticeably older and has been given a garden setting appropriate to an established scholar, with an array of tea service, porcelains, and antique bronze vessels such as a Suzhou antiquarian might own. The colophons again trumpet his praises, but some of them hint that Yang still lived in precarious circumstances, so we must conclude that the gracious setting is an expedient fiction bestowed on him by the painter and that he still depended on the local circle of scholars for support.

The painting was made in the last years of Tang Yin's life, when his brush technique had become so loose and unrestricted that the images threaten to dissolve: a wavering light fills the air, the air invades the surfaces of things, causing them to seem to melt. The rocks on the hillside merge and flow like sea breakers, a cascade pours down the cliff behind the musician, and the figures are nearly transparent. Jiang Zhaoshen believes these motifs continuously moving and modulating in the terrain were intended as a visual metaphor for the effect of music.[61] The sacrifice of naturalistic detail in return for the impression of music itself evidently struck the painter as a good trade, for it put Yang before his public as an artist, not just a personality. Yang's figure has been similarly idealized, with an austere, fine-drawn face and a taut pose, as if he were possessed by his music (fig. 26). If we compare this romanticized image to the portraits of Yang made by the Wen painters, it is evident that these features were also imagined by the painter.

Wen Zhengming and his nephew Wen Boren (1502–1575) both made formal portraits of Yang Jijing, which also seem to have been intended to

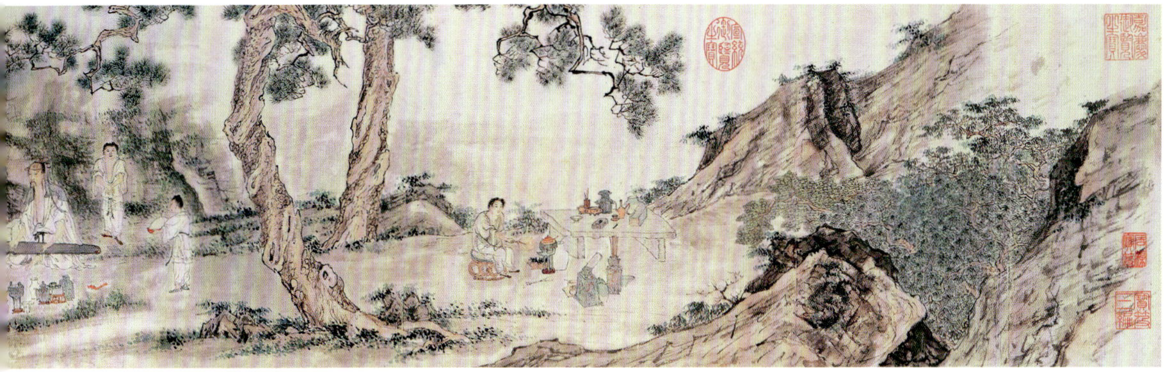

attract commissions.[62] They represented him as he would appear giving a recital in a music-lover's garden. Wen Boren's version of 1526 is a quite literal treatment, a *baimiao* figure curiously lacking expression. Wen Zhengming's, titled *Playing the Lute among Rocks and Banana Palms* (fig. 27), was executed in 1528 and, not unexpectedly, took up the historical aspect of the *qin*. On the upper section of the scroll he wrote out in fine *kaishu* (standard script) the whole of Xi Kang's *fu* on the *qin*. Later regarded as the patron saint of *qin* players, Xi Kang (223–262) was one of the Seven Sages of the Bamboo Grove, a connoisseur of *qin* music, poetry, wine, and the elegant air.[63] Wen's intention was to remind Yang's audience that he was, like some of them, an antiquarian and historian of ancient music as well as a performer.

In these four portraits executed by Wu school masters over a period of some twenty years, we recognize one of the major roles of commemorative painting—to aid a class of persons who could not easily advance themselves, but who were felt by members of the elite to contribute to the cultural wealth of Suzhou.

We have seen already in the career of Yang Jijing how a musician lacking private means fared in sixteenth-century Suzhou: he depended for almost his whole life on the assistance of patrons and fellow artists. Suzhou painters, doctors, and tutors without independent means were in the same situation. They constantly sought friends and patrons to underwrite their work and cultivated the acquaintance of persons who might use their services. Their situation was not very different from the literary specialists of the period who on request composed epitaphs, accounts of conduct, prefaces, colophons, explanations of *biehao*, and the many kinds of honorific writing called for in social exchange. Most literati could produce poems on request at social and literary gatherings, but the most admired writers in Suzhou constituted a small circle of which Zhu Yunming (1461–1527), Lu Can (1494–1551), and Wu Kuan, when he was in residence, were the stars. At least three of the painters—Shen Zhou, Tang Yin, and Wen Zhengming—were also members, regularly responding to requests for written as for painted memorials.

25 Tang Yin (1470–1524). *The Lute Master* (*Hui qin tu*). Handscroll; ink and light color on paper, 29.2 × 197.5 cm. National Palace Museum, Taipei. See also figure 26

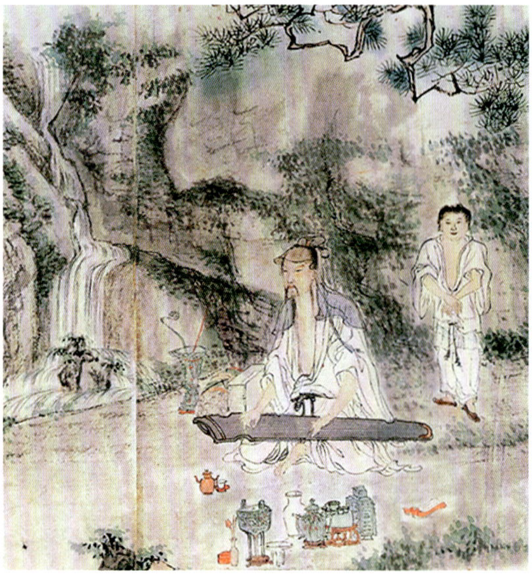

Over the last several years there has been increasing discussion of whether Chinese literati were paid or otherwise reimbursed for works of art, whereas it has long been understood that professional artists were paid as a matter of course. According to an old but unreliable tradition, a gentleman practiced his art only for self-improvement and personal discipline, but that rule had been breached many times since the Tang dynasty by authors of honorific prose and poetry. Ming literati without private means, like Zhu Yunming, Tang Yin, and Lu Zhi (1496–1576), not to mention several Yuan masters, were forced to rely on both their writing and painting for a living. Clear evidence of monetary exchange is hard to come by because no one wished to flout an old and honorable principle that he felt ought to be an inviolable rule. But evidence is beginning to accumulate that in Yuan and Ming times money was the preferred instrument of exchange. So far I have unearthed only one clear-cut example: when his father died, Wen Zhengming wrote to Wu Kuan, his father's close friend, requesting an epitaph. Wu answered, asking Wen to send the necessary information for the epitaph and then scolded him in advance, saying that he must not try to pay for it, for Wu would not allow it.[64] Actual practice regarding reimbursement held that exchanging gifts and favors was common and acceptable, but only relatives and close friends were exempt from obligation of some kind. The nature of the payment was never stated or discussed. The same rule may be applied to paintings generally and to biographical paintings in particular, because they originated in biographical literature and followed the customs of honorific writers.

An artist's obligations to a regular patron with whom he was on close terms included attendance at important affairs in the patron's private and official life at which his rank was marked by an assembly of noteworthy literati. His birthdays, receptions, and departures were recognized and required a written piece and sometimes a painting. Tang Yin's foremost patron was Wang Ao (1450–1524), who in 1506 was appointed grand secretary, then the highest office in the Ming government. Tang made up one of the company who attended him part of the way on his return to court. The party paused at the Great Wind Tower (*Gefeng tai*) at Peixian in Jiangsu, a famous historical site where Liu Bang (256–195 BCE), the founding emperor of the Han dynasty, had raised an army in the third century BCE to attack the Qin. Here Liu Bang received the jubilant people beside a well and composed "The Great Wind Song" preliminary to his advance into Qin territory:

26 Tang Yin (1470–1524). *The Lute Master* (*Hui qin tu*). Detail of figure 25

A great wind arises — billowing clouds fly;
His majesty dominating all within the seas,
he returns to his old home town.
Where can he find brave warriors to guard
the four directions?[65]

Subsequently a pavilion was built at the site of the ancient well in Peixian, and a stele set up engraved with "The Great Wind Song." By the sixteenth century, most of the characters on the stele had been obliterated, but that was of no consequence to the members of Wang Ao's party, as they knew it by heart and were overcome by nostalgia at the thought of the heroic poet who had composed it. Tang Yin sketched the site and explained its significance in an inscription written across the upper margin in a work titled *The Wind Song Tower at Peixian* (fig. 28).[66] His words remind us of Gao Qi, another Suzhou traveler who found moral lessons at ancient sites: "In response to the place, one thinks of the person and seeks an explanation of his successes and failures, his rise and fall. One cannot but be moved by it."[67]

Tang Yin's sketch has a striking immediacy, as if he intended that it should appear spontaneously rendered at a moment's notice, and yet he has clearly marked the specific passages that tell the story. The entrance to the courtyard, the ancient well where Liu Bang stood, and the base of the ruined memorial stele are forcefully drawn, in contrast with the dim, blurred brushwork of the rest of the scene. The sharp focus on these few points signals their importance: they are the signs essential to recognizing the place and its role in history. Thus this seemingly casual sketch is a topographical account, a mood study, and a meditation on history directly connected with

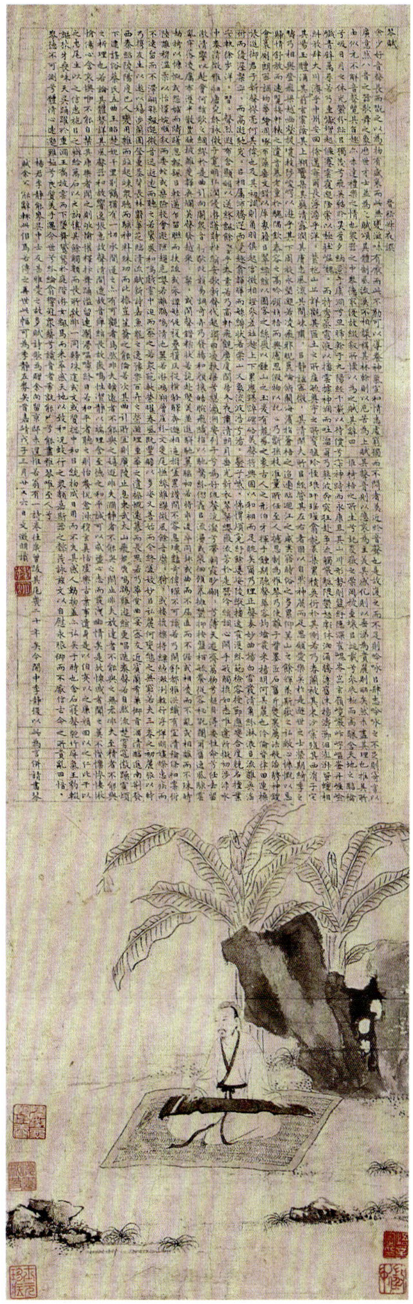

27 Wen Zhengming (1470–1559). *Playing the Lute among Rocks and Banana Palms* (*Portrait of Yang Jijing*), 1528. Hanging scroll; ink on paper, 84 × 27.2 cm. Formerly Wuxi City Museum

the experience of the artist and his patron. It was sketched in situ—an unusual procedure for a Wu school landscapist—and conveys an extraordinary sense of the reality of the occasion to the members of Wang Ao's party but lacks any trace of the ingratiating charm which Tang Yin could so easily summon up.

Of the ten or so paintings he made for Wang Ao over a period of thirty-five years, all were topical, or topographical, or portraits of the patron.[68] They treated places of interest to him or that figured in the Suzhou gazetteer (for Wang Ao was editor of that publication), as well as events in his private life and his very successful public career. The pictures still extant are couched in simple, straightforward, descriptive terms that do not wander from the subject at hand, although Tang Yin liked nothing better than to load a painting with literary and idealistic baggage. But he refrained from doing this in the pictures for Wang because he was well aware that Wang was of an existential and practical turn of mind, that he was an accomplished statesman at an unstable court, and that, when he returned to Suzhou, he concerned himself with local matters of public importance. When Tang painted for him, he was not speaking for himself or his own tastes but for the preferences and obligations of the grand secretary. It was intrinsic to the commemorative painting that it express the views, and hence the personality and mind, of the person honored; the painter was expected to remain in the background.

Despite their pervasive optimism and their inclination toward the ideal, the memorial painters were prepared to deal with subjects of adversity and even disaster, which they also accepted as real experience, the price paid for living and therefore to be recorded. These paintings too were saved in family archives so that descendants might know the true history of their ancestors. Elegiac paintings mourning the death of relatives and friends were fairly common, because they had been for centuries a major subject in literary biography. In Ming times, the devastating floods that repeatedly ravaged Jiangnan were recorded in paintings with a full complement of poems describing the particular calamity.[69]

The worst catastrophe that befell southeast China was the civil war that broke out during the 1350s and 1360s, when Zhang Shicheng and Zhu Yuanzhang fought for possession of Suzhou, their soldiers pillaging the farms and living off the land. In Jingxi, on the north shore of Lake Tai, a wealthy family named Wang found themselves caught

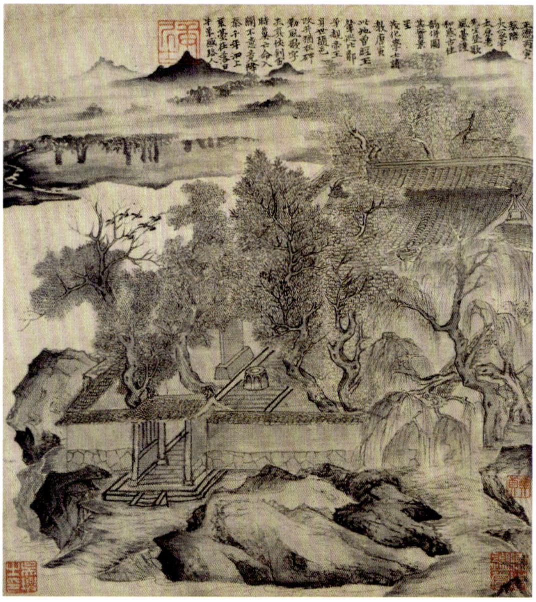

28 Tang Yin (1470–1524). *The Wind Song Tower at Peixian* (*Peitai shi jing ye*), 1506. Album leaf; ink on paper, 26 × 23.7 cm. Palace Museum, Beijing

between the battle lines of the opposing forces on an estate which had been in their family for three hundred years. The son of the family, Wang Yuntong (active mid-fourteenth century), realizing that they must soon seek refuge, commissioned the young painter Chen Ruyan (ca. 1331–1371) to make *View of Jingxi* (*Jingxi tu*) (fig. 29), so that the family might have a record of their estate.[70] In a colophon on the painting Ni Zan declares it the earliest surviving work by Chen Ruyan. The style is interesting chiefly for its deliberately prosaic rendering of the town: the compound of the Wang family is shown in the lower left corner among the trees on the near side of the Zhanqiao Bridge, which joins the two shores of the inlet. In this strangely impassive rendering, the only expressive feature is the disquieting emptiness and silence of the town.

Shortly before Zhu Yuanzhang took Jingxi in 1356, the Wang family at last abandoned their house and fled to safety within the walls of Suzhou.[71] Over the next two or three years, Wang Yuntong gathered twelve colophons from friends and relatives, many of whom had lived at Jingxi and took refuge with the Wang family. One of them was Ni Zan, who speaks of Jingxi as a site possessed of a "genius of place." The fine scenery and healthy air drew great people to settle there: Buddhist and Daoist monks who built temples, scholarly men who came seeking reclusion. The idea of a place having a felicitous nature sympathetic to man is a very old one in China, and this nature was thought to influence the mental and moral fiber of the inhabitants of the place. Ni Zan asserts the Wang family had benefited from this spiritual force, and so felt it the more keenly when they were driven off the land.[72] The colophons

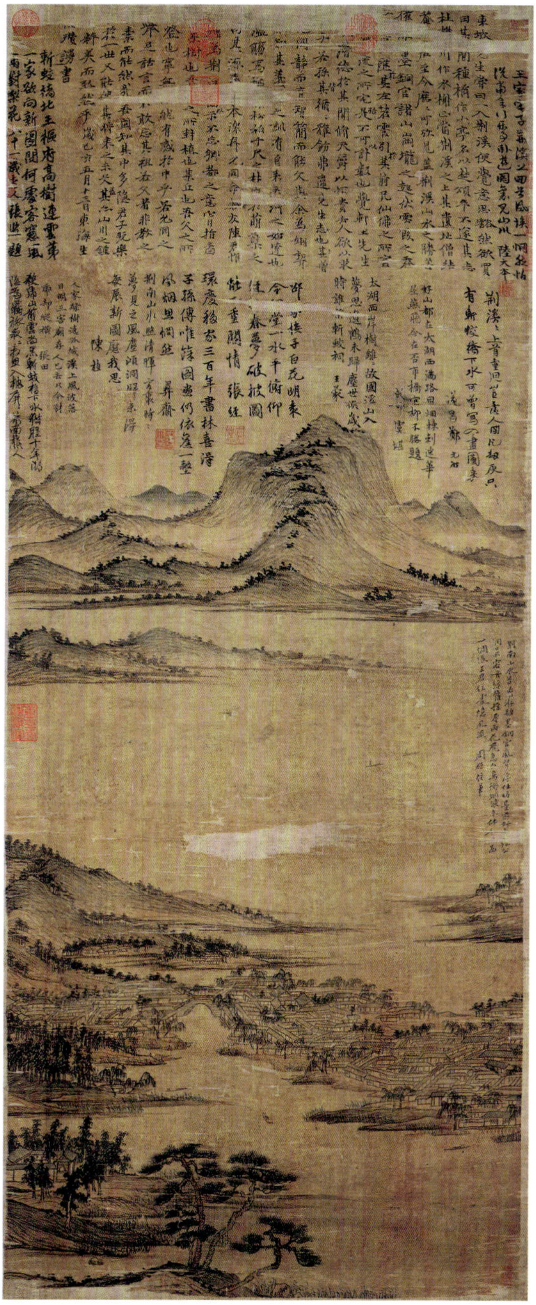

29 Chen Ruyan (ca. 1331–1371). *View of Jingxi* (*Jingxi tu*), 1359. Hanging scroll; ink on silk, 129 × 52.7 cm. National Palace Museum, Taipei

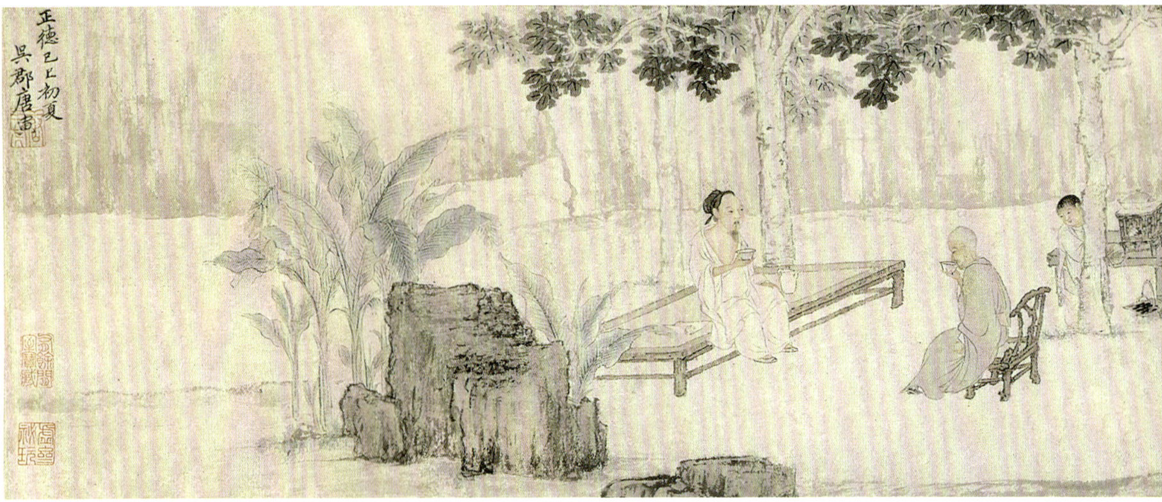

mourn their loss; in a poem, a cousin of the family describes the ruined buildings:

Colophon 4.
By good fortune its libraries had been passed down
through generations of sons and grandsons.
Now this painting is all that remains of them.[73]

書林喜得子孫傳。
惟餘圖畫仍依舊。

Another poem sounds a last ominous note alluding to the warring armies:

The Sanhai Temple still remains, but Zhou Chu
is already gone;
Now there are only the wolf and tiger crossing
paths.[74]

三害廟存人已去。
只今豺虎却縱橫。

Zhou Chu was a hero of the Eastern Han who had slain a water monster preying on the people of Jingxi. The poet laments that now there is no hero to defend them.

Claims for reclusion became increasingly formulaic in the Ming dynasty, which enjoyed peace for an extended period, and reclusion was often invoked simply to withdraw to private life without incurring disapproval. But withdrawal often had real meaning in the late Yuan dynasty, when the civil war sent many country families even deeper into the hinterland or to safety within the walls of Suzhou. Disasters like that at Jingxi were recorded in pictures and text, and the records preserved. But it should be remarked that the full horror and violence of civil war and the dreadful details of destruction are not disclosed in either the painted or the written record, nor are the particulars of the floods. Commemorative art exercised an unspoken rule of decorum limiting the direct expression of extremes of emotion.

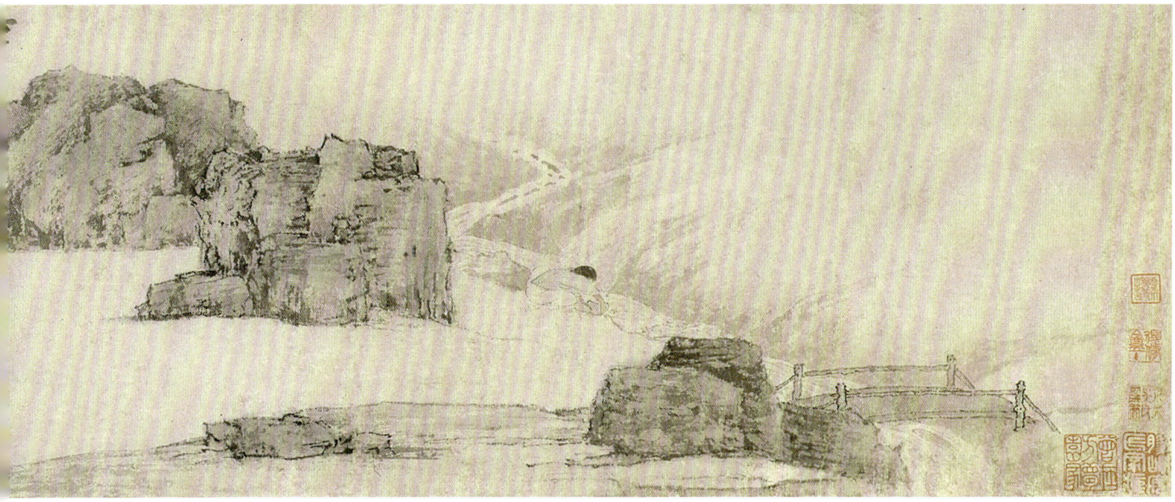

The question of the artist's expressive role in commemorative art looms larger as we consider in turn different kinds of memorial painting and their functions in Chinese cultural life. This question is quite separate from the matter of his artistic personality, his command of form, which he seeks to imprint—indeed cannot avoid imprinting—on the painting. He may, like Chen Ruyan, have been involved in the painting as a close friend of the Wang family, in the same predicament and suffering the same dangers. But the young artist of this mute painting suppressed any response he may have had to the experience of war. In the Yuan and Ming periods did the painter ever inject his own feelings or views into his work? Did he create such paintings in his own behalf? A partial answer can be derived from *The Bamboo Stove* (*Zhu cha lu*), or *Tea Drinking Under the Tong Tree* (fig. 30), a combined elegy and eulogy in prose, poetry, calligraphy, and painting, composed jointly by Zhu Yunming and Tang Yin to honor the memory of a man they both greatly admired and to whom both were indebted.[75] The subject of the scroll is Wu Kuan, the son of a Suzhou family of merchants who had prospered in the textile business and sent him to win lasting fame for them in the civil service. He spent thirty years in office in Beijing, and when at home in Suzhou he taught and sponsored promising students in literature and the arts. He dedicated his rare leisure hours to the cult of tea flourishing in Suzhou and to his collection of paintings and antiquities. To the Suzhou of his time Wu Kuan was the Confucian ideal of the *junzi* (gentleman).

One of his favorite antiques was the bamboo tea stove (fig. 31) that gave its name to this scroll. The picture originated in a set of poems on tea lore composed by Wu Kuan and sent to Zhu Yunming. Zhu answered him with a matching set of poems celebrating the tea sessions Wu Kuan shared with Binghe, a Buddhist monk and his

30 Attributed to Tang Yin (1470–1524). *The Bamboo Stove* (*Zhu cha lu*), 1509. Handscroll; ink and slight color on paper, 23.8 × 116.6. The Art Institute of Chicago, Kate S. Buckingham Endowment Fund, 1941.13. See also figures 31 and 32

"friend in tea." Thus, Wu Kuan was the subject of the memorial, but he was neither the recipient nor the patron. Wu died in Beijing in 1504, while still in office, and Tang Yin did not paint *The Bamboo Stove* until five years later in 1509. It is almost certain that he volunteered to do so or was invited by Zhu, for the two of them were accustomed to collaborate on honorific works and made a specialty of the "triple treasure," a scroll combining poetry, calligraphy, and painting.[76] Subsequently, Zhu copied his poems about tea on the painting's colophon papers, preceded by a brief dedication to the memory of Wu Kuan. Thus *The Bamboo Stove* is a memorial by two colleagues of a man greatly respected by both and—rare among memorial paintings—seems to speak as directly of the feelings of poet and painter as it does to the honor of Wu Kuan. It is cast in subdued elegiac tones appropriate to its purpose; and, as Wu Kuan had many friends and admirers in Suzhou and Beijing, it is quite possible that it was commissioned by a third party. But, as far as we know, the two sets of poems on which it was based, Wu Kuan's and Zhu's written in response, were in Zhu Yunming's possession, and he must have had a proprietary feeling about them. In any case, neither the genre of memorial painting generally nor the theme of tea in particular admitted the expression of intense emotion. Zhu's colophon is addressed to Wu Kuan:

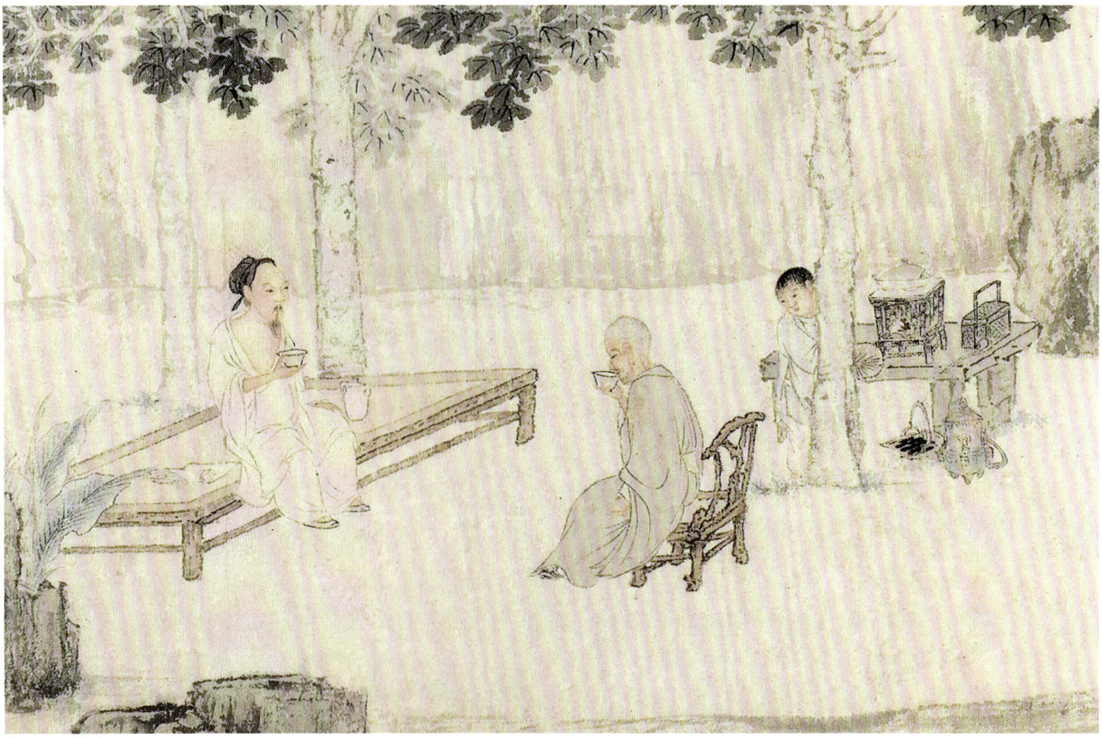

31 Attributed to Tang Yin (1470–1524). *The Bamboo Stove* (*Zhu cha lu*), 1509. Detail of figure 30

Dedication and poems by Zhu.

You sent to me for my comment your poems on *The Bamboo Tea Stove*. Taking them in both hands and reciting them to the last line is like listening to the harmonies of the Shao, filling me with unceasing respect and affection. Disregarding my own incompetence, I follow your rhyme pattern in four quatrains—mere beating on a clay pot compared to your thunder. Feeling most unworthy, I submit them with apprehension for your comment.

Immortal hands dispense the waters of the jade stream.
I call the boy as the water nears the boil in the bamboo stove.
The dark dragons twist and writhe beside the brush rest,
And the many-colored phoenix sings sweetly before the bench.

Binghe composes an inscription catching the spirit of the tea rite;
Paoan, too, searching for the apt word, forgets to sleep.
Often I have wanted to entrust perfection of the idea to a painting,
But feared no painting could do it the justice it deserves.

You have traveled through Jiangnan to seven famous streams
And many times north to brew water drawn from the Jade River.
On the Xiao and Xiang the night rain has fallen on your window,
And in the Jie Valley autumn clouds arose before your chair.

In the Han garden tea once quenched the thirst of Sima,
In the pavilion tea enabled Lao Shao to stay awake.
Lu Tong always knew the appeal of tea,
An appeal so profound it can never be fully known.

The dewy shoots of tea buds mix with the sweet water,
And in the fine bamboo stove brew over a slow fire.
The pure airs of Ruan Ji's music inspired his descendants,
A Xian's supreme virtue derived from a brilliant forebear.

When you pour hot water at the table we forget exhaustion;
In fine mist beyond the screen a crane sleeps beside us.
Serving tea comes not from the skillful hand but from the knowing heart.
If it did not pass through blazing fire it would not reach perfection.

In all your life you never drew near the Stream of Greed.
You draw off only the purest water from the rolling boil.
You surpass Master Lu and his bronze stove,
You excel even Master Han and his stone tripod.

The cup filled with flower dew relieves the lethargy of spring.
Ears cocked to catch the pine wind, you wake from daytime sleep.
The labors of official service do not allow the full reclusive life,
Only you and your descendants will carry it to perfection.[77]

奉教竹茶爐詩。
捧誦之餘，如聞韶濩。令人敬愛之不暇。生不揣踈陋，
踵韻四首，瓦缶雷鳴，不勝惶汗，伏惟政教。

仙掌分來自玉泉。呼童試向竹爐煎。
蒼虬蟠繞筆床外。彩鳳和鳴詩榻前。

冰壑著銘深得趣。匏庵索句久忘眠。
幾回欲付丹青畫。又恐丹青畫不全。

嘗遍江南七品泉。北遊復汲玉河煎。
瀟湘夜雨來窗外。嶰谷秋雲起座前。

翰苑曾消司馬渴。書齋每破老韶眠。
盧仝素識茶中趣。此趣多應識未全。

露芽數朵和甘泉。雅稱筠爐漫火煎。
老阮清風能啟後。阿咸高節有光前。

案頭湯沸人忘倦。簾外烟微鶴傍眠。
不是良工心獨巧。每經烈焰豈能全。

平生端不近貪泉。只取清泠旋旋煎。
陸氏銅壚應在右。韓公石鼎敢爭前。

滿甌花露消春困。兩耳松風驚晝眠。
宦轍難全隱居事。君家子姓獨能全。
祝允明

Much of the iconography of the painting originates in the poems mounted with it and reiterates many of the poetic themes. The setting is a spring on Mount Hui near Suzhou, one of seven springs in Jiangnan famous for the freshness of its water, and Wu Kuan's favorite. That discriminating tea master thought nothing of traveling far into the mountains to obtain the purest water, taking with

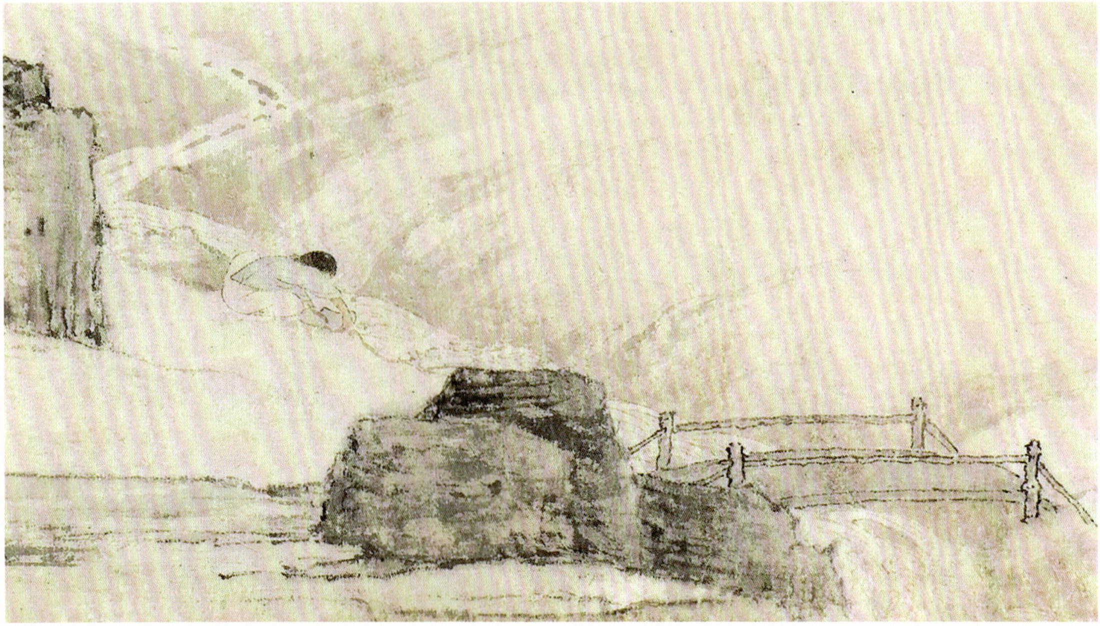

32 Attributed to Tang Yin (1470–1524). *The Bamboo Stove* (*Zhu cha lu*), 1509. Detail of figure 30

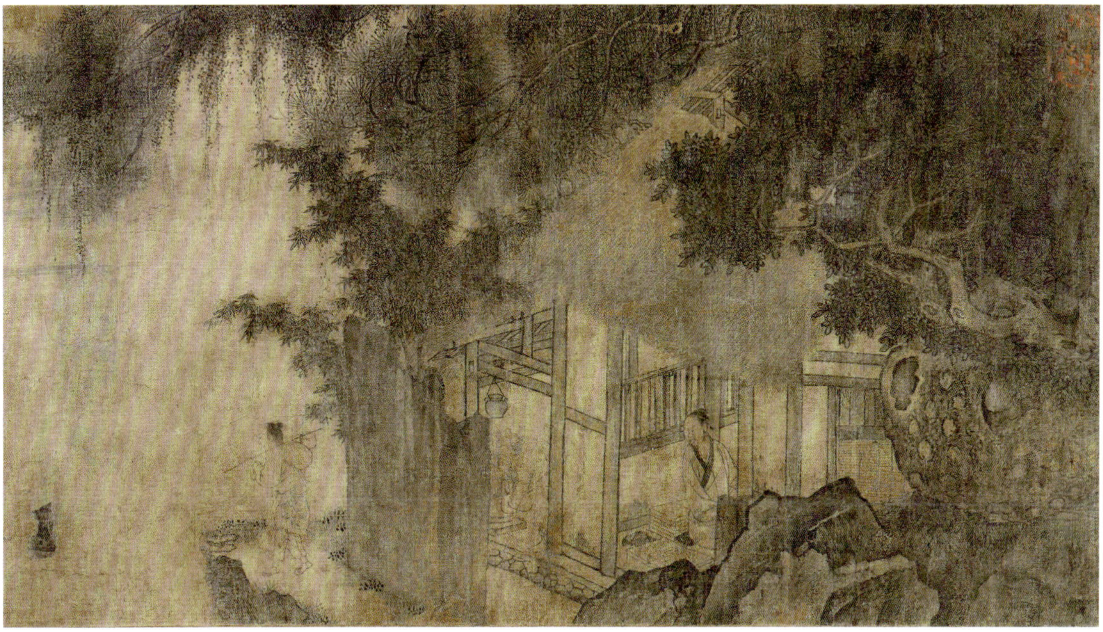

him his tea equipment and his "friend in tea." His stove consisted of a ceramic vessel containing the fire and kettle, and a bamboo casing woven around it for insulation and to render it portable. Especially designed for the peripatetic tea adept, this ingenious contrivance had been in use since the early fifteenth century. Wu Kuan, the antiquarian, cherished arcane techniques, objects that were old, practices that were unusual; in Suzhou his tastes were considered the height of discrimination.[78]

The elegiac note is sounded at the outset of the scroll, where a boy is drawing tea water from a mountain spring issuing from the mist in a passage of pale and icy purity (fig. 32). The stream alludes to the Tang tea master Lu Tong (ca. 775–835), whose *hao* was Yuchuan, Jade Stream. Conventionally considered the founder of the tea cult, he recommended just such a remote mountain stream for brewing the best tea and cautioned that using well water was an offense against tea. Lu Tong speaks of his delight in this wonderful herb in a poem on drinking seven cups of tea, which renewed body and spirit and transported him to the islands of the immortals in a state of euphoria.[79] In the Southern Song period, this iconic scene was celebrated in a painting by Liu Songnian (ca. 1150–after 1225). In the sixteenth century, this work was circulating in Suzhou, where it commanded the attention of many painters and connoisseurs, among them Tang Yin, Du Mu (1459–1525), and probably also Zhu Yunming. It is now lost but may be at least dimly represented by an anonymous copy, possibly of Song date, titled *Lu Tong Making Tea* (fig. 33). Quoting from the descriptions of Liu's original work written by Du Mu and Tang Yin,

33 Anonymous (Song dynasty?). Copy after *Lu Tong Making Tea* (*Lu Tong peng cha tu juan*). Handscroll; ink and color on silk, 24.1×44.7 cm. Palace Museum, Beijing

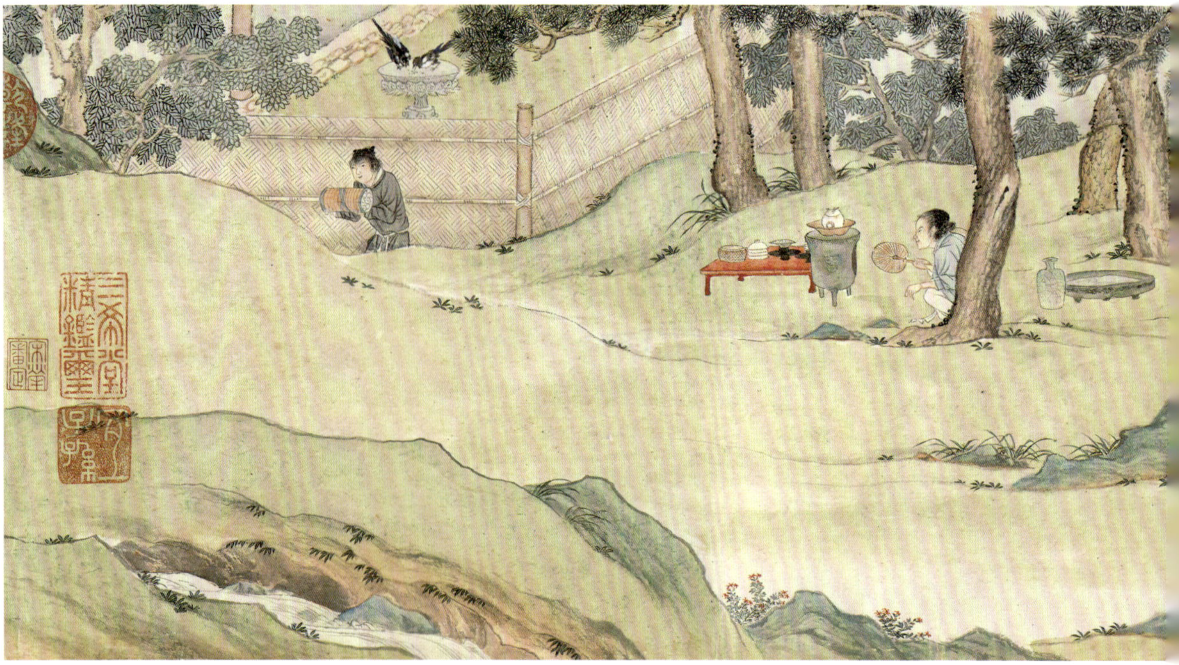

we can recognize the following: Master Lu appears in his house of "a few bays" having just awoken from a "daytime sleep," his head tilted to catch "the sound of the wind in the pines." In the kitchen a young maid "is fanning the kettle" on the stove. She wears her hair over her face and is a bit daft but has a way with tea. An older maid is outside, going to fetch water from a "jade stream" with a broken jug. Tang Yin's two boy servants are loosely modeled on the shabby maids, one "fanning the fire in the bamboo stove," the other "dipping up water from the spring." Zhu Yunming's last lines declare that Lu Tong himself knew best the power that tea exerted over its devotees, but so mysterious was it that even he could not fathom all its mysteries.[80]

For his part, Tang Yin added to his painting a dictionary of figurative forms implying a blameless spirit and fine discrimination. The celebrants are separated from the dusty world by a bridge, an old Buddhist symbol signifying escape from corruption to purity. Wu Kuan and the monk are sipping tea in silence under a *wutong* tree, the only tree on which the "many-colored phoenix" of Zhu's poem would roost, on an austere and empty stage marked out by rocks like a Chinese garden. The ideal sought in the design of a Chinese garden is not richness and abundance but serenity. Tea, like the stream, the garden, and the *wutong* tree, does not respond to extravagance or ostentation. In poem and painting alike, each one of these myths and symbols bespeaks the nobility of spirit

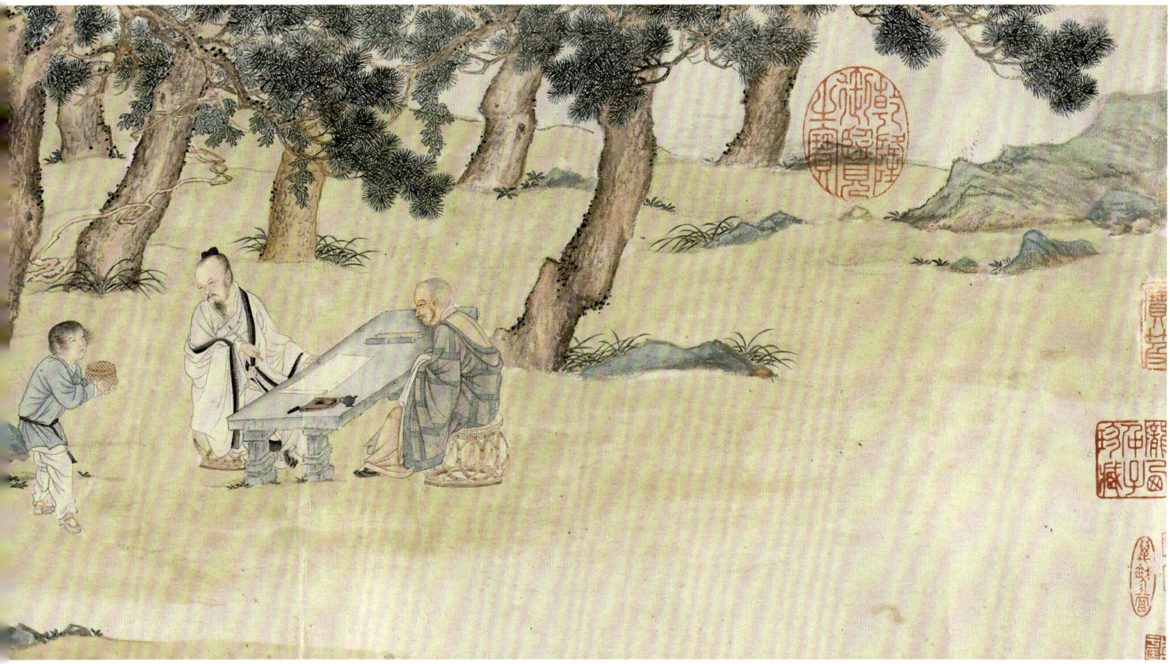

ascribed to Wu Kuan. The entire iconographic assemblage is a metaphorical portrait of the man.

Most of the Suzhou painters of the Ming dynasty had strong historicist leanings and were as much preoccupied with the antiquity of painting as with its practice. The ancient style that they particularly favored to embody commemorative subjects they termed "antique orthodoxy," modeling it on classical Song paintings of narrative and didactic subjects. Transmitted by Zhao Mengfu to the Suzhou Ming masters, it took to itself certain classicizing features and formed the foundation on which Tang Yin, Wen Zhengming, and Qiu Ying (ca. 1495–1552) built many of their memorial paintings. Its special strengths were the capacity to tell a story in a single succinct scene and at the same time to characterize the participants in the plain dignified figure drawing of Li Gonglin. *The Bamboo Stove* may be compared to *Zhao Mengfu Writing the "Heart Sutra" in Exchange for Tea* painted by Qiu Ying in 1542–43 (fig. 34). Both paintings are encomia on celebrated members of the literati class engaged in their favorite pursuits and presented as exemplars of the *junzi*. Zhao Mengfu is shown writing out the *Heart Sutra* for the monk Kong, who had presented him with a gift of tea—the autograph an icon of literati culture and the tea an icon of equal value to the tea connoisseur. Both pictures represent the key scene in their respective narratives, the figures placed in the middle of an open stage, encircled by a few elements of scenery

34 Qiu Ying (ca. 1495–1552). *Zhao Mengfu Writing the "Heart Sutra" in Exchange for Tea*, 1542–43. Handscroll; ink and color on paper, 21.9 × 77.8 cm. The Cleveland Museum of Art. John L. Severance Fund (1963.102)

with an unstressed background, the slow-moving figures drawn as simple silhouettes. Shading and texture are sporadic and restricted to the landscape, nowhere interfering with the figures, and the images are immersed in a pale, even light. Our impression is one of easy naturalism, but in fact the motifs are stringently abbreviated, with spreading voids and detail omitted arbitrarily except where it serves to enhance the figures. The only forms allowed to remain are those that carry the train of the narrative and imply the austere tastes of the participants.

* * *

Several questions emerge from this examination of commemorative landscape paintings. Why did the Chinese have such a marked preference for painting that was supported by the written word? How much of the role played by the patron-recipient was real, how much ideal? In what way and to what degree was the painter engaged in the expressive content of the work? Should we use the term "expressionist" for Chinese painting in the same sense that it is applied to Western art?

Most of the works we have examined are supplied, or were once supplied, with names, places, dates, evocative poetry, and exegetical prose. Why did the participants in Chinese memorials deem it essential that the picture be accompanied by a written explanation and testimonials? It is a Western bias that a work of visual art which requires a written program to be understood is less perfect as art; such a bias never occurred to the Chinese, and for this we must be grateful. In China no art was more highly esteemed than the written word, and history and biography were among its earliest forms. A memorial was felt to be more complete when it was written as well as illustrated: words can render specific and concrete some facts and conditions that the image cannot treat at all. While the image can summon up and intensify moods that words would only dilute, it cannot deal with relationships in time. Moreover, certain figures of speech are so complex that they cannot be translated into visual form; the same is true of symbolic narratives drawn from history. To exclude the literary element not only would break with tradition but would impoverish the work of visual art as a whole.

Some essential parts of a patron's personal history, the ones that he especially wanted to make known, had to be transmitted in words, since he was simultaneously seeking anonymity in the ideal protected role of the recluse. This meant that the description of his history had to be rooted in facts that clearly identified him as the subject of the painting. At the same time, and following his wishes, it had to reveal something of his essential nature and certain beliefs and preferences to which he subscribed. In these ways, the role played by the patron-recipient in the painting was a very real one.

The painter's feelings were not as deeply involved as the recipient's in the facts of the scroll's narrative: when he became engaged in the creation of the painting, it was essentially as an artist. When he chose the style (or was chosen for his style), shaped it to convey the story, and framed that story in a mood, it was his artistic personality that was most prominent. The actual content of the narrative was often supplied by the author of the preface and the colophon writers, who, if they were good at their task, could greatly enrich the viewer's understanding of the scroll. Once the viewer had studied the painting, read the colophons, and grasped the full meaning of the symbolism to the recipient, he was more strongly predisposed toward the recipient than toward the artist, attributing the expressive quality of the image to the personal experience of the recipient that first arrested his attention and aroused his sympathy, rather than to the painter. At the inception of a picture, all the collaborators—painter, poets, commentators—receive the idea of the memorial from the patron. He is the original mover of the enterprise, even though he may not execute any of its parts and even when a third party commissions the scroll for him or when the painter offers it on his own behalf. Thus the painter shares the task of creating a commemorative scroll with the other artists, but all are present chiefly in their artistic personalities. While they may be familiar with and share the feelings they give voice to, they are essentially speaking for someone else, and their engagement with the expressive aspects of the work was hence restricted.

The evolution of Chinese painting to a more "expressionistic" mode began toward the end of the Song and the beginning of the Yuan period, when its attention shifted from nature to man. Man began to figure largely, even exclusively, in the colophons, while the landscape began to acquire the mild-tempered, withdrawn air conventionally ascribed to the scholar. The landscape setting actually enlarged in extent while the human figure diminished, but at the same time it became a sounding board for human experience and sensibility. The colophons grew longer and more numerous, and the spirit of the painting more subjective as biographical themes became more common. The private patron came increasingly to the fore, a figure who was only beginning to call attention to himself during the Song dynasty, when imperial and sectarian patronage were almost the only kinds known. The patron-recipient gained in parity with the artist—not as creator but as the source of content—and his concerns with the painting were, properly speaking, personal, self-centered, and rooted in the purview of the elite class. His experience of expressionism differed from the Western one, in part because it was shared by his collaborators, who spoke in the inscriptions from the same convictions, and in part because it grew directly from a tradition of literary biography that rested on settled standards of decorum and restraint.

The shift to humanistic themes occurred with relative suddenness in the early Yuan dynasty, owing chiefly to the political crisis, which intensified the literati's consciousness of themselves as bearers of a native culture, in contrast to the Mongols. As the commemorative landscape was usually made by several persons who agreed to pool their talents to honor one of their number, we know that its social function was recognized and approved. From its beginnings, it aimed at a sense of cohesion and collegiality, an impression which it still leaves with the viewer today.

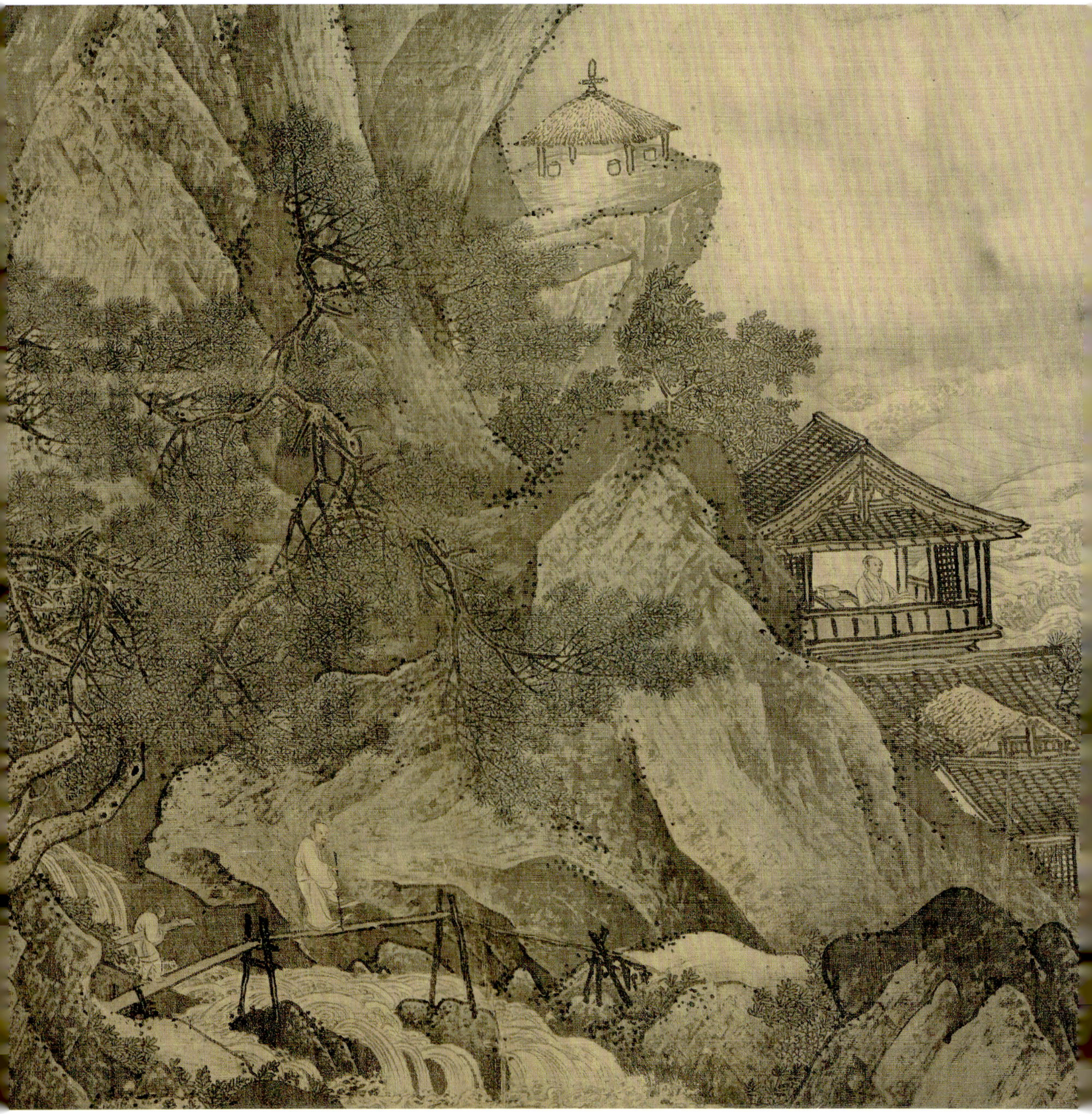

35 Zhou Chen (ca. 1455–ca. 1535). *The North Sea* (*Beiming*). Detail of figure 40

Chapter Three
What's in a Name? The *Biehao* Painting

The practice of naming in Chinese portraiture was peculiar to Chinese culture and has much to say about the highly subjective nature of Chinese painting in the later dynasties. In old China an educated man might have several names: a legal name, a family name, a social name, and one or more *biehao*—pen name, brush name, or literary name. He might take as many *biehao* as he wished and on any occasion that he felt should be marked. The *biehao* differed from his other names in being adopted entirely by his own choice, whereas his other names were more or less decided by family members. Hence the *hao* (or *biehao*) was more personal; only he knew his reasons for choosing it and how it was to be understood. Sometimes it was intended to imply a high moral character or a standard to be aimed at, but it could also be used to sound a deliberately perverse or ironic note implying contradiction of or indifference to convention. Generally, a *biehao* was chosen to set oneself apart from others as a unique individual. It should convey something about him that was private and personal, but that the owner nevertheless desired to make known to his society. The *hao* painting was designed to evoke this name, and, with its introduction, probably in the Yuan dynasty, a new norm of portraiture and a new game of wits emerged in Chinese painting. The *biehao* painting may have first appeared in the early fourteenth century; it certainly had its heyday in the fifteenth and sixteenth centuries in Suzhou, where it became immensely popular among the painters and patrons of the Wu school. Its nature and history are the subject of this chapter.

The *hao* painting is a problem in implication, allusion, insinuation, and personification, all literary devices for substituting a place-name for a person's name, an image for a virtue, weather for a trait of character, an historical personage for an ethical standard. Just as artistic taste in the Yuan and Ming dynasties deplored literal illustration and the pursuit of formal realism in painting, literary taste disdained the obvious, the trite, the commonplace expression of traits and qualities. The literatus thought of his *hao* as a kind of thumbnail sketch of himself that, by the use of metaphor, synecdoche, and periphrasis, would call up a mental image, a frame of mind, a shade of personality showing him in a truer light than a portrait describing merely surface appearances. The *hao* painting was the more highly valued if it could accomplish its purpose with a display of wit, ambiguity, double entendre, or playfulness, qualities which often spill over into the painting. The viewer was expected to appraise the picture with both literary and pictorial criteria in mind. The program of the *hao* picture was a conundrum, a mystery story contrived to attract attention, arouse the intellect and the wit, and, in the end, be exposed. No one could understand it except the initiated, who already knew the subject's name or discovered it by reading the colophons, and they, of course, constituted most of the audience to whom the painting was directed. Like commemorative scrolls generally, the *hao* painting was a class genre, designed for the exercise and entertainment of the scholar class, most of whom were writers accustomed to exhibit their verbal talents in social exchange.

The first mention of such pictures in literary records that has come to light so far suggests the early Yuan dynasty and the Mongol court as the point of origin of the *hao* picture and the circle of Zhao Mengfu and Gao Kegong (1248–1310) as its inventors. The genre of *hao* painting is so deeply imprinted with the habits and aptitudes of writers that it is no surprise to learn that it originated in a literati circle. It is exactly described in the epitaph of a scholar named Huang Yiqing (1263–1337), who lived and wrote in seclusion without benefit of civil appointment, while his good friend Li Meng (1255–1321) flourished at court.[81]

Huang Yiqing took the *hao* "Autumn River," and Li Meng took the *hao* "Autumn Valley." Among Li Meng's poems are the lines: "You (Huang) fish for the moon in the autumn river; I (Meng) plow the clouds in the autumn valley. You jeer at me for escaping fame; I cry shame on you still eating fish. Everyone in and outside the court repeated this poem, passing it from mouth to mouth [enjoying its wit]." Thereupon Zhao Mengfu of the *Hanlin* committed these ideas to painting(s), saying "Under a just rule we should not neglect talent like this but should bring it forward."[82]

君以秋江自號，而李公自號秋谷，遺君詩有「君釣秋江月，我耕秋谷雲，逃名君笑我，伴食我慚君」之句，朝野傳解誦滿口。內翰趙文敏公既寫以為圖，且謂不宜使清時有遺才，力薦之。

Li Meng's poem is couched in an ironic tone, facetiously casting his friend as an impoverished rustic scraping by on fish and himself as a plodding bureaucrat cheated of fame. (Actually he served three Yuan emperors in succession.) Double meanings, mock derision, sarcasm — all sorts of fleeting, lighthearted figures of speech make their way into *hao* painting by way of language, brought there almost unconsciously by the literatus who paints as he speaks and as he composes poems.

We observe that the *hao* names of Huang and Li are paired, chosen by their owners to express mutual friendship, and that they use simple descriptive terms taken from the poetry of landscape. It was especially important to the painter that the phrases "fishing for the moon in the autumn river" and "plowing the clouds in the autumn valley" are vivid pictorial images, easily projected in the mind's eye. As Zhao actually painted them, they may have constituted either a single picture or a matched pair.

It could not have been a coincidence that the friends Zhao Mengfu and Gao Kegong were both engaged with *hao* paintings at the same time. In 1297 Gao had made two such paintings, one for himself and one for an impoverished friend,[83] and in 1302 Zhao painted *Water Village*, a masterpiece of the type (see fig. 16). Which one of them initiated the idea of basing a picture on the owner's name? This is not known with certainty. Gao Kegong did not begin to paint until about 1290, when he first met Zhao Mengfu.[84] Although he was older than Zhao and reached higher official rank, in artistic matters he seems to have been content with the position of follower. I suspect the idea of the *hao* painting originated with Zhao, from whom emanated so many inspired ideas of a brilliant period.

Zhao Mengfu's genius shone again in his grandson Wang Meng (ca. 1308–1385), who inherited the talents and traditions of a family famous in the fine arts. Wang was too young to have trained with his grandfather but evidently missed

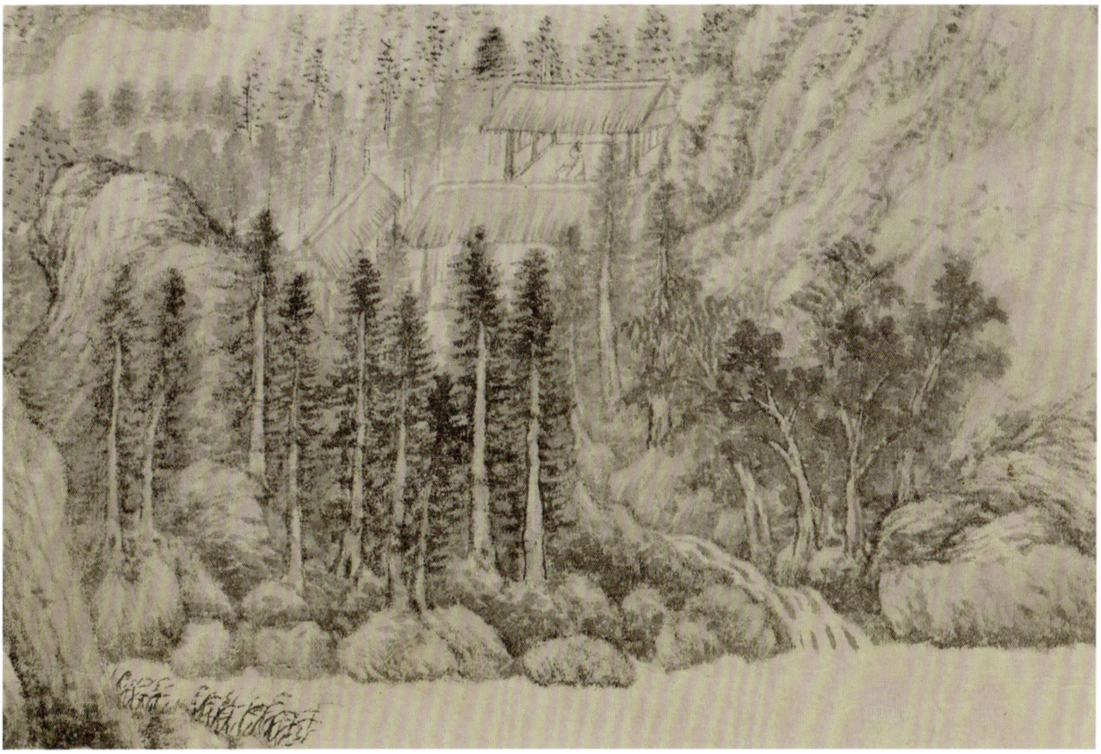

36 Wang Meng (ca. 1308–1385). *Small Retreat of Master Cloudy Woods* (*Yunlin xiaoyin tu*). Detail of figure 37

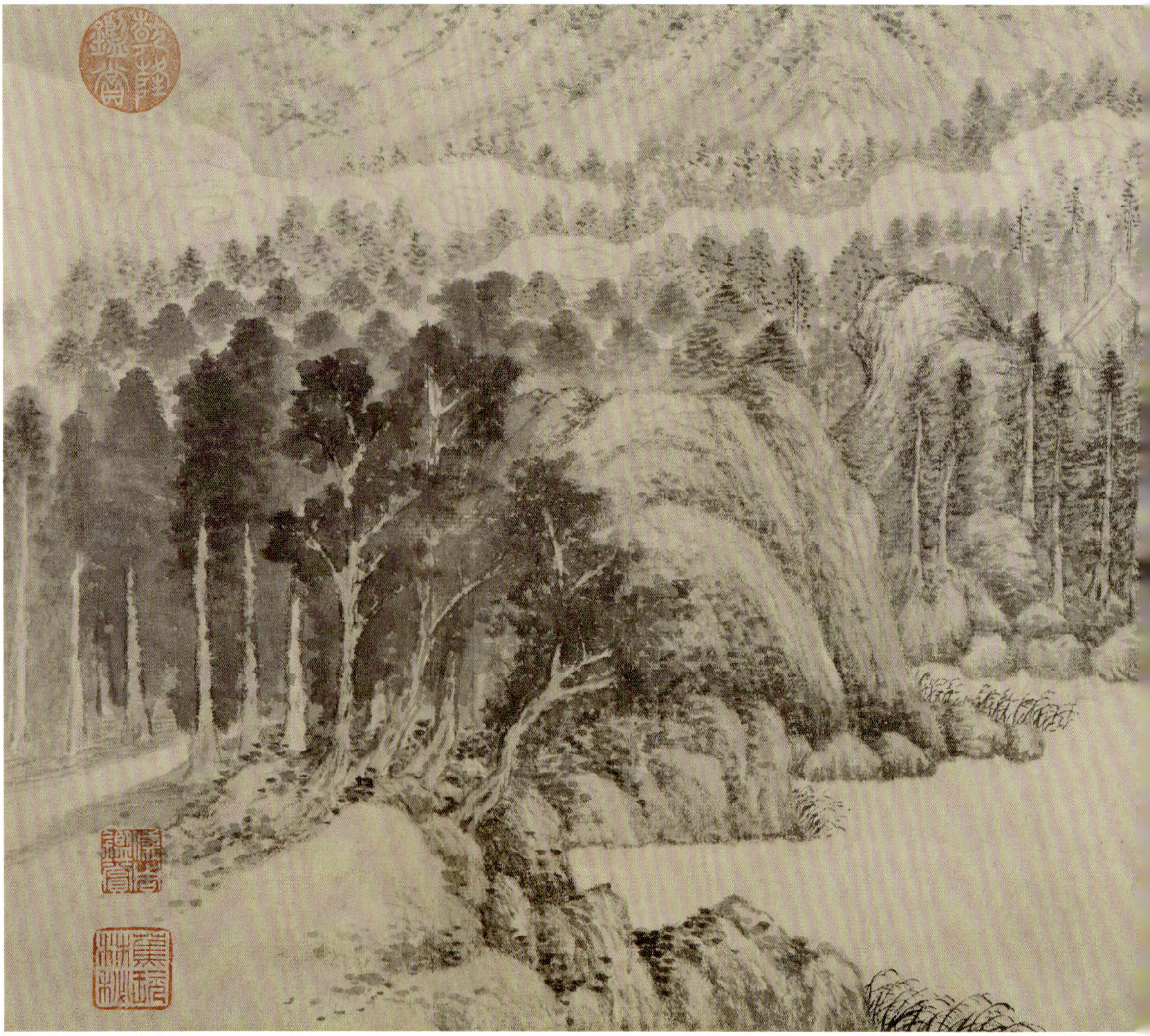

nothing essential thereby: all his work is striking for its originality and, especially in the late phase of his career, he made a large number of memorial paintings for private persons and family members. The little-known handscroll titled *Small Retreat of Master Cloudy Woods* (*Yunlin xiaoyin tu*) (fig. 37)[85] is remarkable for its fine balance of mild temper, powerful brushwork, and an unusually abstract composition. Wang preferred the style of Dong Yuan, misleadingly ordinary in appearance but capable of the rich textures and the stark formal patterns he favored in his late works. Moreover,

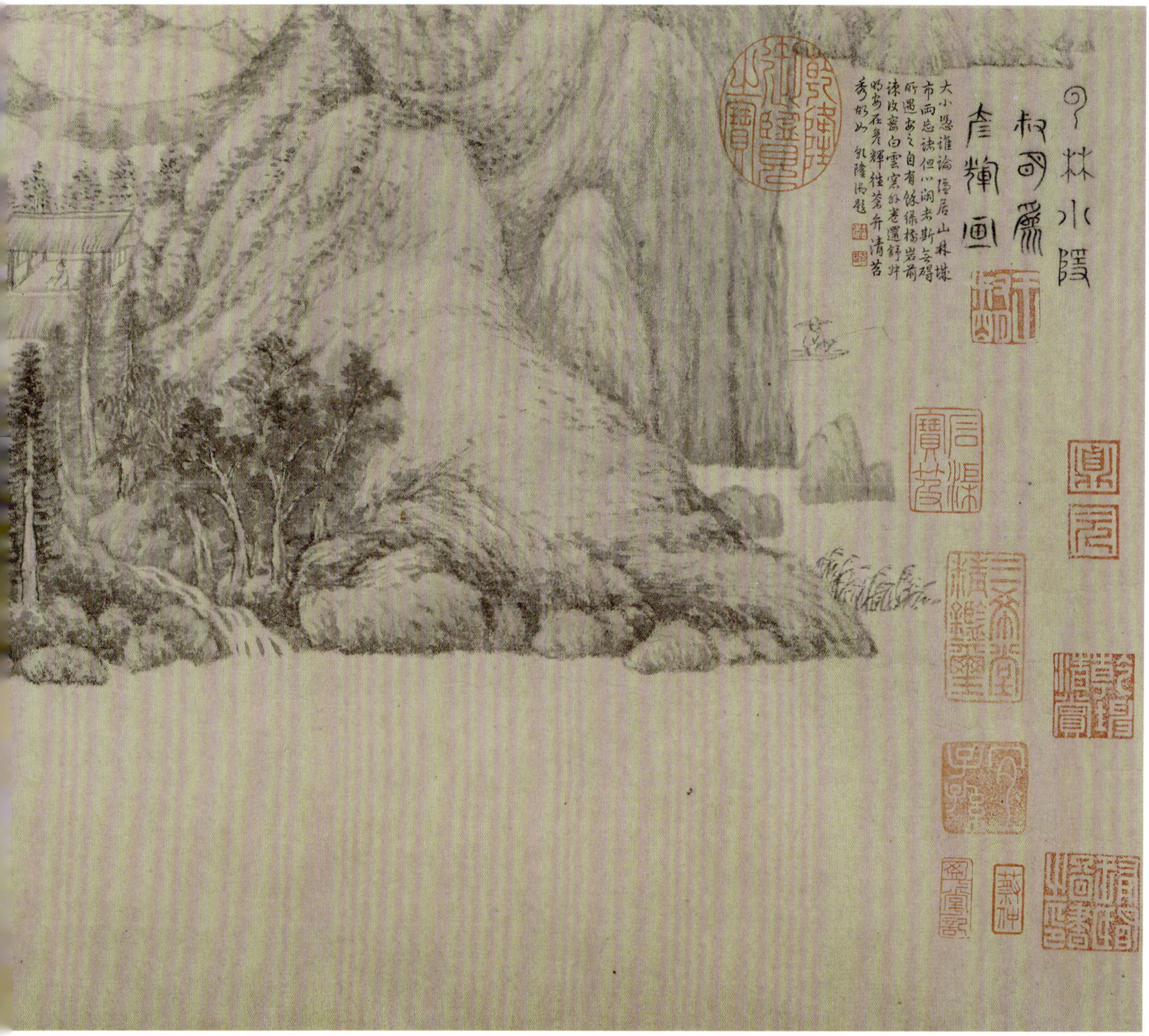

Dong's style could summon up the humid climate of southeastern China, which was called for by the setting of *Yunlin xiaoyin tu*, the story of the Small Retreat of Master Cloudy Woods. Wang made it for his nephew, Cui Yanhui, a private scholar happily free of worldly ambitions, a man of spirit and an artist by nature, who gathered herbs as he wandered through the mountains in rustic dress. He dabbled in painting and liked to practice calligraphy to supply his house with name plaques for the rooms. Cui called himself a small recluse content with a small retreat. His

37 Wang Meng (ca. 1308–1385). *Small Retreat of Master Cloudy Woods* (*Yunlin xiaoyin tu*). Handscroll; ink on paper, 27.3 × 64.8 cm. Private collection. See also figure 36

friend and biographer Xu Yikui, at the behest of Cui's friends, narrates the story of his discovery of the cloudy woods in the Bian Mountains:

For generations the Cui family of Qiantang [present-day Hangzhou] has lived in the busy town, where carts, men, and horses crowd together in confusion; the din resounds all day like thunder, and the air rises thick with dust like mist. Master Yanhui decided he could not bear it and planned how he might escape Qiantang and find another home. As he was related on his mother's side to the Zhao family of Wuxing, he traveled up and down the Zhe River [in Wuxing]. Gazing at the mountains by the river rising high into the clouds and shining in the sunlight, he longed constantly for deep seclusion [among those mountains] but had not yet found a suitable dwelling site. One day as he was walking in the foothills of the Bian Mountains he saw some five or six *li* in front of him a great valley covered with cryptomeria, oak, pine, and cassia standing in ranks, their upper branches entangled together. At the time, rain was clearing, and the clouds had not wholly dissipated. The treetops climbed piercing the clouds and leaping upward like coiling dragons, clouds and trees casting the valley into light and shade. Yanhui lingered and could not bring himself to leave. Sighing, he said, "Is this not fit for my dwelling place?"

Then he used the timber to build a house of three or four bays, arranging in order a hall, a study, a fireplace, a bath. He brought his wife and children to live there. Then he had the fields cleared and rice planted, started an orchard, put in vegetables, dug a pond and raised fish to support his family. He spent his leisure taking up the books of the old writers to scan some lines. As he is fond of the large and small seal scripts, he wrote tablets for the house in the styles of Li Si [d. 257 BCE] and Li Yangbing [721/2–785]. When he finished writing, he would again put on his rustic cap and dress and wander about under the overarching trees. Gazing up he saw the clouds coming at random and going without a trace. He began to feel he had joined with them, forgetting all material existence. Thereupon he took as his *hao* "The Small Hermit of Cloudy Woods." His thought was: "The great recluses are to be found in the towns and the court. I have no such talents. I will live as a small hermit."[86]

[...]

In antiquity, historians discussing the ranking of hermit scholars generally spoke of three classes. The recluse of the highest level is able to help the whole world. He realizes his distinction but feels out of place in the ordinary world and would rather decline fame and high rank than be bothered with them. The next rank is less firm of character but impetuous in spirit. On examining his inner worth, he finds his talents insufficient for worldly use. But he can find contentment among the hills and valleys, thus winning constant respect from others for a high spirit. As for those who are willing to serve but cannot rise in rank: their angling for fame and hunting for praise to gain advantage and wealth is what a Han writer called "recluses who steal an empty reputation," and a Tang man called "taking a shortcut to the capital" [from Shaoshi Mountain near Luoyang].[87] They constitute an inferior class.

I appreciate Yanhui, who deplores them but says nothing, while he defers to the upper rank but does not consort with them. Is it possible that Yanhui considers himself to belong to what I have termed the second class? His many friends respect him because, although most worldly people covet fame and profit, he has the force of will to rise above them. Therefore his friends have requested me to write the record of

"The Small Hermit," and I have composed this essay for him. Many of his ancestors were recluses of great virtue, and Master Wenmin, Zhao Mengfu, was his grandfather on the mother's side.

Xu Yikui of Shifeng[88]

錢唐崔氏，世居闤闠中。閭閻比轃，人馬雜沓，竟日聲囂若雷，氣滃如霧。至彥暉氏，有敻塵之思，不堪處也。謀去此而他焉。彥暉之外家蓋吳興趙氏，往來霅上。見霅上諸山干青雲，而耀白日。恆欲深隱其間，而未得其勝。一日步自弁之麓，猶夷澗谷之間，五六里許，前見大壑，杉櫧松桂，大木森立，枝柯相繆，時新雨霽，宿雲未盡，斂木末上，穿雲氣，如蛟螭騰起，而與雲會，壑為晝陰。彥暉躊躇不去，歎曰「此不足以居我耶。」遂具材木，作屋三四楹，室堂煬湢，以次具挈妻孥往居焉。治畬種稻，藝圃種蔬，鑿池種魚，以自給暇。則取古人書，閱三數行，又嗜篆(篆)籀，或取斯冰篆法作□匾，書已復，山巾野服，逍遙乎穹林之下，仰觀乎雲來也，無心雲去也，無迹悠悠，然若與為忘形交者，遂自號曰雲林小隱。其意以為大隱在市朝。吾以非才，姑處其小者耳。

古之為史者，論隱之品，大概有三。蓋謂上焉者，負濟世之具。自視甚高，而與世柄鑿。寧辭名位，而不屑就。次焉者，質弱氣沖，內審其材，不足以用世。寧甘心林壑，使人常高其風。至於欲仕無階，漁名獵譽，以徼利祿，如漢世所謂處士，純盜虛聲。唐人所謂終南捷徑，少室高價者，斯為下矣。余雅彥暉彼下焉。固其所斥而不道。而上焉者，亦其所讓而不居。然則彥暉之所以自處，其殆吾之所謂次焉者歟。其友以世俗多嗜聲利。而彥暉獨有高世之志，可尚也。請即其小隱為之著記，為著於篇。彥暉之上世多隱德，而文敏公孟頫則其外曾大父云。始豐徐一夔記。

Cui Yanhui had recently moved his household to a beautiful site in the Bian Mountains, where he built his house in a pine forest wrapped in clouds, as shown in the painting (see fig. 36). In a moment of intense feeling he was inspired to take the *hao* Yunlin (Cloudy Woods), as if the name would make him one with the place. And, remembering Bai Juyi's poem, "The great *yin* [recluse] is at court or in the city, / the small *yin* is on a hillside plot," he declared himself to be a "small yin," declining to compete in the great world or with the great hermits.[89] He is barely visible high in a pavilion, his back against a mountainside and a wall of trees in front of him, obstructed from view by the forest and obscured by mist. As we have seen, in some of Ni Zan's paintings the human figure has actually disappeared. In Wang Meng's, figures are barely visible, as if the recipient, being fully explained in the preface, sinks back into the role of recluse in the picture. Even if his figure is not banished completely, it is increasingly abstracted into a puppetlike form. Eventually, in Shen Zhou's paintings, figures are reduced to ironic mannequins.

As so often in commemorative paintings, conspicuous seclusion is the primary theme, but on close viewing it is contradicted by a clear sign of access to the pavilion. On the left a path leads through the forest to the dwelling. (The loss of a few inches of silk has deprived it of its original force.)[90] The master is isolated and protected, yet accessible to those who know the way. Reclusion in the Yuan and Ming periods meant discrimination in social relations, never loneliness and deprivation.

When Cui Yanhui and his friends set out to assemble this memorial, he told the story of discovering the pine forest to Xu Yikui, intending that it should be incorporated in the painting as an explanation of the origin of his *hao* and a record of his love of the land. The *hao* is embodied in the shreds of clouds drifting through the pines, seeming so natural that at first glance they are scarcely noticed. When we learn that Cui Yanhui's *hao* was Cloudy Woods, they suddenly begin to speak. The *hao* painting turns on a kind of pun, a visual-verbal irony giving the motifs in the picture two meanings. The pun demands that certain pictorial motifs be privileged above others so that the viewer will recognize their significance and appreciate the equivalence of word and image. The figure of the fisherman half cut off by the right cliff is also an instance of irony. It forces a second scale on the painting, which baldly contradicts the scale of Yanhui's blurred little figure in the study and signals to the viewer that the scene does not belong to the real world and is not to be taken at face value. The taste for irony and ambiguous meanings is more common in literature than in the figurative arts but entered painting with a surge via the *biehao*. It offered an invitation to an open break with visual naturalism in which the literary element might possibly overwhelm the pictorial. But it was an invitation the Chinese painter declined. Commemorative painting of the Yuan and middle Ming periods never lost its balance or gave up its partial, but deeply felt, attachment to relatively natural appearances in landscape. So the pun is almost concealed, and the assemblage of motifs reads chiefly as a landscape of pine woods adrift in clouds. But the image still hints faintly at further meaning.

This distinguished painting demands a date, but the painter inscribed on it only the title and his signature in his characteristic "small seal" script. Fortunately, Cui Yanhui was an indefatigable collector of colophons, gathering twenty-seven for the scroll. The few dated colophons establish the period of execution as being between 1370 and 1381. Zhou Fang's second colophon states that he first knew Cui in 1366, when he joined Cui's household in Hangzhou to serve as his tutor in Confucian studies.[91] They discussed Confucian doctrine, sat up at night writing poems and drinking tea, and thus spent "several years." "Several" probably means at least three or four years after 1366; thus the earliest date for the execution of the painting would be about 1370. The date 1378 is given in a colophon by Wang Yu in which he records his pleasure at being shown Wang Meng's *fu* poem and Xu Yikui's "Record of the Small Retreat of Master Cloudy Woods," but he does not mention the painting, only the inscription. All three were definitely finished by 1381, when Cui Yanhui, on his travels with the painting in hand, met Wang Lian and elicited from him a poem that was duly mounted on the scroll. That same year, Cui also sent an agent with the finished painting to another friend, Dong Cun, to request the same favor.[92] From this we may infer that Cui Yanhui made the trip of discovery to Wuxing between 1370 and 1381 and that Wang Meng painted the picture during this same period.

Thus the Wang Meng scroll is not, strictly speaking, a Yuan painting, but it is a late work of the Yuan master, continuing Zhao Mengfu's *hao* painting type into the Ming dynasty in the Suzhou area. This subtype of memorial painting reached its greatest currency in the fifteenth and sixteenth centuries, when it flourished among the patrons and painters of that region. As an essentially biographical form of art, it could easily slip into an autobiographical form if the patron or recipient chose to take a larger hand in its creation. The patron or recipient determined the theme because that depended on his name, but he might also dictate details of setting and architecture and request specific literary or pictorial allusions of significance to himself. I have not been able to find concrete evidence of exactly how the recipient and the painter decided what should be represented, but it is self-evident that the main points of the subject matter originated with the recipient and that the participants in the scroll must have exchanged views. Usage governing the making of memorial landscape painting in literati circles began to coalesce and clarify during the Yuan dynasty. Colophon writers studied the painting if it already existed, gave thought to the earlier colophons, not only for a poetic rhyme scheme to be matched but also for themes of interest to the owner, and bore in mind that their ultimate purpose was to do him honor.

The style of *Master Cloudy Woods* is unpretentious and pacific in the extreme: it does not reflect the political and military disasters that preceded it, but the longing of its owner for present relief from the discomfort of Qiantang. The motifs are simplified in three dominant patterns that stand out cleanly against the void of water. The forms chosen are slow-moving, melting, and deliberately unfocused, and the image is possessed by an unnatural stillness. Evidently the theme and the mood of the painting were decided by the moment in the forest when Cui Yanhui realized his *hao*. But in the 1370s Wang Meng was a mature master of strongly marked artistic personality. Here the force of his genius almost obscures the narrative of Cui Yanhui's experience in the Bian Mountains. We may find ourselves gazing at the image for quite a long time before we ask what its original meaning was. This was the fate of many commemorative landscape scrolls when they were first studied by Western art historians intent on the history of style rather than the part they played in the social life of their time.

The painting called *Friend of Pines* (*Yousong tu*) (fig. 39) originally carried colophons by contemporaries in honor of the recipient.[93] Now only a single colophon by Wen Boren remains, giving the subject's name but no other particulars, leaving the scroll shorn of its history and unrecognizable as a *hao* painting. Fortunately, the writer Zhang Chou (1577–1643), who saved so much of Ming painting history for us, was able to reconstruct the past of this scroll, too.[94] Du Qiong (1397–1474), a senior member and founding teacher of the Wu school, put his seals on the painting proper, but no signature or dedication. Zhang Chou points

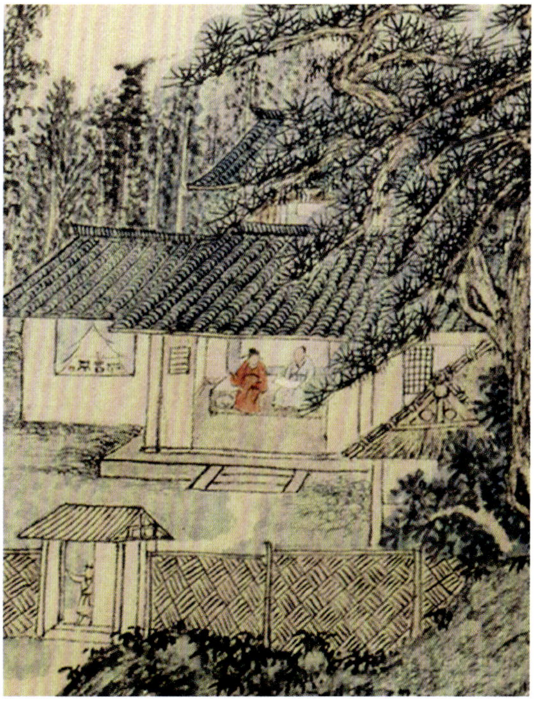

38 Du Qiong (1397–1474). *Friend of Pines* (*Yousong tu*). Detail of figure 39

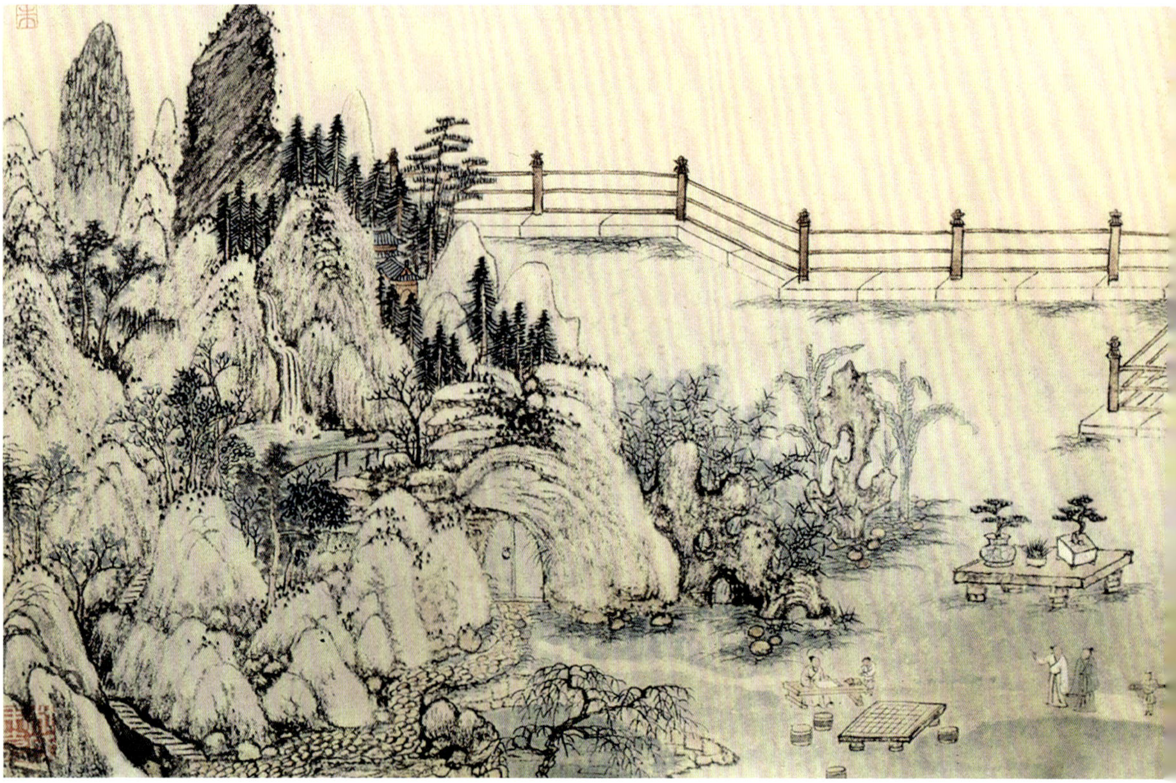

out that Du made the scroll at the request of his brother-in-law, Master Wei, whose *hao* was Yousong (Friend of Pines), a name inspired by his affection for the pine trees in his garden. Since the artist made the painting for a member of his family, signature and inscription were unnecessary. Du Qiong seems to have been familiar with the garden and its owner. With a touch of whimsy, he represents Master Wei seated in his library, showing the actual scroll to a guest while they wait for tea (see fig. 38).

Many *hao* names were concrete, descriptive terms that referred in some way or other to the practice, or at least the ideal, of reclusion—seeking refuge from the tainted world in the moral purity of nature. But during the Ming dynasty, active officials were tied to the city, and retired officials and unappointed scholars rarely withdrew far from it. The claim to reclusion was therefore more often a social convention than a reality. The role of the recluse could be a pretext for leading a private life, and reclusion filled many purposes. In the Yuan dynasty, it served as refuge from disorder and violence; in the Ming, it gave leeway for individual preference or family convenience. But the promise of personal freedom at the end of one's

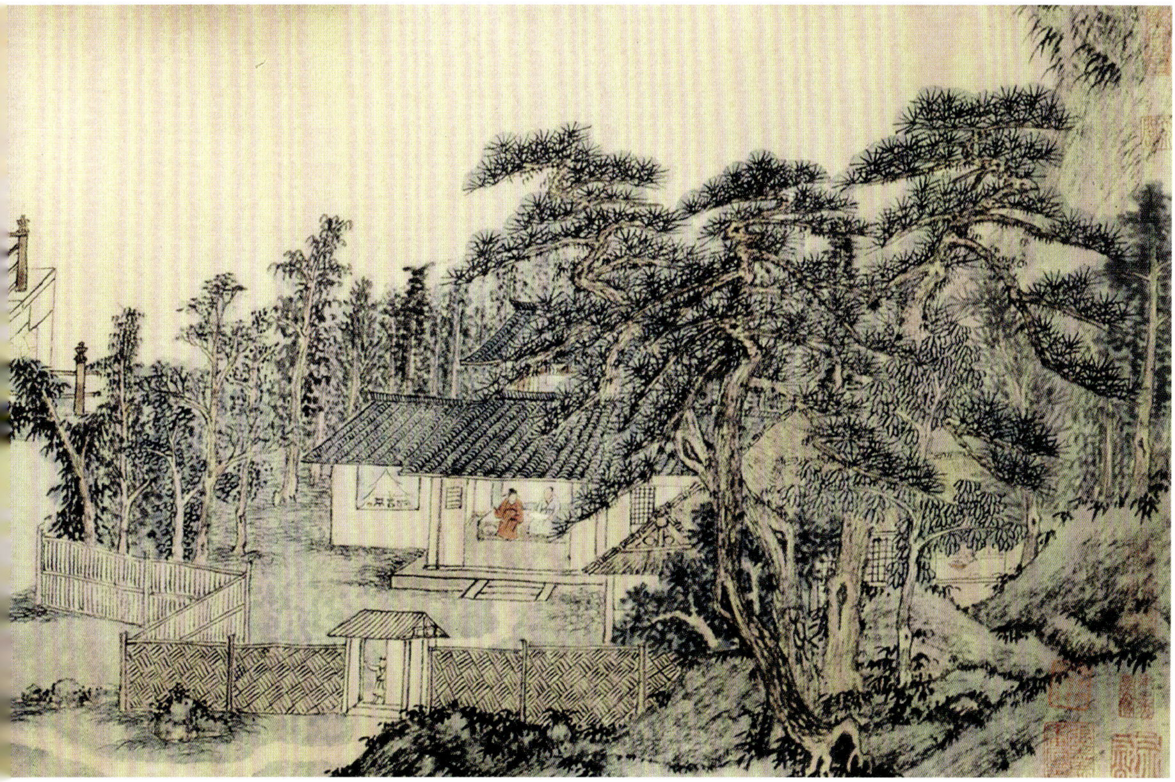

life continued to exert a powerful attraction on the Chinese mind. In the Tang dynasty and before, this ideal was vaguely associated with the magical land of the immortals. After the Song dynasty, the theme of the immortals is absorbed into a more sophisticated vision of the ideal man in a private garden disguised as a wilderness landscape. The garden was designed as a microcosm of the world, with additions from Daoist mythology, as seen in the miniature mountainscape that belonged to Wei Yousong and still to be seen in Suzhou gardens today. Paths, bridges, and water courses wander through it; toy buildings rise among the mountains; the closed door of an underground cave hints at the vanished fairyland. And everywhere are the scholar's favorite plants and playthings: pine trees and banana palms, Taihu rocks and a table loaded with *penjing* (bonsai).

Although the *hao* painting was the creation of the literati, it did not remain their exclusive preserve for long. It was soon taken up by professional masters too, especially in Suzhou, where scholarly tastes had permeated the merchant ranks as well as the elite class. There were many eager patrons seeking either to present or to be the subject of an honorific scroll. Zhou Chen

39 Du Qiong (1397–1474). *Friend of Pines* (*Yousong tu*). Handscroll; ink and color on paper, 28.8 × 92.5 cm. Palace Museum, Beijing. See also figure 38

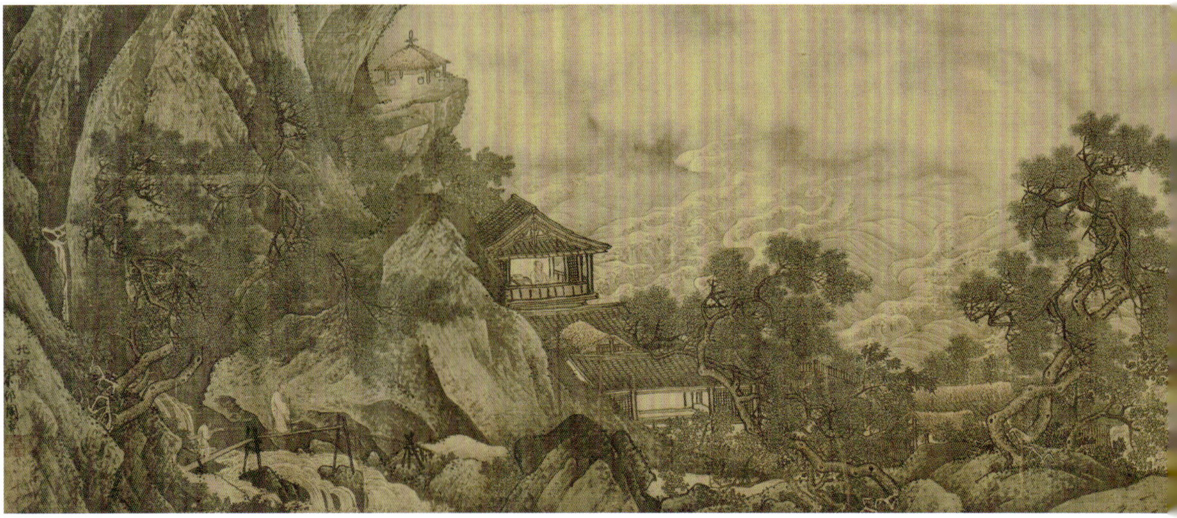

(ca. 1455–ca. 1535) and his most successful student, Qiu Ying, as well as others, filled these commissions. I would assume that the literati discussed the interpretation of themes and iconography with them, for it was essential that word and image should agree. The circle of artists in Suzhou was small, and they all knew one another even if they did not frequent the same parties. Moreover, painters, poets, and prose writers of honorific works were accustomed to collaborating with one another, and professionals just as much as amateurs were keenly interested in their colleagues' practice.

Zhou Chen's masterpiece, *The North Sea* (*Beiming*) (fig. 40), is a *hao* painting made for a man who had elected the name Beiming.[95] The artist signed the scroll with his name and the title, but that is all that is known of its origins; the colophons and inscriptions that once explained it are missing. Some years ago, Lawrence Sickman remarked that this painting might be an illustration of the patron's *hao* (pen name).[96] A second glance reveals certain anomalies in the illustrated narrative that confirm his opinion.

The picture tells two stories at once (a common effect in *hao* paintings). The conventional story depicts a scholar seated in his study and gazing into the distance while he waits for a guest who comes across a bridge, followed by a boy carrying a *qin*—the stuff of a thousand honorific paintings (see fig. 35). A quite independent and more sensational story describes a storm raging above the figures, who are wholly unaware of it. This story, from the first chapter of *Zhuangzi*, narrates how a great fish rose from the North Sea, transforming itself into a bird with enormous dark wings.[97] The bird soared southward, borne on the current of a cosmic storm, its heroic flight convulsing the sea and mountains around the pavilion. The image of a bird riding southward on the wind is a trope for a scholar of high ambition launched on the road to success and so must be a metaphor for

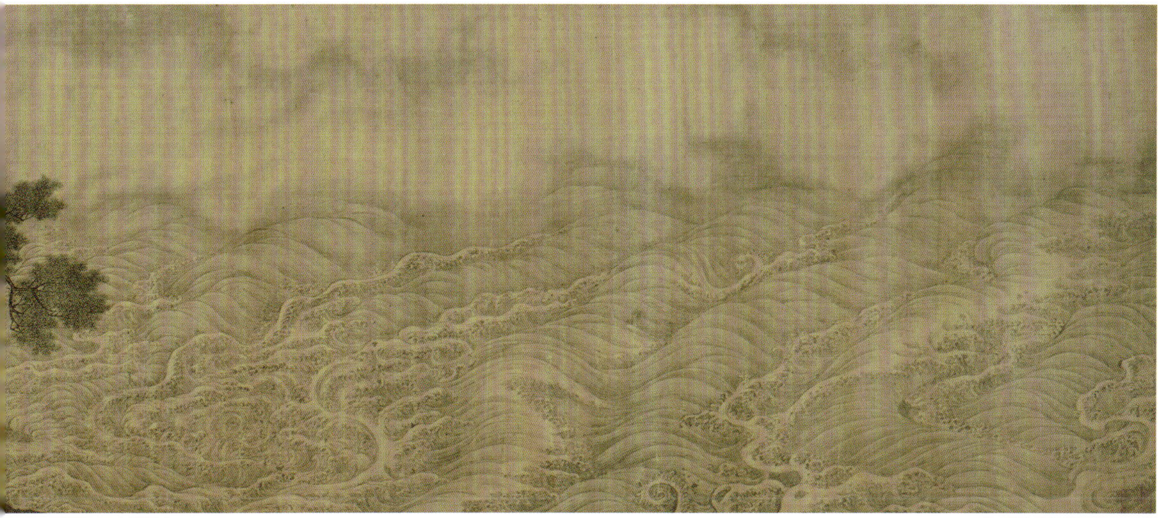

the patron. Zhou Chen depicts Master Beiming twice, once in the literal form of a scholar in a pavilion about to receive a guest and again by the turbulent clouds and waters alluding to the force of his ambition. But there is a sharp disjuncture between the figures and the landscape: the storm must be the setting for a dramatic narrative, but in fact it has no visible effect on the figures. Master Beiming awaits his guest, oblivious of the cataclysm; the guest arrives unperturbed by the uproar around him and intending to perform on the *qin* in the midst of it. They are playing roles in a commonplace social event quite separate from the storm. Moreover, the storm stands for only one aspect of the master's character—his indomitable will and purpose. The apparent anomalies and discrepancies are peculiar marks of the *hao* painting and clues to a second level of meaning that is directly relevant to the intellectual and spiritual nature of the patron, even though its outward form seems entirely unrelated to him. Paintings based on literary allusions become more common in the Ming dynasty, and the sources they refer to range widely over Chinese literature. Pictures and *hao* designed by literary men assumed their audience to be fully literate, intellectually agile, and quite prepared to digest two stories in a single image.

The same thing may be said of the selective revival of styles in the Ming dynasty: the viewer was invited to perceive and place motifs "quoted" from antique styles, just as he recognized illustrations of passages from ancient literature. *The North Sea* is again exemplary: Zhou Chen was a close student of Song styles of the eleventh and early twelfth centuries, especially Li Tang (ca. 1070s–ca. 1150s), the Song dragon painters, and other Southern Song artists rarely mentioned today. One of these little-known masters was a southerner, Zhao Fu (or Fei, active 1131–1162), who lived near the estuary of the Yangzi and seems to have devoted much of his career to recording

40 Zhou Chen (ca. 1455–ca. 1535). *The North Sea (Beiming)*. Handscroll; ink and light color on silk, 28.3 × 135.9 cm. The Nelson-Atkins Museum of Art, Kansas City, Missouri. Purchase: William Rockhill Nelson Trust, 58–55. See also figure 35

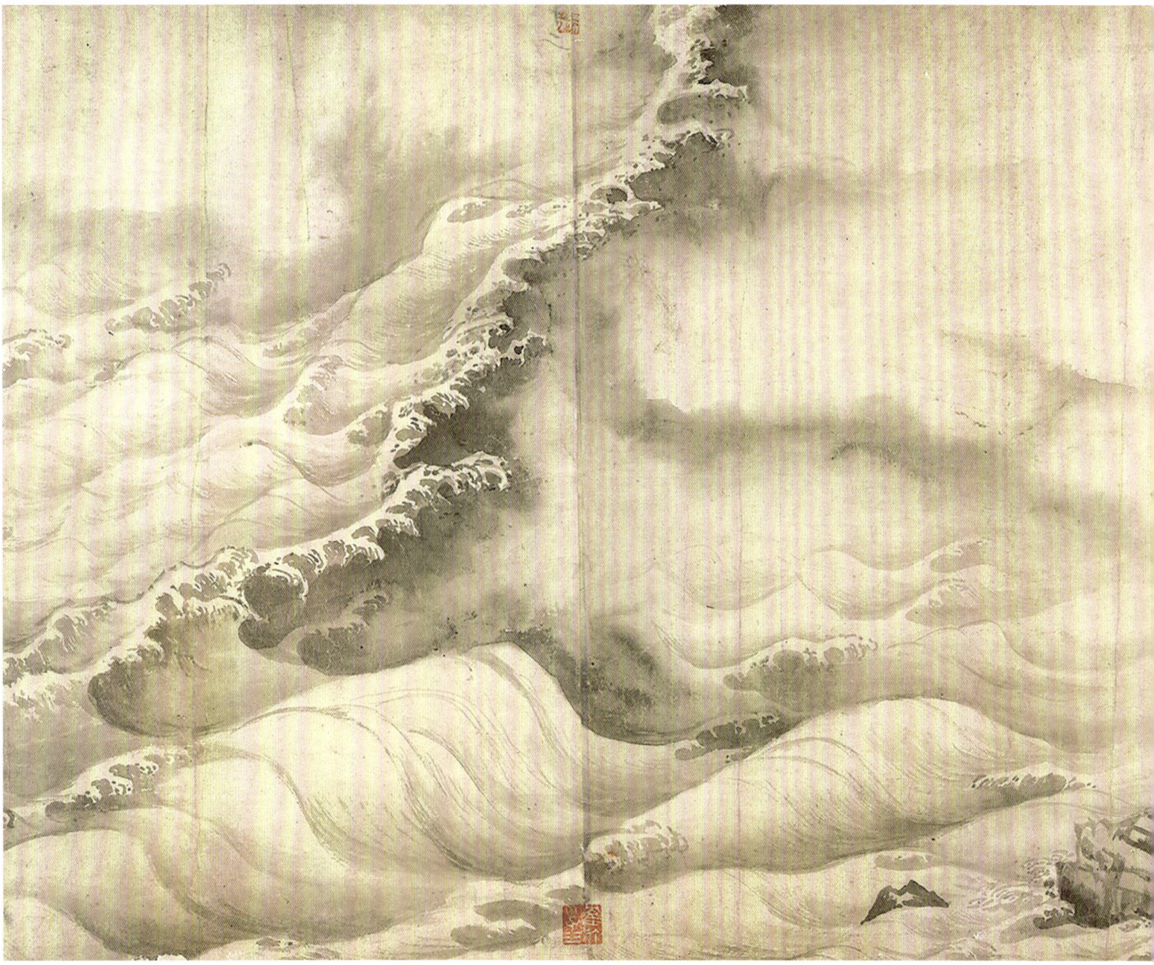

the scenery and moods of the river. His only surviving work is the sensational *Ten Thousand Li on the River* (fig. 41), which was in two Wuxing collections in the fifteenth and sixteenth centuries, and is now in the Palace Museum, Beijing. It was greatly admired by the Ming colophon writers, who praised in prose and poetry the tremendous force of the *dao* conjured up by Zhao Fu in the headlong rush of the river to the sea.[98] It seems likely that this painting came to the attention of Zhou Chen when he was casting about for a mythical storm to represent the heroic character of Beiming. He took the great wave from the last passage, where the river meets the sea, but moved it to the opening of his scroll and translated the primal energy of the sea into an intricate and

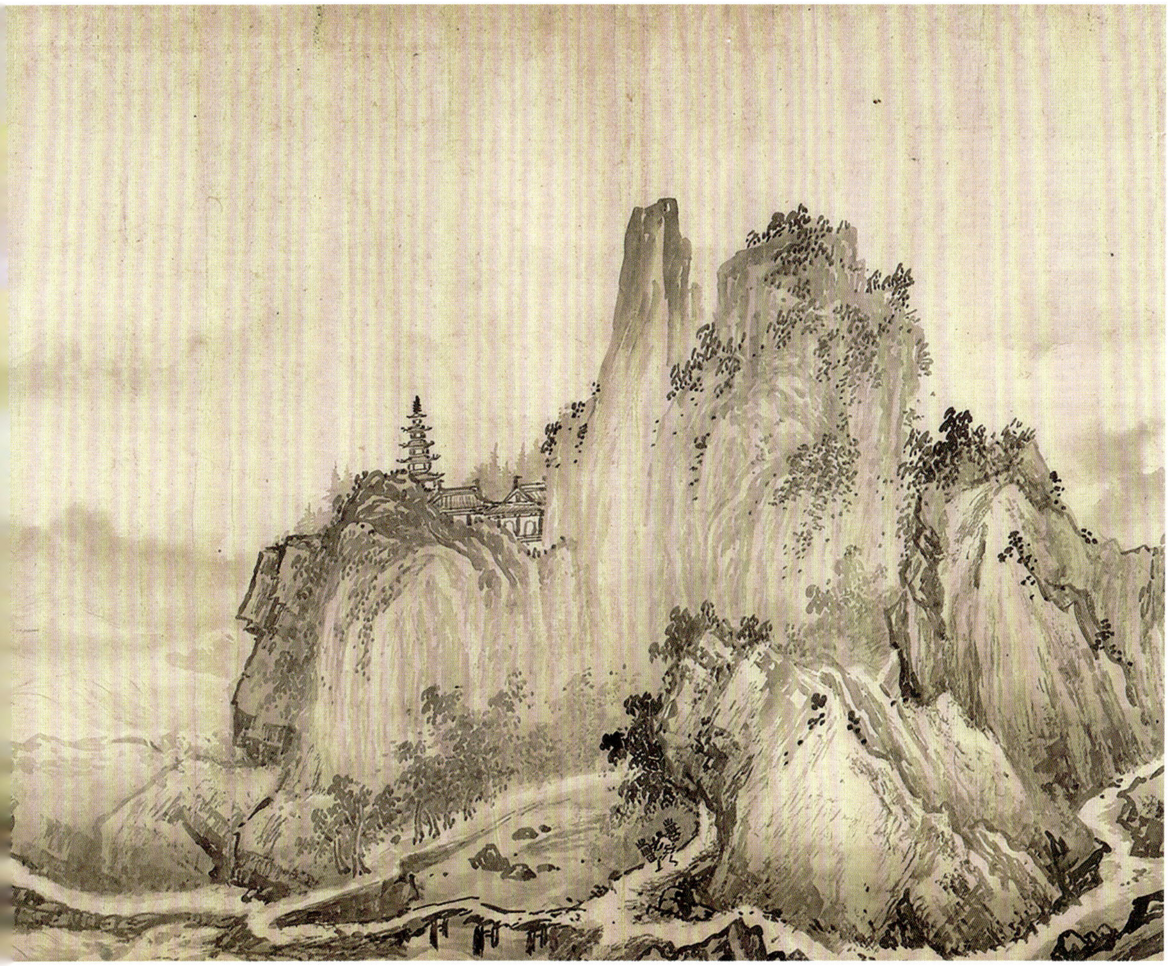

manneristic calligraphy of waves more suited to a symbolic context. He studied the rocks in Li Tang's work and the painting of clouds in Zhao Fu's and the dragon masters'.

The *hao* painting subtype of commemorative art was always intended to eulogize the subject and could also serve to advertise him in a discreet way. To many potential patrons this was a matter of importance, especially to musicians such as Yang Jijing, who, as we have seen, benefited from the assistance of the painters. A glance at the recipients of honorary scrolls in Suzhou shows that a large number of them were doctors and apothecaries. The medical profession was on the rise in the early Ming period, and doctors sought to advance from the level of herb-gatherer

41 Zhao Fu (active 1131–1162). *Ten Thousand Li on the River* (*Jiang shan wanli tu juan*). Detail of last section. Handscroll; ink on paper, 45.1×992.5 cm. Palace Museum, Beijing

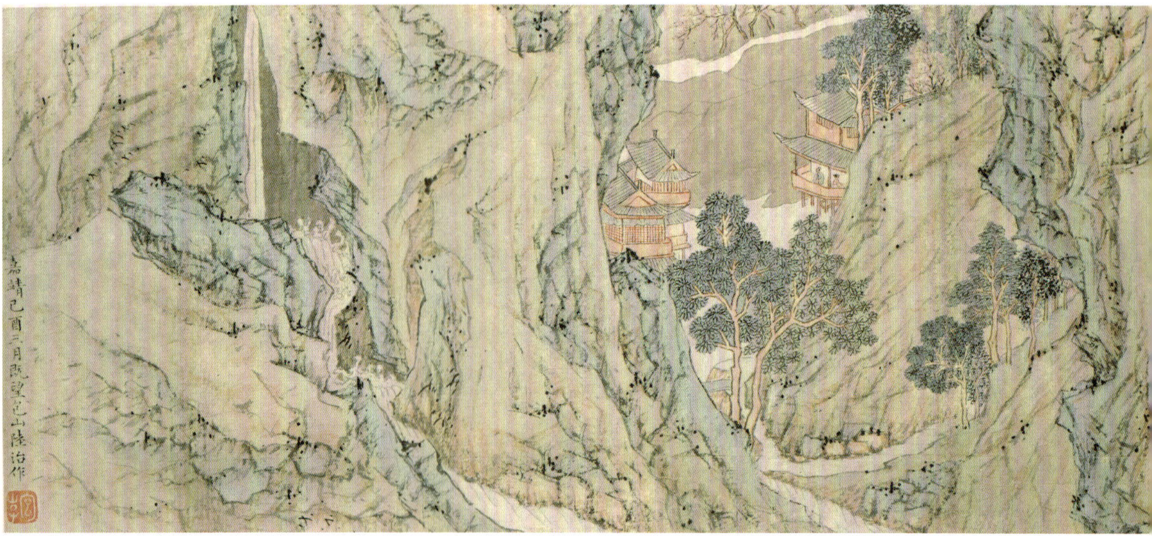

and druggist to equality with the scholar-official. Certainly the doctors collected paintings for the pleasure of looking at them but also for the social cachet they conferred and as a sign of the improved status of their profession. Moreover, they had begun to realize that art is a powerful instrument for the publication of professional skills and services, all the more powerful in the hands of a great master. Suzhou's most famous painters—Shen Zhou, Wen Zhengming, Tang Yin, Lu Zhi (1496–1576)—all dedicated paintings to doctors.

The most delightful and inventive of such paintings is *The Jade Field* (*Yutian*) by Lu Zhi (fig. 42), painted in 1549 at the request of the doctor Wang Laibin. It once carried a poem by Lu Zhi, a set of poems by Suzhou scholars, and a record explaining that Doctor Wang's *biehao* was Yutian. The original inscriptions were separated from the painting and replaced with forgeries,[99] but the quality of the painting is so fine, and it fits in Lu Zhi's oeuvre so convincingly, that its authenticity has never been questioned. The name seems to have fired Lu Zhi's imagination in the execution of the painting. He takes flight in an ingenious conceit celebrating the magic potency of jade which in ancient China had a legendary capacity to protect against illness and mortality. The name Jade Field was especially appropriate for a medical man, and Lu Zhi's pictorial celebration of its virtues can easily be read as a eulogy of Doctor Wang's technical expertise.[100] The image of *yutian* that Lu Zhi conceived and committed to paper in no way resembles the real carved jade objects known to us in Chinese decorative art, but a freely imagined vision of garden rocks—enlarged to fill the picture frame, pierced with bizarre holes, and dyed a transparent green. The viewer is deliberately disoriented by an incoherent spatial structure and a distorted scale which offer nothing

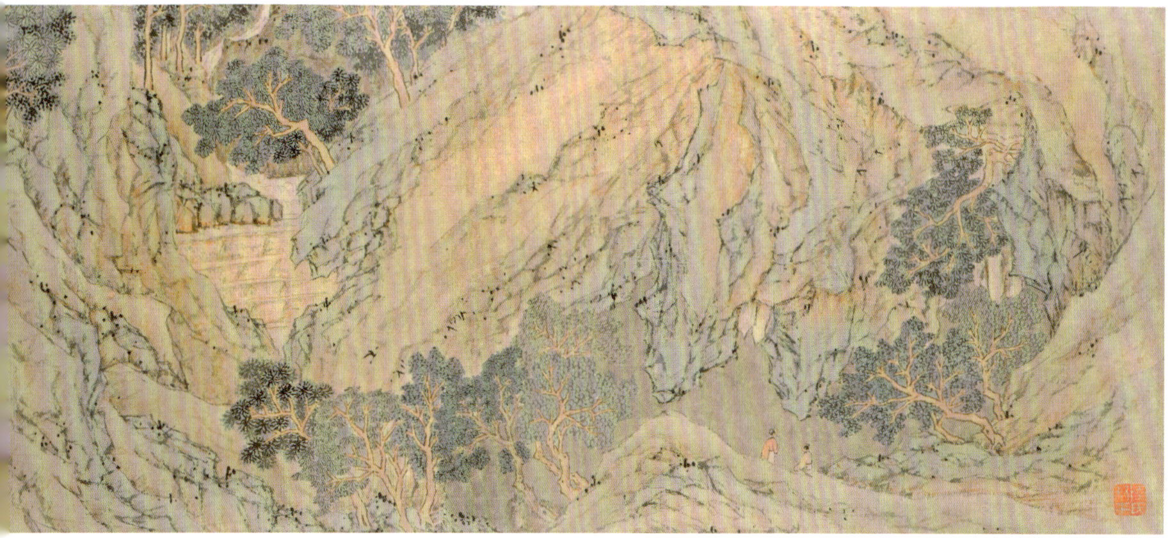

familiar but induce a sense of trance or dream. The rocks are implausible, seeming more like heaving surf than stone, and the stalactite cave is a memory of Zhang Gong's grotto, a geological wonder in Wuxing. How could such a confection be explained if the preface (no longer included on the scroll) did not tell us that it was all cooked up in honor of a doctor who wanted to publicize his superior professional talents?

One of the great charms of Wu school painting is the imaginative perception with which the painters were able to disguise the sometimes prosaic and monetary aspect of their art. The illustration of a *biehao* often acted on them as a stimulus for the invention of fresh pictorial imagery. The image, first aroused in the artist's mind by language, led away from nature in the painting toward abstract and even mildly fantastic forms. But although Lu Zhi had a taste for fantasy and allowed it more play than his contemporaries did, he never resorted to extremes of distortion or hinted at aggression.

The Suzhou painters and writers were adept at mutual collaboration and in the sixteenth century played the great game of word and image with relish and ever more buoyant flights of imagination. Place-names played an important part in the discourse of commemoration: of all the devices employed to voice the symbolism of the *hao*, the most widely used and the most apt to deal with the double meaning of the genre was the place-name. This device came easily to scholarly practice because in ancient China famous men were called by the name of the district in which they lived. The famous tenth-century painter Li Cheng, from Yingqiu, was called Li Yingqiu; his follower in the eleventh century, Guo Xi, was called Guo Heyang (as present-day Henan was then known). An admired personage became known by his domicile rather than his *ming* (name), and to be

42 Lu Zhi (1496–1576). *The Jade Field* (*Yutian*), 1549. Handscroll; ink and color on paper, 24.2 × 136.1 cm. The Nelson-Atkins Museum of Art, Kansas City, Missouri. Purchase: William Rockhill Nelson Trust, 50–68

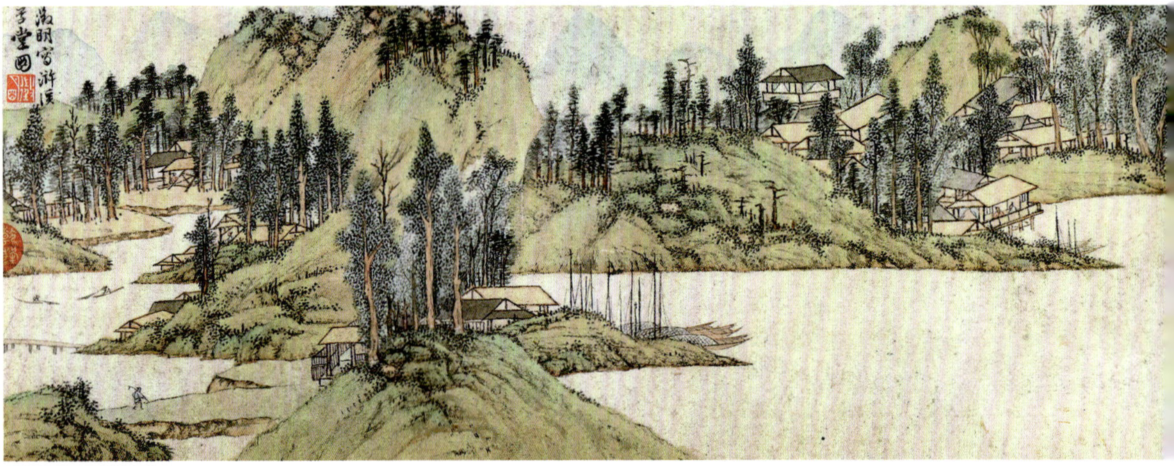

called by the name of one's domicile was a mark of respect. By Song times it was commonplace to refer to a person by the name of his estate or study pavilion, e.g., Su Dongpo and Li Longmian, and these names became *hao*, too. Place-names used as *hao* are distinctly ambiguous, because, depending on the context, the name may refer either to the man or to the place where he lived. Yet Chinese writers treated person and place as identical, and most commemorative paintings adopted the name of the pavilion as a metonym for its owner, the implication being that his intellectual labors there were the real measure of his quality as a man. Hence the great and lasting symbol of the recluse and the reclusive life became the library, recast as a thatched hut to imply the absence of pretension in its owner.

A painting that treats the identity of man and place, and the man's loyalty to the place, is *Thatched Hut at Huxi* (*Huxi caotang tu*) (fig. 43), executed by Wen Zhengming in collaboration with the writer Lu Can (1494–1551).[101] The handscroll was commissioned in 1535 by a scholar, Master Shen, making plans for his retirement. According to Lu Can's preface, it is a topographical painting representing an actual place, a farming community west of Suzhou named Huxi. However, it is really a panegyric on the moral character of Master Shen, whose family owned ancestral land in Huxi. Forty years earlier, Master Shen had given up his patrimony to his brothers to pursue Confucian scholarship at a school in Suzhou. Now about to retire, he longed to return to his native Huxi but was unwilling to ask for a share of the land from his brothers. Lu Can explains his dilemma:

Thirty *li* west of Wu city (Suzhou) there is a place called Hushu [also Huxi] on the main north–south road. There boats and carriages gather as at a hub; cottages and wells crowd as densely as a wall. Yet broad fields spread out on all sides, and the landscape is fragrant and orderly—indeed a lovely place. The family of my friend, Shen Tianmin, has dwelt there for many generations. When Master Shen took up

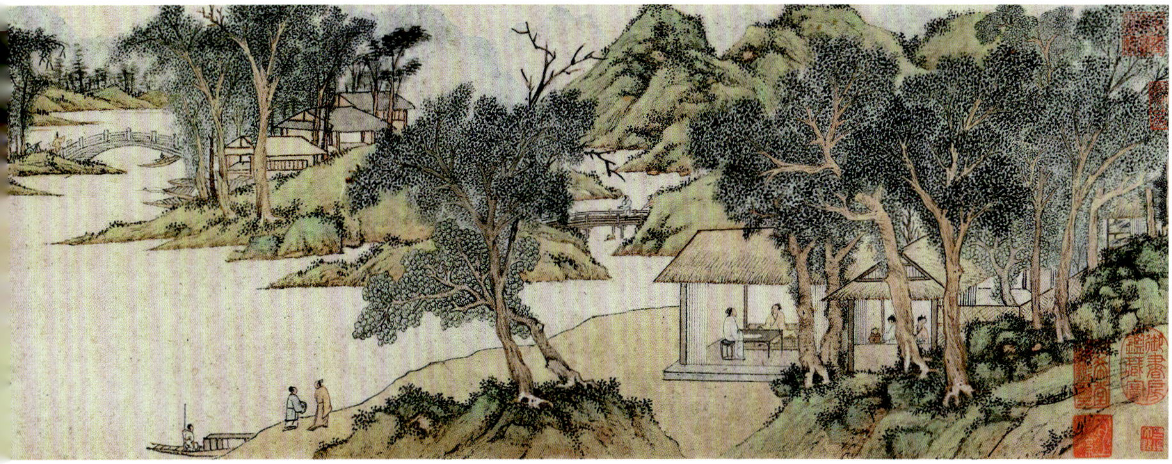

scholarship and entered the Confucian school, he moved his residence several hundred paces east of the college for convenience in his studies. He was unfortunate: he sat several times for the civil service examination seeking office but did not succeed. This year he retired and was awarded the honor of an imperial decree and ceremonial dress.

He said to me: "From my childhood on I have devoted myself to books, and I have now lived in the city for forty years, always gazing westward at my old village and thinking affectionately of it, as if all the places where my ancestors planted trees, fished, wandered in the country, and where they were buried, were right before my eyes. I returned every year to visit their tombs and never for a single day forget to think of it. Therefore I have taken Huxi as my *hao* to declare my longing and have also named my house [in Suzhou] Huxi. The *Taishi* Master Hengshan (Wen Zhengming) has honored me by making a picture of Huxi like a poem. Could you not record this meaning of the name Huxi for me?

[...]

When I first moved here [to Suzhou] I left the old farm to my brothers and their families so they might plow the land and live by it. If now I should take it back for my own convenience they and their children would lose their dwelling place and livelihood. I cannot bear to do that. I will grow old in town."

I [Lu Can] yielded, sighing, and said: "In this you are worthy beyond other men. To remember your roots is filiality; to behave unselfishly is *ren*. Filial conduct is to be devoted to family; benevolence is to be generous to the clan. On these two principles the ancients modeled their conduct.

Those today, capped, robed, and called *junzi*, cannot always live up to this [standard]. Thus you are worthy beyond other men. I am insignificant, and my words carry no weight, so I cannot make an example of your conduct for the benefit of the world. But I will write a word to show to your sons and grandsons so that your conduct may not be forgotten. I composed this "Record of the Huxi Thatched Hut" on the first day of the ninth month of autumn in 1537—Lu Can of Chenhu.[102]

43 Wen Zhengming (1470–1559). *Thatched Hut at Huxi* (*Huxi caotang tu*), 1535. Handscroll; ink and color on paper, 27 × 143 cm. Liaoning Provincial Museum

吳城之西三十里，有地曰滸墅，當南北之衝，舟車輳集，廬井聯絡，與城郭不殊。而其間田疇寬衍，泉石芳潔，固樂土也。友人沈君天民，家於茲累世矣。君既業儒為校官弟子，乃遷居學宮之東數百武，以便肄習。而君數奇，屢試有司不利。頃以年至得謝去。且遇詔例有章服之榮。間語予曰：自吾結髮讀書，僑居城市者，今四十年矣。每西望故里，慨然興思。凡吾先人種樹釣遊之處，與其體魄之藏焉者，恍若在目焉。雖歲時不廢展省，而猶不能一日忘於懷也。因自號滸谿，以著吾志。且以名所居之堂。而太史衡山先生辱為之圖若詩矣。子盍為我記。[...] 誠有意於復其故業，誰能禦者。君曰：然。是吾心也。抑自吾之始遷而來也。先人之舊田廬，既以讓吾兄弟若子姓。俾耕而食其中久矣。今將復取之，苟便於身，而俾兄弟子姓之失所。吾不忍也。吾老於城市矣。予退而嘆曰：君於是乎賢遠於人。夫不忘其本孝也。不私其有，仁也。孝能篤於親，仁能厚於族，斯二者，古之人則行之。而今之衣冠而稱君子者，乃往往有愧焉。君於是乎賢遠於人，顧予賤，且言不足信，不能彰之以勵夫薄俗也。姑為書之以示其子孫，俾無忘焉。作滸谿草堂記。嘉靖丁酉秋九月朔日。前進士東胡陸粲書。

Shen Tianmin had discovered to his chagrin that the path to scholarship was long and hazardous. He had studied in Suzhou as a *shengyuan*, the lowest rank of student-scholar receiving a regular stipend from the government. He was legally committed to remain a student-scholar until he passed the provincial examination or retired. He never passed. When at last he accepted retirement, the emperor granted him a decree conferring on him the rank and dress of a scholar and exempting him from corvée labor.[103] Despite his disappointment, Master Shen demonstrated his filial affection and declared his loyalty to his ancestors by renouncing reclusion in his old home in the country, accepting instead "reclusion in the city," a figure of speech introduced in the Song period to accommodate the host of scholars who had private reasons for preferring town life. He assuaged his homesickness by renaming his Suzhou house Huxi and adopting that name as his *biehao*. To remind his descendants, and the world, of this occasion, he requested a painting from Wen Zhengming, a record from Lu Can, a set of poems from friends witnessing this rite of passage, and a formal title for the assembled work from Wang Guxiang. He clearly commissioned the scroll so that a formal account of his retirement might be placed in the family record. Lu Can duly explains the history of the family with many exclamations of admiration and, in the moralizing tradition of social biography, attributes their continuing good fortune to Shen's generosity and filial affection.

Wen Zhengming's painting does not represent the new Huxi in the bustling city of Suzhou, nor even the old Huxi in the country, a working plantation from which the Shen family derived its income. Rather he conceives an ideal place of classical calm and serenity: simplified, sublimely ordered, all the thatched houses from the same mold, the shorelines horizontal and parallel, and the trees vertical and uniform. The geometric formality of the structure and the fastidious ordering of the terrain were favorite devices of Wen Zhengming when he wished to convey a state of ideality. In the opening passage, the meticulous discipline relents only enough to allow the trees immediately surrounding the Shen family dwelling to incline slightly so as to draw attention to it. Wen Zhengming may have had in the back of his mind a memory of the old myth of the islands of the immortals adrift in a blue-green mist. But he has given it a modern Ming face, secularized and peopled with Suzhou scholars transported to the country on a perpetual sabbatical.

This view of the reclusive life is, of course, not what existed, but what was longed for. The purpose of commemorative art, as also poetry, was to determine the high values in life, to embody them in visible form, and to set them, even if temporarily, before the owner of the scroll.

The most sought-after painter of *hao* subjects in Suzhou was Tang Yin, who was, strictly speaking, a professional painter dependent on commissions for a living. But he was also a man of letters, having earned the *jinshi* degree and then seen it rescinded in an examination scandal. He commanded the aptitude and the imagination of a writer and was happiest when he could load his picture with literary baggage. He pursued a successful career in Suzhou for twenty-five years, mostly dedicated to producing commemorative paintings and writing honorific prose.

Tang Yin's neighbor in Suzhou, a Master Chen,[104] was a zealous practitioner of the fine art of serving and drinking tea. He adopted the *hao* Shiming (Serving Tea), which embraced his pleasure in tea and his philosophy of life. He invited the painter to make a picture of him as he awaited a guest invited for tea and contemplated the significance of the occasion (fig. 44).[105] He and Lu Can both had a taste for literary complexity, so he asked Lu to write the *bian*, the explanation of the origin of a *hao*. The essay is cast in the form of a dialogue between Lu Can, who defends his friend, and a visitor who attacks him, debating whether Master Chen is guilty of being obsessed with tea. (In the Confucian view obsession was an excessive indulgence in emotion that depleted a person's mental energy, and was hence a threat to the balanced mind.)

VISITOR: Does Master Chen value tea too greatly?
LU CAN: No.
VISITOR: Is he obsessed with it?
LU CAN: How could he be obsessed with it? Rather he finds in it a way to lodge his [feelings]. Everyone in the world accepts the idea of tea, but who truly understands it? Master Chen truly understands it. That is what "lodging" really means.
VISITOR: How does he engage in the practice of tea?
LU CAN: He places the utensils in order by a lattice window, lays out the water [jar] and the [tea] scoop, lights the pine branches, and boils the water until "crab's eyes" [small bubbles] rise. For these [trivial things], he has warm feelings. He gathers close friends together and shares with them a fine aesthetic experience.
VISITOR: If [the service] is like this, is it not close to obsession?
LU CAN: [Characters missing].... The proof of this lies in Yumeng's case.[106] So Master Chen is truly engaged in the practice of tea, serene when things are proper, compliant when they are not. That is not obsession. Master Chen is not given to obsession. The service of tea has its Dao. If [you try it yourself], you will realize that it does. How could Master Chen find mere relaxation in serving tea? [Lu Can then offers a second instance of Chen's detachment.] The way Master Chen plays the *qin* preserves the art of Zhou of Yongmen.[107] At that time, Zhou's followers excelled but could not reach his level. Thus we know that Master Chen does not expend all his powers on tea; rather he engages in it without exhausting his abilities. And this practice is true "lodging" [of his feelings].

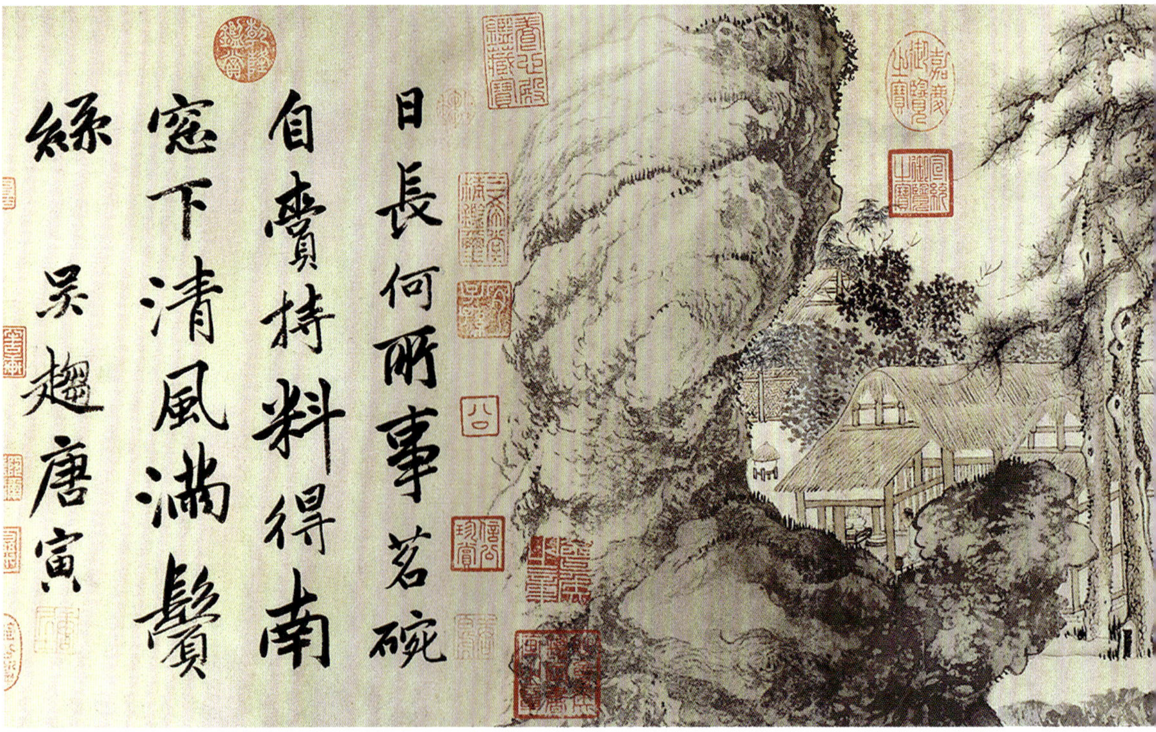

VISITOR: And does he not fully expend his powers in playing the *qin*?

LU CAN: There are none who do not eat and drink, but few who know flavor.[108] The ancients set this as their model. Those who enter into the Dao come near it. Of Master Chen we can say that he knows tea, but does he therefore in serving it disclose all he knows of it? Truly its virtues are inexhaustible. In everyday life Master Chen is courteous and inoffensive, upright and resolute, scrupulous in everything he does, and in using tea as lodging.

The visitor agreed and retired, saying: "Only now do I understand Master Chen's [*hao*], Shiming."

Mid-autumn 1535—Lu Can, Pingyuan[109]

客曰陳子尚乎。予曰否。陳子溺歟。曰曷溺哉。陳子寓也。天下莫不由之，孰則知之。陳子誠知之。斯寓爾然，則陳子曷事。曰列具綺寮，分江貯月，然松明瀹蟹眼，爰發幽抱，廼集良友，酬嘉風物，于于然也。若是幾於溺矣。曰□徵諸羽濛哉。夫誠深於茗，恬於直，遂於厄非溺耶。陳子弗為也。事必有道，由是而知，道之有矣。陳子豈安茗哉。陳子操縵有雍門之遺，一時學者頡頏未逮。知其弗究於茗也，弗究而事固寓也已。曷弗於縵。曰莫不飲食，鮮能知味，先民則之。入道者迩焉。陳子謂知茗也。將淵其意於茲乎。是益不可以究矣。陳子平居，抑抑不抗，篤信質直，介然有為，故於事事亶乎。其寓也，客唯唯謝曰，今而後知陳子事茗。嘉靖乙未孟秋之吉。

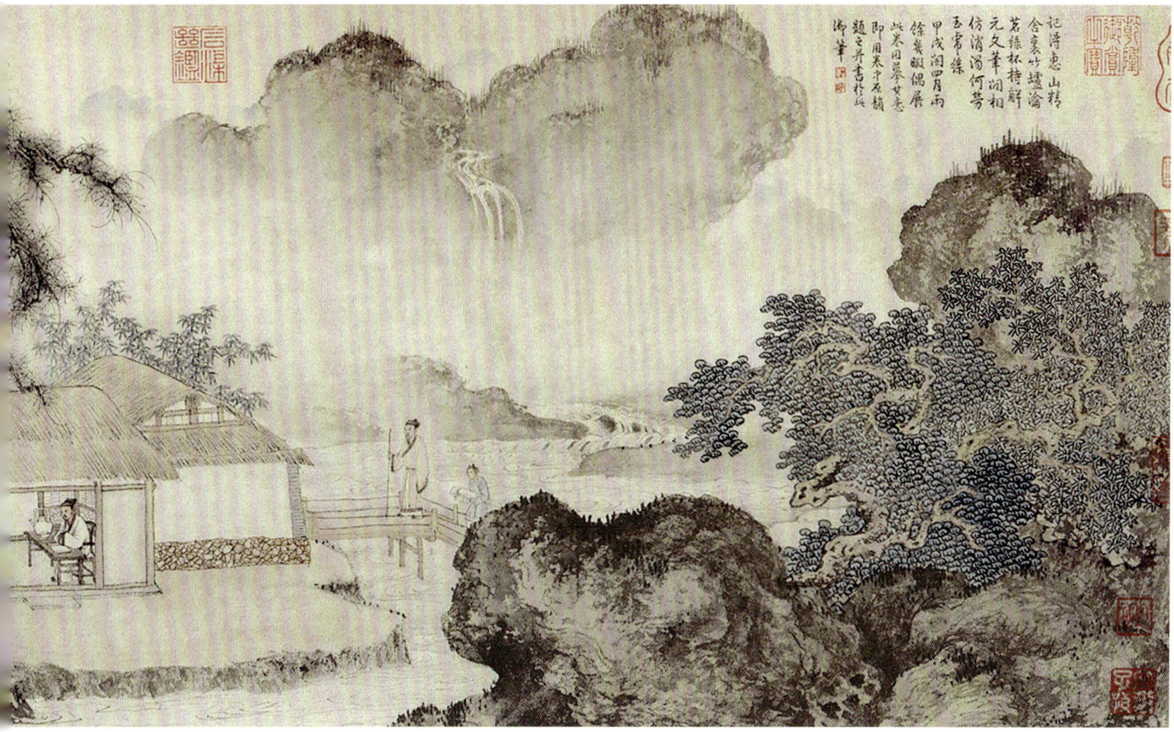

44 Tang Yin (1470–1524). *Shiming Serving Tea* (*Shiming tu juan*). Handscroll; ink and color on paper, 31.2 × 106.9 cm. Palace Museum, Beijing. See also figure 45

Lu Can explains that Master Chen is guided in the service of tea by the study of Dao. In serving tea he attains the abstemious and temperate spirit that is the very opposite of obsession. Possibly Master Chen bore in mind Lu Yu's (733–804) essay on tea, in which the Tang master cautions devotees of tea against extreme practices: "Moderation is the very essence of tea. Tea does not lend itself to extravagance. If a tea is insipid and bland, it will lose its flavor before even half a cup has disappeared. How much more so in the case of extravagance in its use."[110]

This discussion of the *hao* is moralized, like the account of Huxi: Lu Can defends Shiming against the charge of obsession by arguing that he is not consumed by attention to the technique and manners of the tea rite—he merely enjoys it as a civilized and convivial pleasure that offers a temporary expression of feeling. But in this instance he presents the patron as one who has already penetrated the Dao, and through his experience of the Dao has gained a detachment that he brings to all his activities, including the practice of tea and the mastery of the *qin*. The artist's task, then, was to make a painting that would intimate something of this abstruse character.

Tang Yin presented him with this strange and beautiful picture. We would expect to see, as we do, Master Chen in his study and the guest arriving with a boy servant carrying a *qin* (fig. 45). The boy with a *qin* is sometimes a stock figure standing for music generally but is required here as the *qin* is specifically mentioned as one of Master Chen's pursuits. For the same reason the kitchen is glimpsed through a gap in the rocks so the preparation of tea can be noted, even though it will not be examined in depth, and Chen Shiming acknowledged a master. Equally, the white teapot on his desk proclaims him a connoisseur of tea equipage. But the setting (which was actually near Tang Yin's house, outside the north wall of Suzhou) has been transferred to some flawlessly pure and perfect place swimming in a pale light and unbroken peace. Only the boiling black rocks do not belong to the characterization of Chen Shiming but rather serve as a proscenium which formally separates the tea scene from the real world.

It was the writer's task to extend the meaning of the *hao* beyond the owner's tastes and pastimes, which could be illustrated and endowed with feeling, to the final eulogistic role of praising moral character. Of all human traits, this one most resists transformation into imagery, demanding

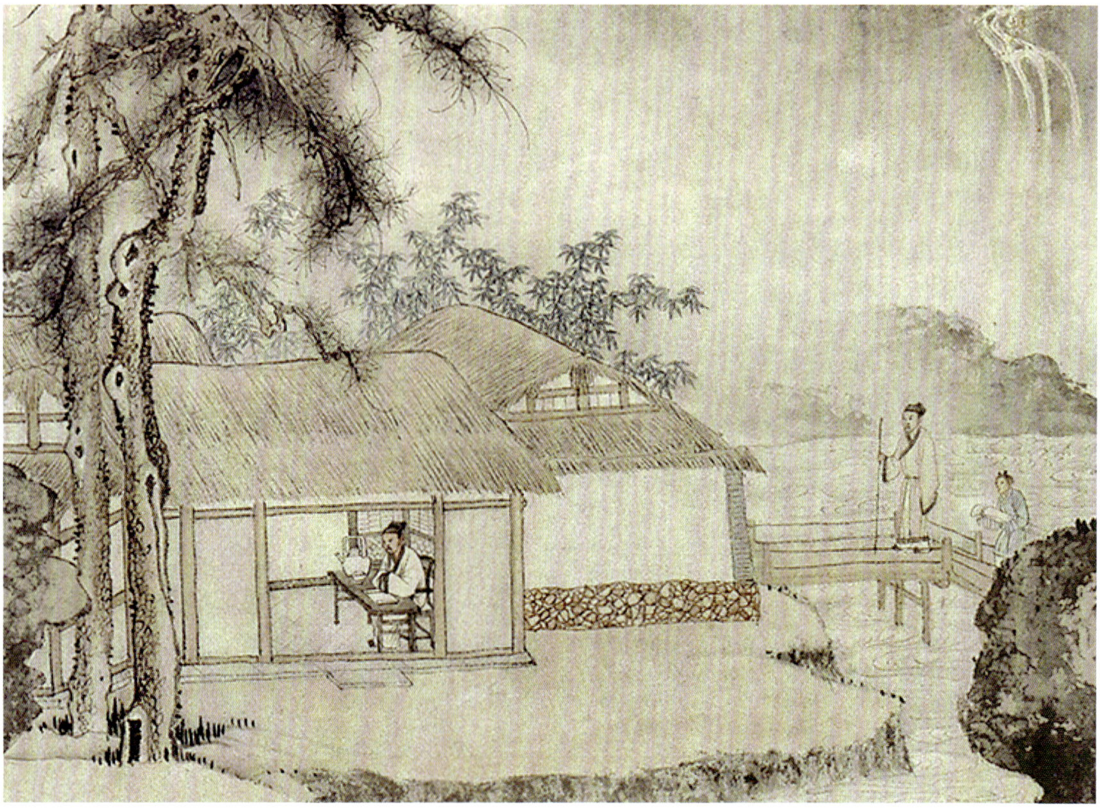

45 Tang Yin (1470–1524). *Shiming Serving Tea* (*Shiming tu juan*). Detail of figure 44

the most in periphrasis, subtlety of invention, and psychological context, and thereby causing the painter to fall back on the written word. The clue to the painted image was buried in the inscriptions, which came to serve as an exegesis for the picture, as we have just seen in the portrait of Chen Shiming. Hence the multitude of records, prefaces, forewords, and explanations on the colophon papers of memorial paintings, starting in the Yuan dynasty and continuing undiminished in the Ming.

Both the literati painters and the professional masters of Suzhou adopted this genre, to the delight of their friends and patrons, and proceeded with enthusiasm to expand the idea beyond the reclusion themes and the simple place-names inherited from the Yuan period. The meaning and implications of the *biehao* were enlarged to include the owner's personal preoccupations, such as the tea cult, sites of special significance, subjective experience like dreams, and professional ambitions disguised in many shades of metaphor.

The Suzhou writers and painters especially sought and found ways to describe models of human excellence and philosophical allegiance of sometimes quite singular kinds. A case in point is a *hao* painting contrived jointly in 1531 by two distinguished citizens of Suzhou, Wen Zhengming and a younger friend of his, Yuan Bao (1499–1576). One of the "Six Talents of the Yuan Family," Yuan Bao was a bibliophile and art collector who had taken as his literary name Woxue, "Sleeping during the Snow."[111] By choosing this *hao*, he meant to declare his admiration for the Confucian worthy Yuan An, whom he had chosen as a model of conduct. Yuan An had died in 92 CE after an eminent career in the Han government and was acknowledged as the founder of the powerful Yuan family. His story, as it was told throughout the history of Chinese painting, was based exclusively on a single episode in his early life when he was a clerical functionary in Henan, quoted in the *Hou Han shu*:

At the time, a great blizzard occurred, accumulating several feet of snow. The magistrate of Luoyang himself went out to investigate the crisis. The people had dug [their houses] out of the snow and were begging for food. When he reached Yuan An's gate and saw no path there, he feared Yuan An was dead. He ordered his men to dig a path and open the door. There they found Yuan An stretched out on the bed asleep. When the magistrate asked why he had not come out for help, Yuan An answered, "The people were starving in the blizzard. It would not have been right to trouble them further." The magistrate judged Yuan worthy and recommended him for the title "filial and incorruptible."[112]

時大雪積地丈餘。洛陽令自出案，行見人家皆除雪，出有乞食者。至袁安門，無有行路。謂安已死，令人除雪。入戶見安僵臥，問何以不出。安曰大雪，人皆餓。不宜干人。令以為賢，舉為孝廉也。

At the time of this event, Yuan An was a young officer in corvée service in the provincial government of Henan, with, as yet, neither means nor reputation. Awaking in his cottage one night during a disastrous blizzard, he took what seemed the most practical and dignified action and went back to sleep instead of rushing outside for help. The magistrate was impressed by his kindness in not troubling the people and by his presence of mind, and he recommended him to the emperor for further official appointment.

Throughout his career as an imperial minister, Yuan An was remembered for this incident and the character it reflected. He came to personify three major virtues: he was scrupulous in his treatment of the people; he would not beg, as unbefitting his dignity; and he was so imperturbable that he could sleep soundly through the worst crisis. At the peak of his distinguished service, long after the incident of the snowstorm, Yuan An exhibited courage and ingenuity in curbing the power of the feudal families who opposed the throne, and the emperor again acknowledged his loyalty. Yuan Bao adopted the *hao* Woxue out of respect for these sterling qualities.

After the Han dynasty, the story of Yuan An developed a history of its own, used to exemplify the virtuous emperor worthy of loyalty and the faithful official who serves him. A Song emperor, dispatching a governor to Nanjing, presented him with a painting titled *Yuan An Sleeping during the Great Snow* (*Yuan An woxue*), composed of eight contiguous hanging scrolls, together with a command to display it in a prominent place where officials and commoners both might profit from its teachings.[113] The emperor's intent was to broadcast a message commanding loyalty to the throne and promising humane government. Emperors of succeeding dynasties in every century from the eighth to the sixteenth ordered their court painters to represent this story. Such famous painters as Wang Wei in the Tang dynasty, Huang Quan and Dong Yuan in the tenth century, Fan Kuan and Li Gonglin in the eleventh, Li Tang in the twelfth, and Zhao Mengfu in the fourteenth century all took up this subject matter.[114] The theme of Yuan An resounded for so long because it was both an imperial commitment to good government and an exhortation to and commendation of the men who made the government work.

Wen Zhengming had strong historicist leanings and was as much preoccupied with the antiquity of painting as with its practice. Of all the past masters, he most admired Zhao Mengfu, a painter who commanded many styles and whom Wen sought to emulate in order to enlarge his own repertory. From Zhao he learned the figure style termed "antique orthodoxy," evident in the tea paintings of Tang Yin (see figs. 30, 44) as well as in Qiu Ying's *Zhao Mengfu Writing the "Heart Sutra"* (see fig. 34). By "antique orthodoxy" Wen meant the idealized naturalism of Tang and Song narrative and figure painting, which had been used for centuries to illustrate old tales and didactic Confucian stories. Although small in scale and elegant in execution, it was especially favored during the Ming dynasty for the representation of heroic themes and admired personalities of the past. Wen, who eagerly copied any work by Zhao he could find, adopted it to illustrate the story of the ideal minister. He tells us how he made such a painting for his friend Yuan Bao, who called himself Woxue (fig. 46):

In the winter of 1531 after a snowfall, Master Yuan Yuzhi [Yuan Bao] came to pay a call at the Tingyun Pavilion [Wen Zhengming's study]. On that occasion we reminisced about Master Zhao Mengfu of the Yuan dynasty who once made a painting for Yuan Jingchun [Yuan Yi, 1262–1306] titled *Yuan An Sleeping during the Great Snow*. So, following Master Zhao's style, I made a painting on that theme [for Yuan Bao]. The next year I borrowed from the Zhu family of Songjiang [for study] an antique painting by Zhao Mengfu with terse and aloof brushwork, restrained and elegant design. Only then did I grasp that his is the ability of the great masters, and I felt ashamed of my own banal dabblings. But Master Yuan did not think it poor. So he had it mounted on a roller and brought it to show me. Then I wrote out Yuan An's biography and had it mounted with the painting....[115]

嘉靖辛卯冬月雪後，袁君與之過余停雲館。因憶勝國時趙文敏公為袁靜春作汝南高士圖。遂仿像為之。明年從松江朱氏借觀松雪舊圖。筆力簡遠，意匠高雅，真得古人能事。始覺區區塵冗可媿也。而袁君不以為劣，裝池成軸，攜來相示。遂抄袁公本傳系之。

Wen and Yuan Bao were discussing an occasion two centuries earlier, when Zhao Mengfu had made a version of *Yuan An Sleeping during the Great Snow* for Yuan Jingchun. Exhilarated by the recollection, they determined to commemorate that event by reenacting it in Wen's study, the Tingyun Pavilion. Yuan Bao's motive was that he shared two names, possibly three, with the personalities in the story. His *hao* alluded to the central act in the Yuan An narrative (sleeping during a blizzard); his family name was the same as Yuan Jingchun's and Yuan An's; and Jingchun may well have been his ancestor. It is also possible that the Yuan families of the Yuan and Ming dynasties claimed descent from Yuan An himself, the founder of the clan. In any case, Yuan Bao's fascination with his namesake persisted, because eleven years later, in 1542, he persuaded Wen Zhengming to paint a second picture of the same subject. Together they examined a genuine work by Zhao Mengfu, were consumed with admiration, and Wen again "copied" it for him, making yet another version to which he freely added motifs to make "the mood lonely, lofty, and detached."[116]

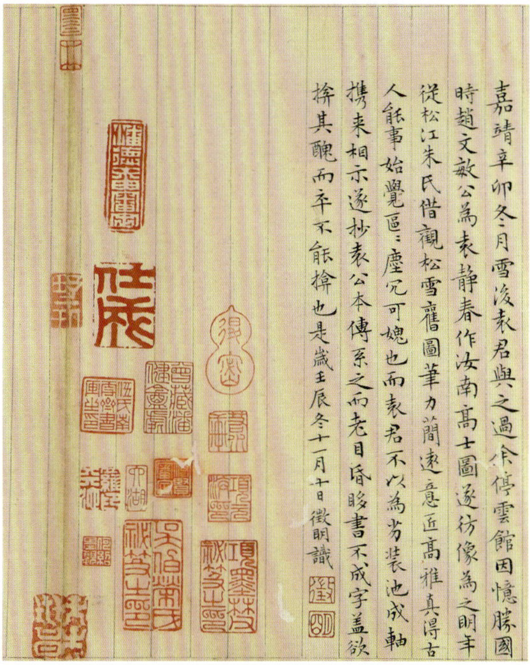

46 Wen Zhengming's colophon, last section, from *Yuan An Sleeping during the Great Snow* (*Yuan An woxue*). See also figure 47

In these and the many other snowscapes he executed during his long career, Wen seems to have been particularly attracted by the formal and expressive effect of snow, which, he explains in a colophon, conveyed to him a sense of moral purity:

In ancient times eminent men and retired officials would play with the brush to paint landscapes for their amusement. They often painted snow scenes, using this theme to convey the idea of a person who is singular, detached, and beyond the ordinary. [117]

古之高人逸士。往往喜弄筆。作山水以自娛。然多寫雪景者。蓋欲假此以寄其孤高拔俗之意耳。

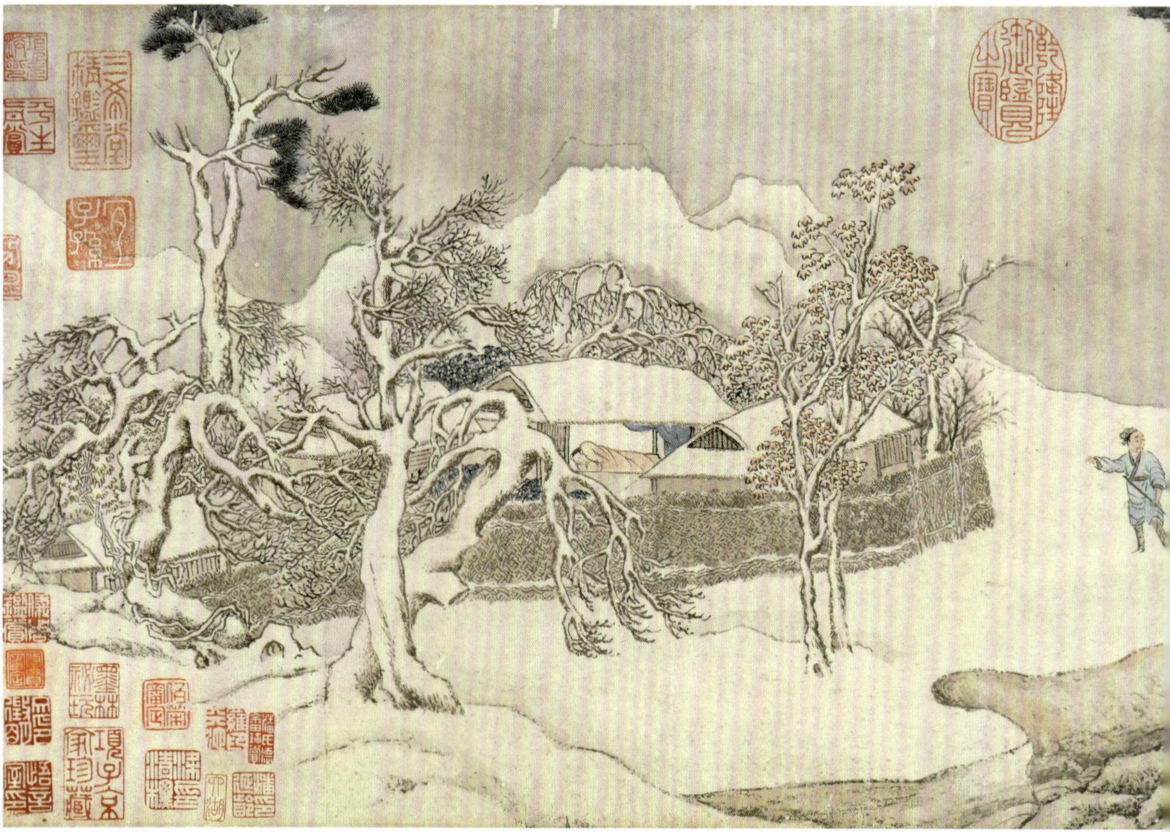

He then lists eight famous snow scenes by the leading masters in Chinese art history, among them Zhao Mengfu's *Yuan An Sleeping during the Great Snow*.[118] In his own *Yuan An* painting (fig. 47), Wen was consciously likening the sharp, clear-cut lines, the strong black-white contrasts, and the capacity of snow to obliterate detail and simplify complexity to Yuan An's uncompromising moral principles. The harsh, pure temper of the winter season is turned into a metaphor for the incorruptible official. Wen had a rare gift for abstraction, to which the snow scene by its nature was especially fitted. It is characteristic of much Wu school painting that when it remakes landscape as a reflection of human character and feeling, the image drifts almost imperceptibly away from nature toward a new level of abstraction and clarity of form. We are reminded again that "antique orthodoxy" is a classicizing style deliberately chosen by painters of honorific pictures because it relates a narrative simply and directly, while idealizing the setting and the personage being honored.

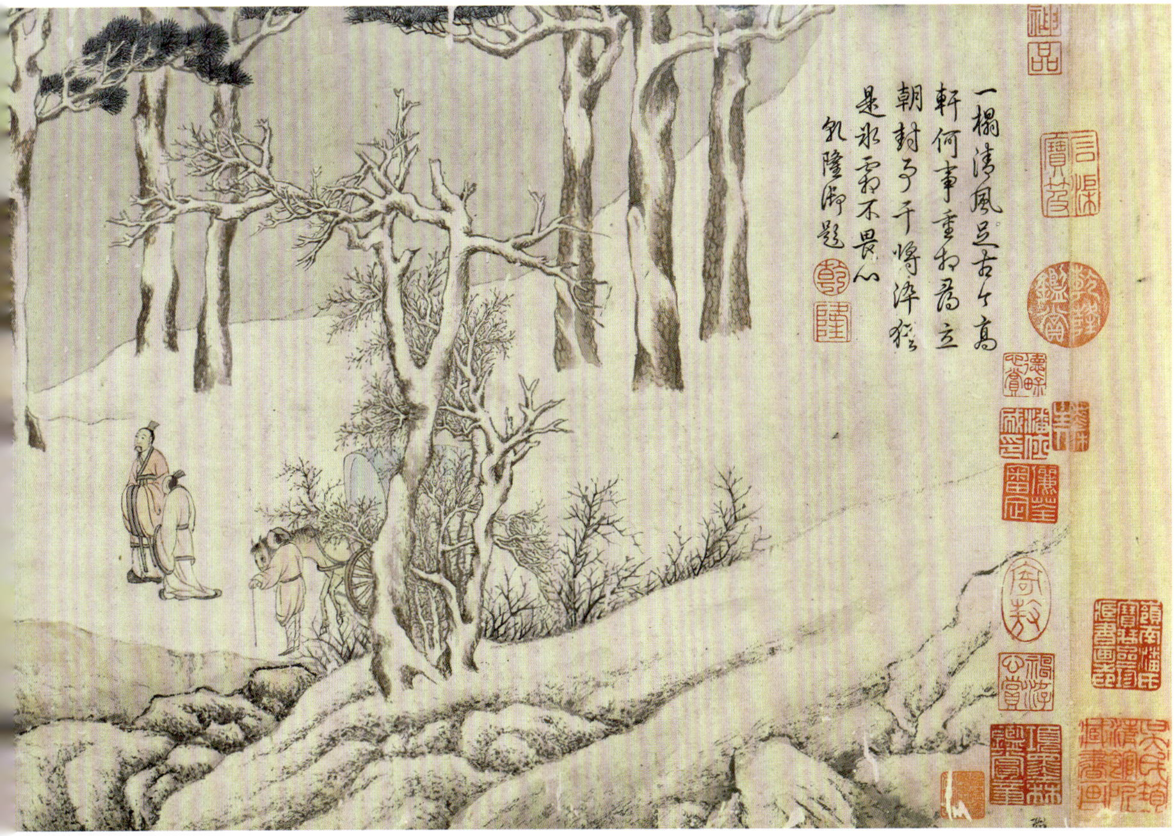

The *biehao* functioned in many ways to introduce new iconography to Chinese painting. In the Yuan An narrative, it was a bridge to the past by means of a name which summoned up old Luoyang, a familiar Eastern Han story about a paragon who was the minister of state. It conveys more about the personalities of Yuan Bao and Wen Zhengming, excavating antiquity for a model of an ethical standard for the present, than it does about Yuan An, who had all but disappeared under layers of mythology and moralizing. The Ming masters used history as if it were a language that spoke of seasons, personalities, places, and events signifying moral principles. To the artists, writers, and patrons who invoked the device of the *biehao*, it was yet another means to apprehend the past and make it live again.

The foundations for the invention of the *hao* painting already existed in the Song dynasty: it is one of several subtypes of biographical painting concerned with the recipient of the painting. It is distinctive by its dependence on the written preface, without which it would not be fully comprehensible. Its verbal conventions are old

47 Wen Zhengming (1470–1559). *Yuan An Sleeping during the Great Snow* (*Yuan An woxue*), 1531. Handscroll; ink and light color on paper, 27.3×78.1 cm. Private collection. See also figure 46

and well tried. The rebus with its double verbal and pictorial meanings is known from Han times on and was widely practiced in the Song dynasty.[119] At first, the pun and *hao* may seem trite, facile, and popularized (they have that reputation in the West in modern times). But to the painters of honorific scrolls in the Yuan and Ming dynasties, they were the visual counterparts of such literary figures of speech as irony, metonymy, metaphor, and periphrasis, all of which afford an indirect means of referencing. These figures were no longer the exclusive prerogative of writers, but became visual substitutes for the literal, the prosaic, and the commonplace, intended to light the painter's invention anew and to seize the viewer's attention as the unexplained image cannot. They simplify and sharpen the meaning of the painting, shedding irrelevancies and stressing singleness of theme.

Beyond its popularity with patrons, the *hao* painting offered to the Ming painter two immeasurable benefits. It lent itself to the theme of landscape, with which the Chinese painter had long been engrossed and which by the Ming dynasty had developed into an indestructible tradition; and landscape reinforced by the written word allowed the painter to treat human will and personality as the real content of art and, finally, to touch on questions of moral virtue. The *hao* picture restored to the iconology of Chinese painting intellectual interest and originality and a degree of individualism unknown before: the Ming painter called his patron quite literally by his name.

* * *

Although commemorative landscape was made as a form of biography intended to be preserved for generations by the honorand's family, it was not made as a fully public monument accessible to everyone. In scale, the images are by no means monumental. The handscrolls are seldom more than a meter in length, as that was ample to support almost any desired number of colophons. The hanging scroll format was rarely used, because it could not accommodate the literary component. Restraint and nuance characterize the preferred styles, which were usually limited to monochrome ink during the Yuan dynasty, whereas subdued color was used in the Ming. The written component of the scroll was understandable only to those who were sophisticated in prose, poetry, and the conventions of honorific biographical writing. This was an art like chamber music, addressed to a limited audience of the initiated but always intent on conveying an exact tone of meaning.

Commemorative landscape paintings, especially those dedicated to the elucidation of the recipient's *hao*, were often cast in styles decided by some event in his real or imagined experience, as *Master Cloudy Woods* was, and were often determined by considerations of his character or a projected state of mind, like *Yuan An woxue* and *Beiming*. These are surprisingly personal declarations, and, perhaps by way of compensation, their style often betrays an intentional degree of removal from the real world—the content of the painting is idealized, and the form becomes abstracted, as if to militate against charges of egoism, sensationalism, or sentimentality, dangers to which a highly subjective art is especially exposed. The figural style of "antique orthodoxy" learned from the Song painters is an example of this. Its slightly impersonal air interposes a certain distance between the subject and the viewer that has the effect of relieving the subject of too close a scrutiny.

The historical outlines of commemorative landscape painting are vague and sporadic in the Song period. They begin to clarify only in the early Yuan dynasty, when paintings of the genre started to resemble one another, clearly implying that artists, writers, and patrons have become conscious of it as a distinct genre and are testing standards for it. By the middle Ming period, it became an institution of social exchange like honorific poetry, familiar to all literati, many of whom specialized in composing explanatory prefaces and colophons for the scrolls. The genre was readily accepted in the Yuan dynasty because it had only a short history of its own in the Song and so was less restricted by precedent than older forms of memorial art like the true portrait. By Song times the portrait had become the almost exclusive vehicle of the ancestor cult, the Buddhist and Daoist churches, and the imperial authority. In each of these cases, it was restricted by prescriptive rules and traditions that resisted change. By contrast, commemorative landscape broke a new path, in which landscape was the apparent subject, but a person, whether represented or not, was the real focus. A landscape setting was required by the three oldest subjects: departure; literary gathering; and house, estate, or study. But the scholar's experience dealt with a much broader range of occasions—travel, anniversary, appointment, promotion, eulogy and elegy, various forms of social support, and advertisement, indeed almost any occasion a patron might conceive. These occasions did not all require a landscape background. Nonetheless, with a remarkable degree of unanimity, all these occasions too were supplied with natural settings, suggesting that the painters and patrons had compelling reasons for preserving landscape. Their reasons may have been purely aesthetic: the forms of landscape are less subject to rules of perspective, more malleable and more easily abstracted. There were no set rules governing the oldest categories of house, departures, and literary gathering. Ni Zan could paint a departure scene that omitted the traveler, and Duan Muzhi could combine occasions of retirement and anniversary into one. The theme of the memorial landscape was rooted in literature, but its visual form and details mutated according to ad hoc artistic circumstances.

The collection of preface and colophons was also only lightly controlled: they were made at the will of the honorand and could be undertaken spontaneously or with deliberation. In some scrolls the components were assembled over many years, as in *Water Village* and *Master Cloudy Woods* (figs. 16, 37); in others components were omitted, as in *Beiming* (fig. 40). In most cases, the painting preceded the colophons, affording the writers a preview of the subject; but this cannot be taken as a firm rule. In some instances, the recipient seems to have begun by collecting written pieces, only later deciding to add a painting as a centerpiece. If he had a motive other than self-interest to seek such a tribute, it would have been a sense of filial duty: to leave a formal record of his loyalty to and achievement in the family name, which would lend prestige to his descendants. None of the writings on the paintings examined here mention motives more personal than that, and even these compliments are conveyed through another speaker.

The mounting popularity that memorial landscape painting enjoyed in the Yuan dynasty can be partly accounted for by its relative freedom from pre-established rules. Such paintings were not conferred on the individual by an official public authority (except perhaps at the village level), and neither did they place the recipient under obligation to the state or the civil service. The makers themselves decided on the form the paintings took and chose the occasion for declaring, commissioning, or awarding them. As a social institution, the making and giving of memorial paintings was resilient and relatively free of restraint: any educated man could initiate such a gift, and it could be adapted to almost any set of particulars — hence the sense of freedom it offered to scholars seeking a channel of expression independent of government, encumbered by only a moderate weight of tradition, dedicated to and dominated by themselves.

Notes

1. Stephen Owen, ed. and trans., *An Anthology of Chinese Literature: Beginnings to 1911* (New York: W. W. Norton, 1996), 374–75.

2. Ibid., "The Song of the Yang Pass" (also called "Song of Weichen" [Wei City]).

3. Herbert A. Giles, trans., *Chuang Tzu: Mystic, Moralist, and Social Reformer,* 2nd rev. ed. (Shanghai: Kelly and Walsh, Ltd., 1926), chap. 1, 1–5. Zhuangzi originated the figure of the phoenix (*rukh* in Giles) soaring southward in a cosmic storm. Zhou Chen's *Beiming* (see fig. 40) illustrates the same passage.

4. For Qionglin, see R. H. Matthews, *A Chinese-English Dictionary* (Shanghai: China Inland Mission, 1931), 177.

5. Miyeko Murase, "Farewell Paintings of China: Chinese Gifts to Japanese Visitors," *Artibus Asiae* 32, nos. 2/3 (1970): 211–36.

6. Ibid., 220.

7. Shih Shou-chien, "'Yuyu chunshu' yu Mingdai zhongqi Suzhou zhi songbietu," in *Fengge yu shibian: Zhongguo huihua shi lunji,* Meishu kaogu congkan 4 (Taipei: Yuncheng wenhua shiye gufen youxian gongsi, 1996), 226–55.

8. Susan Bush, *The Chinese Literati on Painting: Su Shih (1037–1101) to Tung Ch'i-ch'ang (1555–1636),* Harvard-Yenching Institute Studies 27 (Cambridge, MA: Harvard University Press, 1971), 8–9.

9. Max Loehr, "Chinese Paintings with Sung Dated Inscriptions," *Ars Orientalis* 4 (1961), 244. The colophons are in Wu Rongguang, *Xinchou xiaoxia ji,* Yishu shangjian xuanzhen ji series (Taipei: Hanhua wenhua shiye gufen youxian gongsi, 1971), *juan* 2: 21.

10. Elizabeth Brotherton, "Two Farewell Handscrolls of the Late Northern Sung," *Archives of Asian Art* 52 (2000–2001): 49; *Tuhui baojian, juan* 4: 102 in *Huashi congshu,* vol. 3 (Shanghai: Shanghai renmin meishu chubanshe, 1963).

11. Julia K. Murray, "Ts'ao Hsün and Two Southern Sung History Scrolls," *Ars Orientalis* 15 (1985): 1–29. Also, Murray, "A Southern Sung Painting Regains Its Memory: *Welcoming the Imperial Carriage* (*Ying-luan t'u*) and Its Colophon," *Journal of Sung and Yuan Studies* 22 (1992): 109–24.

12. Murray, "A Southern Sung Painting Regains Its Memory" (note 11 above), 119.

13. Robert E. Harrist, Jr., "Art and Identity in the Northern Sung Dynasty," in *Arts of the Sung and Yüan: Papers Prepared for an International Symposium Organized by the Metropolitan Museum of Art in Conjunction with the Exhibition Splendors of Imperial China: Treasures from the National Palace Museum, Taipei,* ed. Maxwell K. Hearn and Judith G. Smith (New York: The Metropolitan Museum of Art, 1996), 147–63. For a comprehensive history of Li Gonglin's *Mountain Villa,* see Robert E. Harrist, Jr., *Painting and Private Life in Eleventh-Century China: Mountain Villa by Li Gonglin* (Princeton: Princeton University Press, 1998).

14. The bizarre style must also be the result of repeated copying by imitators who failed to grasp Li's original intention.

15. *Song Liao Jin huajia shiliao* (Documentary Materials on Painters of the Song, Liao, and Jin Dynasties), comp. Chen Gaohua (Beijing: Wenwu chubanshe, 1984), 459.

16. Ronald C. Egan, "Poems on Paintings: Su Shih and Huang T'ing-chien," *Harvard Journal of Asiatic Studies* 43, no. 2 (1983): 431–33.

17. Loehr, "Chinese Paintings with Sung Dated Inscriptions" (note 9 above), 258. See also Max Loehr, "Fishing Village at Hsi-sai Mountain," in *Chinese Calligraphy and Painting in the Collection of John M. Crawford, Jr.*, ed. Laurence Sickman, exhib. cat. (New York: Pierpont Morgan Library, 1962), 61–65.

18. Wen C. Fong, *Beyond Representation: Chinese Painting and Calligraphy, 8th–14th Century* (New York: The Metropolitan Museum of Art; New Haven: Yale University Press, 1992), 249–56.

19. Charles Lachman, trans., *Evaluations of Sung Dynasty Painters of Renown (Liu Tao-ch'un's Sung-ch'ao ming-hua p'ing)* (Leiden and New York: E. J. Brill, 1989), 62–63, *juan* 2: 6r.

20. Susan Bush and Hsio-yen Shih, comps. and eds., *Early Chinese Texts on Painting* (Cambridge, MA: Harvard University Press, 1985), 154–55. See also Richard M. Barnhart, *Wintry Forests, Old Trees: Some Landscape Themes in Chinese Painting*, exhib. cat. (New York: China House Gallery, China Institute in America, 1972), for metaphorical uses of natural forms in Chinese painting.

21. The best reproduction of this dark handscroll is in *Jin Tang Liang Song huihua: Shanshui louge*, ed. Jin Weidong et al. (Shanghai: Shanghai kexue jishu chubanshe; Hong Kong: Shangwu yinshuguan, 2004), 94–99, pl. 11, colophons 257–60. Good plates and some critical comments also in the Hanhai Auction Co. catalogue, Beijing, October 1995: unpaginated, approx. twenty pages of text and plates. Selected texts in *Shiqu baoji xubian*, comp. Wang Jie et al. (1793), facsimile repr. in *Bidian zhulin Shiqu baoji hebian* (Taipei: Guoli gugong bowuyuan, 1971), vol. 3, 1510.

22. Zhou Mi's Record does not include Hu Yuan's original preface. See note 32 below.

23. Richard E. Strassberg, *Inscribed Landscapes: Travel Writing from Imperial China* (Berkeley: University of California Press, 1994), 134–37.

24. "A Single Sail," in *Jin Tang Liang Song huihua: Shanshui louge* (note 21 above), 258. "Milky Way" alludes to the myth of the weaving maid and the herd boy who followed her along the Huanghe (Yellow River) and up into the stars.

25. The themes of the ten poems, from right to left as inscribed on the scroll, are: (1) Zhang Wei's response to the prefect's invitation to a literary gathering; (2) the crane; (3) a jade butterfly; (4) a single sail; (5) (partially effaced at upper margin); (6) returning swallows; (7) the sound of beating clothes; (8) ninety years; (9) farewell to the *xiucai;* (10) weaving at night. See *Jin Tang Liang Song huihua: Shanshui louge* (note 21 above), 257–58.

26. Ibid., 258. The Tiao River is in Wuxing, Zhejiang Province.

27. Ibid.

28. Hanhai Auction Catalogue (note 21 above), pp. 1 and 5.

29. The commentator in *Zhongguo huihua quanji* dismisses the attribution to Zhang Xian as "traditional" (vol. 3, 7). Xu Bangda accepts it in the Hanhai Auction Catalogue (note 21 above), p. 1.

30. Scarlett Jang, "Representations of Exemplary Scholar-Officials, Past and Present," in *Arts of the Sung and Yuan: Ritual, Ethnicity, and Style in Painting*, ed. Cary Y. Liu and Dora C. Y. Ching (Princeton: The Art Museum, Princeton University, 1999), 56–58.

31. Ibid., 51.

32. Zhou Mi et al., *Qidong yeyu* (preface dated 1291), annot. Li Deqing (Shanghai: Huadong shifan daxue chubanshe, 1987), 385–87.

33. Strassberg, *Inscribed Landscapes* (note 23 above), 134–37; Ellen Johnston Laing, "Real or Ideal: The Problem of the 'Elegant Gathering in the Western Garden' in Chinese Historical and Art Historical Records," *Journal of the American Oriental Society* 88, no. 3 (1968): 419–35. For *Five Old Gentlemen of Suiyang*, see Thomas Lawton, *Chinese Figure Painting*, exhib. cat. (Washington, D.C.: Freer Gallery of Art, 1973), nos. 41, 42; and Li Lin-ts'an, "The Five Old Men of Sui-yang," *Gugong jikan* 7, no. 5 (November–December 1973): 1–21.

34. Richard Vinograd, "Family Properties: Personal Context and Cultural Pattern in Wang Meng's *Pien Mountains* of 1366," *Ars Orientalis* 13 (1982): 11.

35. David Nivison, "Aspects of Traditional Chinese Biography," *Journal of Asian Studies* 21, no. 4 (August 1962): 457–63.

36. Ibid., 463.

37. Ibid., 457. Endymion Wilkinson gives an exacting account of the many kinds of commemorative writing current in the Song and Yuan dynasties in his *Chinese History: A Manual*, 2nd ed. (Cambridge, MA: Harvard University Asia Center in association with Harvard University Press, 2000), 120–28.
38. Chu-tsing Li, *Autumn Colors on the Ch'iao and Hua Mountains: A Landscape by Chao Meng-fu* (Ascona: Artibus Asiae, 1965), 53ff.; James Cahill, *Hills beyond a River: Chinese Painting of the Yüan Dynasty, 1279–1368* (New York: Weatherhill, 1976), 45–46. Colophons: *Shiqu baoji*, comp. Zhang Zhao et al. (1745), facsimile repr. in *Bidian zhulin Shiqu baoji hebian* (Taipei: Guoli gugong bowuyuan, 1971) pt. 1, vol. 1, 577–85.
39. Qian Dejun's *fu*: *Shiqu baoji*, pt. 1, vol. 1, 579–80.
40. Qian Dejun's two *ji* dated 1315: *Shiqu baoji*, pt. 1, vol. 1, 579, 581.
41. See John C. Ferguson (Fu Kaisen), *Lidai zhulu huamu* (Taipei: Taiwan Zhonghua shuju, 1968), vol. 2, 387–96.
42. Colophon by Qian Liangyou: *Shiqu baoji*, pt. 1, vol. 1, 582.
43. David Sensabaugh, "Life at Jade Mountain: Notes on the Life of the Man of Letters in Fourteenth-Century Wu Society," in *Chūgoku kaigashi ronshū: Suzuki Kei Sensei kanreki kinen* (Tokyo: Yoshikawa Kōbunkan, 1981), 44–69. See also idem, "Guests at Jade Mountain: Aspects of Patronage in Fourteenth-Century K'un-shan," in *Artists and Patrons: Some Social and Economic Aspects of Chinese Painting*, ed. Chu-tsing Li et al. (Lawrence, KS: Kress Foundation Department of Art History, University of Kansas; Kansas City: Nelson-Atkins Museum of Art, in association with University of Washington Press, 1989), 93–100.
44. Sensabaugh, "Life at Jade Mountain" (note 43 above), 59.
45. For colophons, see *Gugong shuhua lu* (Taipei: National Palace Museum, 1965), vol. 3, *juan* 5: 271–72.
46. F.W. Mote, *The Poet Kao Ch'i, 1336–1374* (Princeton: Princeton University Press, 1962), 94–98.
47. Ibid., 98–99.
48. *Gugong shuhua lu* (note 45 above), vol. 3, *juan* 5: 271–72.
49. Ibid., 272. Lü Min was a sometime Daoist and occasionally wore Daoist dress and took refuge in the Daoist community. The "Crane and Gourd Study," otherwise unidentified, may have been his.
50. Zhou Zimei is not further identified.
51. For information on Ni Zan's life, see Wen C. Fong et al., *Images of the Mind: Selections from the Edward L. Elliott Family and the John B. Elliott Collections of Chinese Calligraphy and Painting at The Art Museum, Princeton University*, exhib. cat. (Princeton: The Art Museum, Princeton University, in association with Princeton University Press, 1984), 105ff. For his biography, see also *Dictionary of Ming Biography, 1368–1644*, ed. L. Carrington Goodrich and Chaoying Fang (New York: Columbia University Press, 1976), 1090–93.
52. For Ni Zan's poem, see *Zhongguo huihua quanji*, vol. 8, *yuan*, 34. See also "Chao Yin Shih," in David Hawkes, trans., *Ch'u Tz'u: The Songs of the South, an Ancient Chinese Anthology* (New York: Oxford University Press, 1962), 119–20.
53. Unidentified as yet, but his history is almost certainly discussed in the many inscriptions on the colophon papers (illegible in the plates). See *Chūgoku kaiga sōgō zuroku*, comp. Suzuki Kei, vol. 4 (Tokyo: Tōkyō Daigaku Shuppankai, 1982–83), no. 30–274.
54. Reproduced and recorded in Yang Xin, ed., *Gugong bowuyuan cang Ming Qing huihua* (Beijing: Zijincheng chubanshe, 1994), no. 9.
55. Mary Ann Rogers, "Visions of Grandeur: The Life and Art of Dai Jin," in Richard M. Barnhart, et al., *Painters of the Great Ming: The Imperial Court and the Zhe School*, exhib. cat. (Dallas: Dallas Museum of Art, 1993), 127–94.
56. *The Zhenshou Tang* by Tang Yin is reproduced with all seventeen colophons in *Zhongguo gudai shuhua tumu*, vol. 20 (Beijing: Wenwu chubanshe, 1999), no. 1–1383; also in Gu Wenbin, *Guoyun lou shuhua ji* (preface dated 1882) (repr., Taipei: Hanhua wenhua shiye gufen youxian gongsi, 1971), *juan* 4: 14–16.
57. *Tiewang shanhu* records a *zhenshou tang* memorial of 1366 to which Wang Meng contributed a poem. See Du Mu (1459–1525), *Tiewang shanhu*, Yishu shangjian xuanzhen series (Taipei: Guoli zhongyang tushuguan, 1970–), *juan* 10, p. 787.
58. For the exam scandal of 1499, see Anne de Coursey Clapp, *The Painting of T'ang Yin* (Chicago: University of Chicago Press, 1991), 2–8.
59. See Jiang Zhaoshen, "Wupai huajia bixia de Yang Jijing," *Gugong jikan* 8, no. 1 (Autumn 1973): 57–70 (Chinese), 35–47 (English); Wu Sheng (18th century), *Daguan lu* (preface dated 1712), Yishu shangjian xuanzhen series (Taipei: Guoli zhongyang tushuguan, 1970), vol. 4, *juan* 20:

23–25; An Qi (b. 1683), *Moyuan huiguan* (preface dated 1742), *juan* 4: 246 in *Yishu congbian*, ed. Yang Jialuo (Taipei: Shijie shuju, 1962–67), vol. 17.

60. See Jiang Zhaoshen, "Wupai huajia" (note 59 above), 61–66; and James C. Y. Watt, "The *Qin* and the Chinese Literati," *Orientations* 12, no. 11 (November 1981): 38–49.

61. Jiang Zhaoshen, "Wupai huajia" (note 59 above), 59.

62. Wen Zhengming's portrait, formerly in the Wuxi City Museum, is recorded in *Shuhua jianying*, vol. 2, *juan* 21: 9. Wen Boren's portrait is in the National Palace Museum. See Jiang Zhaoshen, "Wupai huajia" (note 59 above), 57–70, pl. 4B.

63. For Xi Kang, see Audrey G. Spiro, *Contemplating the Ancients: Aesthetic and Social Issues in Early Chinese Portraiture* (Berkeley: University of California Press, 1990), 76–81, passim.

64. Wen Zhengming, *Wen Zhengming huigao* (Shanghai: Shenzhou guoguangshe, 1929), *juan* 9: 107. See also Craig Clunas, *Elegant Debts: The Social Art of Wen Zhengming, 1470–1559* (Honolulu: University of Hawai'i Press, 2004), passim.

65. Victor H. Mair, ed., *The Shorter Columbia Anthology of Traditional Chinese Literature* (New York: Columbia University Press, 2000), 241.

66. The *Great Wind Tower* and its inscription, now in the Palace Museum, Beijing, are reproduced in Gugong bowuyuan, ed., *Mingdai Wumen huihua* (Beijing: Gugong bowuyuan zijincheng chubanshe; Hong Kong: Shangwu yinshuguan,1990), no. 33.

67. Mote, *The Poet Kao Ch'i* (note 46 above), 185.

68. Clapp, *Painting of T'ang Yin* (note 58 above), 33–37.

69. For floods, see Clapp, *Painting of T'ang Yin* (note 58 above), 33–37, 254, nn. 35, 36.

70. Claudia Brown, "Ch'en Ju-yen and Late Yuan Painting in Suchou" (PhD dissertation, University of Kansas, 1985), 118–22, app. 309–16. The painting is reproduced in *Gugong shuhua tulu*, vols. 6, 7 (Taipei: Guoli gugong bowuyuan, 1991). For the colophon, see *Gugong shuhua lu* (note 45 above), vol. 3, *juan* 5: 271.

71. Phillip Bloom, "Mapping Violence in the Late-Yuan Jiangnan Landscape," unpublished manuscript, 18.

72. Brown, "Ch'en Ju-yen and Late Yuan Painting in Suchou" (note 70 above), 309–10.

73. *Gugong shuhua lu* (note 45 above), vol. 3, *juan* 5: 275.

74. The Sanhai Shrine was built to honor Zhou Chu; see Bloom, "Mapping Violence" (note 71 above), 11.

75. Published in Charles Fabens Kelley, "A Chinese Painting of the Ming Dynasty," *Bulletin of the Art Institute of Chicago* 36, no. 3 (March 1942): 34–36. For the colophons, see Pang Yuanji (1864–1949), *Xuzhai minghua lu* (preface dated 1909), Yishu shangjian xuanzhen sanji series (repr., Taipei: Hanhua wenhua shiye gufen youxian gongsi, 1971), *juan* 4: 5–8.

76. Clapp, *Painting of T'ang Yin* (note 58 above), 52–56.

77. For Zhu Yunming's poem, see Pang Yuanji, *Xuzhai minghua lu* (note 75 above), *juan* 4: 5–6. For names and terms, please see the Glossary.

78. Pang Yuanji, *Xuzhai minghua lu* (note 75 above), *juan* 4: 7.

79. For Lu Tong and his poem on tea, see *Tang shi jianshang cidian*, comp. Xiao Difei et al. (Shanghai: Shanghai cishu chubanshe, 1983), 1036–38. For Lu Yu, see "The Autobiography of Instructor Lu," in Mair, ed., *The Shorter Columbia Anthology of Traditional Chinese Literature* (note 65 above), 452–55; and *Zhongguo wenxue jia dacidian*, vol. 1 (Taipei: Shijie shuju, 1974), no. 1516.

80. The same version is described by Du Mu in *Tiewang shanhu* (note 57 above), *juan* 4: 86–87; and by Tang Yin in *Shiqu baoji sanbian*, comp. Hu Jing et al. (1817), facsimile repr. in *Bidian zhulin Shiqu baoji hebian* (Taipei: Guoli gugong bowuyuan, 1969), vol. 2, 905.

81. For Huang Yiqing, see *Yuanren zhuanji ziliao suoyin*, ed. Wang Deyi et al. (Beijing: Zhonghua shuju, 1987), vol. 3, 1481. For Li Meng, see ibid., vol. 1, 461–62.

82. *Yuandai huajia shiliao*, comp. Chen Gaohua (Shanghai: Shanghai renmin meishu, 1980), 65–66. When one is poor, one eats fish.

83. Ibid., 15–16, 12.

84. James Cahill, *Hills Beyond a River: Chinese Painting of the Yüan Dynasty, 1279–1368* (New York: Weatherhill, 1976), 48.

85. For the colophons, see Lu Xinyuan, *Rangliguan guoyan xulu* (supplement) (Wuxing: Yigutang, 1891), *juan* 3: 13a–29a; reproduced in Xie Zhiliu, *Tang Wudai Song Yuan mingji* (Shanghai: Gudian wenxue chubanshe, 1957), pls. 105, 106.

86. Cui Yanhui may have found his match in the poem by Bai Juyi quoted by Li Chi in his article "The Changing Concept of the Recluse in Chinese Literature," which surveys a spectrum of types of recluse from the Zhou dynasty to the eighteenth century; see

Harvard Journal of Asiatic Studies 24 (1962–63), 243. The poet speaks sardonically, Cui in earnest.

87. "Empty reputation" is possibly quoted from Ban Gu in the *Hanshu*. I have not identified "Shortcut to the Capital" by a Tang writer.

88. Lu Xinyuan, *Rangliguan guoyan xulu* (supplement) (note 85 above), *juan* 3: 14b–16a. I am indebted to Richard Vinograd for his translation of this passage by Xu Yikui in his dissertation, "Wang Meng's 'Pien Mountains': The Landscape of Eremitism in Later Fourteenth Century Chinese Painting" (PhD dissertation, University of California, Berkeley, 1979), 223–40, 259–64. Translation adapted slightly from Vinograd.

89. See Li Chi, "The Changing Concept of the Recluse in Chinese Literature" (note 86 above), 243.

90. Lu Xinyuan, *Rangliguan guoyan xulu* (supplement) (note 85 above), *juan* 3: 28a. In Wang Shizhen's (1526–1590) opinion, the left margin had been trimmed a few inches by a mounter.

91. For Zhou Fang's second colophon of 1381, see Lu Xinyuan, *Rangliguan guoyan xulu* (supplement) (note 85 above), *juan* 3: 27a–27b.

92. For Wang Yu's colophon dated 1378, see Lu Xinyuan, *Rangliguan guoyan xulu* (supplement) (note 85 above), *juan* 3: 19a–20b. See Joseph Chang's argument for the dating of the painting in his article "From *The Clear and Distant Landscape of Wuxing* to *The Humble Hermit of Clouds and Woods*," *Ars Orientalis* 37 (2009): 39–40. Chang accepts 1375 rather than 1381 as the terminus ante quem for the execution of the painting, based on Zhao Yi's inscription of 1375.

93. Gugong bowuyuan *Mingdai Wumen huihua* (Beijing: Gugong bowuyuan zijincheng chubanshe; Hong Kong: Shangwu yinshuguan, 1990), 211, no. 1; *Zhongguo gudai shuhua tumu*, vol. 20 (note 66 above), no. 1–1000.

94. Zhang Chou, *Qinghe shuhua fang* (preface dated 1616) (repr., Taipei: Xuehai shuju, 1975), vol. 3, *hai:* 6.

95. *Eight Dynasties of Chinese Painting: The Collections of the Nelson Gallery-Atkins Museum, Kansas City, and the Cleveland Museum of Art*, ed. Wai-kam Ho et al., exhib. cat. (Cleveland: Cleveland Museum of Art, 1980), no. 158.

96. Laurence Sickman expressed this opinion to me years ago when I first saw the painting in the Nelson Gallery.

97. See note 3 above.

98. *Zhongguo huihua quanji*, vol. 4 (Beijing: Wenwu chubanshe, 1999), p. 30, nos. 99–105.

99. *Eight Dynasties of Chinese Painting* (note 95 above), no. 181. Colophons possibly once belonging to the Nelson Gallery's scroll are recorded in *Shiqu baoji* (note 38 above), pt. 1, vol. 1, 392–93.

100. Louise Yuhas, "The Landscape Paintings of Lu Chih, Part I," *National Palace Museum Bulletin* 20, nos. 5/6 (November–December 1985, January–February 1986): 16–17.

101. *Liaoning sheng bowuguan canghua ji* (Beijing: Wenwu chubanshe, 1962), vol. 2, 30–31. See also *Shiqu baoji* (note 38 above), pt. 1, vol. 2, 1031–33.

102. *Shiqu baoji* (note 38 above), ibid.

103. Ping-ti Ho, *The Ladder of Success in Imperial China: Aspects of Social Mobility, 1368–1911* (New York: Columbia University Press, 1962), 172–75.

104. Liu Jiu'an, "Wumen huajia zhi biehao tu ji jianbie juli," *Gugong bowuyuan yuankan*, no. 3 (1990): 55. Liu identifies Chen Shiming as Tang Yin's neighbor in Suzhou. His *ming* is not known.

105. Clapp, *Painting of T'ang Yin* (note 58 above), 93–96.

106. Yumeng (Fine Rain, probably a *hao*) is unidentified.

107. Zhou of Yongmen (or Zhou Yongmen) was a celebrated *qin* player of the Warring States period, whose music could move men to tears.

108. James Legge, "Doctrine of the Mean," in idem, *The Chinese Classics* (Hong Kong: Hong Kong University Press, 1960), vol. 1, 387.

109. Reproduced in *Zhongguo huihua quanji*, vol. 13 (Beijing: Wenwu chubanshe, 2000), no. 100. Colophons are published in *Shiqu baoji* (note 38 above), pt. 1, vol. 1, 600–1.

110. Lu Yü. *The Classic of Tea*, trans. Francis Ross Carpenter (Boston: Little, Brown, 1974), 111.

111. *Dictionary of Ming Biography, 1368–1644*, ed. L. Carrington Goodrich and Chaoying Fang (note 51 above), vol. 2, 1627.

112. Fan Ye, *Hou Han shu* (Taipei: Dingwen, 1999), *juan* 75: 936. I am grateful to Joseph Chang, who discerned the "Woxue" seal on *Yuan An Sleeping during the Great Snow* when the handscroll was on exhibition at Oberlin College in April 2007. The seal identified the collector for whom Wen Zhengming painted the scroll in 1531. Wang Meng's *Small Retreat of Master Cloudy Woods* (*Yunlin xiaoyin tu*) was also in Yuan Bao's collection in the sixteenth century. See the collection seal "Woxue cang" in Lu Xinyuan, *Rangliguan guoyan xulu* (note 85 above), *juan* 3: 13.

113. Alexander C. Soper, trans. and annot., *Kuo Jo-Hsü's Experiences in Painting (T'u-hua chien-wên chih): An Eleventh-Century History of Chinese Painting, together with the Chinese Text in Facsimile* (Washington, D.C.: American Council of Learned Societies, 1951), 92, 202, n. 684.

114. For Wang Wei, see Susan Bush and Hsio-yen Shih, comps. and eds., *Early Chinese Texts on Painting* (Cambridge, MA: Harvard University Press, 1985), 100. For Huang Quan et al., see Wu Rongguang, *Xinchou xiaoxia ji* (Taipei: Hanhua wenhua shiye gufen youxian gongsi, 1971), *juan* 5: 37.

115. Wen Zhengming, *Wen Zhengming huigao* (Shanghai: Shenzhou guoguangshe, 1929), *juan* 6: 63.

116. Bian Yongyu, *Shigu tang shuhua huikao* (1682) (repr., Shanghai: Jiangu shushe, 1921), vol. 4, 478.

117. *Gugong shuhua lu* (note 45 above), vol. 2, 187–88.

118. Inscribed on the National Palace Museum's handscroll *Crossing a Mountain Pass in Snow* in the style of Wang Wei. Ibid., vol. 2, 188.

119. Qianshen Bai, "Image as Word: A Study of Rebus Play in Song Painting (960–1279)," *Metropolitan Museum of Art Journal* 34 (1999), passim.

Selected Bibliography

An Qi 安岐 (b. 1683). *Moyuan huiguan* 墨緣彙觀 (A Record of Calligraphy and Painting I Was Destined to See). Preface dated 1742. Four *juan* of 1908 edition; repr. in *Yishu congbian,* ed. Yang Jialuo. Vol. 17, no. 161. Taipei: Shijie shuju, 1962–67.

Arts of the Sung and Yüan: Papers Prepared for an International Symposium Organized by the Metropolitan Museum of Art in Conjunction with the Exhibition Splendors of Imperial China: Treasures from the National Palace Museum, Taipei, ed. Maxwell K. Hearn and Judith G. Smith. New York: The Metropolitan Museum of Art, 1996.

Arts of the Sung and Yuan: Ritual, Ethnicity, and Style in Painting, ed. Cary Y. Liu and Dora C. Y. Ching. Princeton: The Art Museum, Princeton University, 1999.

Bai, Qianshen. "Image as Word: A Study of Rebus Play in Song Painting (960–1279)." *Metropolitan Museum of Art Journal* 34 (1999): 57–72.

Barnhart, Richard M. *Wintry Forests, Old Trees: Some Landscape Themes in Chinese Painting.* Exhib. cat. New York: China House Gallery, China Institute in America, 1972.

———, et al. *Painters of the Great Ming: The Imperial Court and the Zhe School.* Exhib. cat. Dallas: Dallas Museum of Art, 1993.

Beasley, W. G., and E. G. Pulleyblank, eds. *Historians of China and Japan.* London: Oxford University Press, 1961; repr., Taipei, n.d.

Bian Yongyu 卞永譽 (1645–1712). *Shigu tang shuhua huikao* 式古堂書畫彙攷 (Notes and Records on Calligraphy and Painting). 1682; repr., Shanghai: Jiangu shushe, 1921.

Brotherton, Elizabeth. "Two Farewell Handscrolls of the Late Northern Sung." *Archives of Asian Art* 52 (2000–2001): 44–62.

Brown, Claudia. "Ch'en Ju-yen and Late Yuan Painting in Suchou." PhD dissertation, University of Kansas, 1985.

———. "Some Aspects of Late Yuan Patronage in Suchou." In *Artists and Patrons: Some Social and Economic Aspects of Chinese Painting,* ed. Chu-tsing Li, James Cahill, and Wai-kam Ho, 101–10. Lawrence, KS: Kress Foundation Department of Art History, University of Kansas; Kansas City: Nelson-Atkins Museum of Art in association with University of Washington Press, 1989.

Bunjinga suihen 文人畫粹編. Vol. 2. *Tōgen, Kyonen* (董源, d. 962), and *Kyonen* 巨然. Tokyo: Chūōkōronsha, 1974.

Bush, Susan. *The Chinese Literati on Painting: Su Shih (1037–1101) to Tung Ch'i-ch'ang (1555–1636).* Harvard-Yenching Institute Studies 27. Cambridge, MA: Harvard University Press, 1971.

Bush, Susan, and Hsio-yen Shih, comps. and eds. *Early Chinese Texts on Painting*. Cambridge, MA: Harvard University Press, 1985.

Cahill, James. "Confucian Elements in the Theory of Painting." In *The Confucian Persuasion*, ed. Arthur F. Wright, 115–140. Stanford: Stanford University Press, 1960.

———. *Hills beyond a River: Chinese Painting of the Yüan Dynasty, 1279–1368*. New York: Weatherhill, 1976.

———. *An Index of Early Chinese Painters and Paintings: T'ang, Sung, and Yuan*. Berkeley: University of California Press, 1980.

———. "Meanings and Functions in Chinese Landscape Painting." In *Three Alternative Histories of Chinese Painting*, 37–69. Lawrence, KS: Spencer Museum of Art, University of Kansas, 1988.

———. *Parting at the Shore: Chinese Painting of the Early and Middle Ming, 1368–1580*. New York: Weatherhill, 1978.

Chang, Joseph. "From *The Clear and Distant Landscape of Wuxing* to *The Humble Hermit of Clouds and Woods*." *Ars Orientalis* 37 (2009): 32–47.

Chūgoku kaiga sōgō zuroku 中國繪画總合図錄 (Comprehensive Illustrated Catalogue of Chinese Painting). Comp. Suzuki Kei 鈴木敬. 5 vols. Tokyo: Tōkyō Daigaku Shuppankai, 1982–83.

Clapp, Anne de Coursey. *The Painting of T'ang Yin*. Chicago: University of Chicago Press, 1991.

———. *Wen Cheng-ming: The Ming Artist and Antiquity*. Artibus Asiae Supplementum 34. Ascona: Artibus Asiae Publishers, 1975.

Clunas, Craig. *Elegant Debts: The Social Art of Wen Zhengming, 1470–1559*. Honolulu: University of Hawai'i Press, 2004.

Contag, Victoria, and Wang Chi-ch'ien. *Seals of Chinese Painters and Collectors of the Ming and Ch'ing Periods*. Hong Kong: Hong Kong University Press, 1966.

Dictionary of Ming Biography, 1368–1644, ed. L. Carrington Goodrich and Chaoying Fang. 2 vols. New York: Columbia University Press, 1976.

Du Mu 都穆 (1459–1525). *Tiewang shanhu* 鐵網珊瑚 (Comments on the Fine Arts). Yishu shangjian xuanzhen 藝術賞鑑選珍 series. Taipei: Guoli zhongyang tushuguan, 1970–.

Edwards, Richard. *The Art of Wen Cheng-ming*. Ann Arbor: University of Michigan Museum, 1976.

———. *The Field of Stones: A Study of the Art of Shen Chou (1427–1509)*. Washington, D.C.: Smithsonian Institution, 1962.

———. "Pine, Hibiscus, and Examination Failures." *University of Michigan Museum of Art Bulletin* 1, nos. 1–2 (1965–66): 15–28.

Egan, Ronald C. "Poems on Paintings: Su Shih and Huang T'ing-chien." *Harvard Journal of Asiatic Studies* 43, no. 2 (1983): 413–51.

Eight Dynasties of Chinese Painting: The Collections of the Nelson Gallery-Atkins Museum, Kansas City, and the Cleveland Museum of Art, ed. Wai-kam Ho et al. Exhib. cat. Cleveland: Cleveland Museum of Art, 1980.

Fan Ye 范曄 (398–445). *Hou Han shu* 後漢書 (History of the Latter Han). 6 vols. Annot. Yang Jialu. Taipei: Dingwen, 1999

Ferguson, John C. (Fu Kaisen 福開森; 1866–1945), ed. *Lidai zhulu huamu* 歷代著錄畫目 (Index of Recorded Paintings of All Periods). 2 vols. Taipei: Taiwan Zhonghua shuju, 1968.

Fong, Wen C. *Beyond Representation: Chinese Painting and Calligraphy, 8th–14th Century*. New York: The Metropolitan Museum of Art; New Haven: Yale University Press, 1992.

———. *Summer Mountains: The Timeless Landscape*. New York: The Metropolitan Museum of Art, 1975.

———, et al., *Images of the Mind: Selections from the Edward L. Elliott Family and the John B. Elliott Collections of Chinese Calligraphy and Painting at The Art Museum, Princeton University*. Exhib. cat. Princeton: The Art Museum, Princeton University, in association with Princeton University Press, 1984.

Franke, Herbert. "Some Aspects of Private Historiography in the Thirteenth and Fourteenth Centuries." In *Historians of China and Japan*, ed. W.G. Beasley and E.G. Pulleyblank, 115–34. London: Oxford University Press, 1961; repr., Taipei, n.d.

Giles, Herbert A., trans. *Chuang Tzu: Mystic, Moralist, and Social Reformer.* 2nd rev. ed. Shanghai: Kelly and Walsh, Ltd., 1926.

Gu Wenbin 顧文彬 (1811–1889). *Guoyun lou shuhua ji* 過雲樓書畫記 (Record of Calligraphy and Painting in the Author's Collection). Yi shu shang jian xuan zhen xu ji 藝術賞鑑選珍續輯 series. Preface dated 1882; repr. Taipei: Hanhua wenhua shiye gufen youxian gongsi, 1971.

Gugong bowuyuan 故宮博物院, ed. *Mingdai Wumen huihua* 明代吳門繪畫 (Wu School Painting of the Ming Dynasty). Beijing: Gugong bowuyuan zijincheng chubanshe; Hong Kong: Shangwu yinshuguan, 1990.

Gugong shuhua lu 故宮書畫 (Catalogue of Calligraphy and Painting in the National Palace Museum). 4 vols. Taipei: National Palace Museum, 1965.

Gugong shuhua tulu 故宫書畫圖錄, ed. Guoli Gugong bowuyuan. 29 vols. Taipei: Guoli gugong bowuyuan, 1989–2010.

Harrist, Robert E., Jr. "Art and Identity in the Northern Sung Dynasty." In *Arts of the Sung and Yüan: Papers Prepared for an International Symposium Organized by the Metropolitan Museum of Art in Conjunction with the Exhibition Splendors of Imperial China: Treasures from the National Palace Museum, Taipei*, ed. Maxwell K. Hearn and Judith G. Smith, 147–63. New York: The Metropolitan Museum of Art, 1996.

———. *Painting and Private Life in Eleventh-Century China: Mountain Villa by Li Gonglin.* Princeton: Princeton University Press, 1998.

Hawkes, David, trans. *Ch'u Tz'u: The Songs of the South, an Ancient Chinese Anthology.* New York: Oxford University Press, 1962.

Hervouet, Yves. *Un poète de cour sous les Han: Sseu-ma Siang-jou.* Paris: Presses universitaires de France, 1964.

Ho, Ping-ti. *The Ladder of Success in Imperial China: Aspects of Social Mobility, 1368–1911.* New York: Columbia University Press, 1962.

Hucker, Charles O. *An Index to Terms and Titles in Government Organization of the Ming Dynasty.* Stanford: Stanford University Press, 1985.

Jang, Scarlett. "Representations of Exemplary Scholar-Officials, Past and Present." In *Arts of the Sung and Yuan: Ritual, Ethnicity, and Style in Painting*, ed. Cary Y. Liu and Dora C. Y. Ching, 38–67. Princeton: The Art Museum, Princeton University, 1999.

Jiang Zhaoshen 江兆申 [Chiang Chao-shen]. *Guanyu Tang Yin de yanjiu* 關於唐寅的研究 (A Study of Tang Yin). Taipei: National Palace Museum, 1976.

———. *Wen Zhengming yu Suzhou huatan* 文徵明與蘇州畫壇 (Wen Zhengming and the Suzhou School of Painting). Taipei: National Palace Museum, 1977.

———. *Wupai hua jiushi nian zhan* 吳派畫九十年展 (Exhibition of Ninety Years of Wu School Painting). Taipei: National Palace Museum, 1975.

———. "Wupai huajia bixia de Yang Jijing" 吳派畫家筆下的楊季靜 (The Wu School Painters and Yang Jijing). *Gugong jikan* 8, no. 1 (Autumn 1973): 57–70 (Chinese), 35–47 (English).

Jin Tang Liang Song huihua: Shanshui louge 金唐兩宋繪畫：山水樓閣 (Paintings of the Jin, Tang, and Song: Landscape and Architecture), ed. Jin Weidong et al. Gugong bowuguan wenwu zhenpin daxi 故宮博物院藏文物珍品大溪 series. Shanghai: Shanghai kexue jishu chubanshe; Hong Kong: Shangwu yinshuguan, 2004.

Kelley, Charles Fabens. "A Chinese Painting of the Ming Dynasty." *Bulletin of the Art Institute of Chicago* 36, no. 3 (March 1942): 34–36.

Lachman, Charles, trans. *Evaluations of Sung Dynasty Painters of Renown (Liu Tao-ch'un's Sung-ch'ao ming-hua p'ing).* Leiden and New York: E. J. Brill, 1989.

Laing, Ellen Johnston. *Chinese Paintings in Chinese Publications, 1956–1968: An Annotated Bibliography and an Index to the Paintings.* Ann Arbor: Center for Chinese Studies, University of Michigan, 1969.

———. "Real or Ideal: The Problem of the 'Elegant Gathering in the Western Garden' in Chinese Historical and Art Historical Records." *Journal of the American Oriental Society* 88, no. 3 (1968): 419–35.

———. "The State of Ming Painting Studies." *Ming Studies* 3 (Spring 1977): 9–25.

Lawton, Thomas. *Chinese Figure Painting.* Exhib. cat. Freer Gallery of

Art, Fiftieth Anniversary Exhibition, vol. 2. Washington, D.C.: Freer Gallery of Art, 1973.

Lee, Sherman E. *Chinese Landscape Painting*. 2nd ed. Cleveland: Cleveland Museum of Art, 1962.

———, and Wai-kam Ho. *Chinese Art Under the Mongols: The Yüan Dynasty (1279–1368)*. Cleveland: Cleveland Museum of Art, 1968.

Legge, James. *The Chinese Classics*. 5 vols. Hong Kong: Hong Kong University Press, 1960.

Li, Chi. "The Changing Concept of the Recluse in Chinese Literature." *Harvard Journal of Asiatic Studies* 24 (1962–63): 234–47.

Li, Chu-tsing. *Autumn Colors on the Ch'iao and Hua Mountains: A Landscape by Chao Meng-fu*. Artibus Asiae Supplementum 21. Ascona: Artibus Asiae Publishers, 1965.

———. "The Development of Painting in Soochow During the Yuan Dynasty." In *Proceedings of the International Symposium on Chinese Painting (1970)*, 483–505. Taipei: National Palace Museum, 1972.

———. "The Role of Wu-hsing in Early Yuan Artistic Development under Mongol Rule." In *China under Mongol Rule*, ed. John D. Langlois, Jr., 331–70. Princeton: Princeton University Press, 1981.

Li, Chu-tsing, James Cahill, and Wai-kam Ho, eds. *Artists and Patrons: Some Social and Economic Aspects of Chinese Painting*. Lawrence, KS: Kress Foundation Department of Art History, University of Kansas; Kansas City: Nelson-Atkins Museum of Art in association with University of Washington Press, 1989.

Li Lin-ts'an. "The Five Old Men of Sui-yang." *Gugong jikan* 7, no. 5 (November–December 1973): 1–21.

Liaoning sheng bowuguan canghua ji 遼寧省博物館藏画集, ed. Liaoning sheng bowuguan. Beijing: Wenwu chubanshe, 1962.

Liu Jiu'an 劉九庵. "Wumen huajia zhi biehao tu ji jianbie juli" 吳門畫家之別號圖及鑒別舉例 ("Illustrations to the Poetic Names of Wu School Painting Masters and Some Examples for Identifying Them"). *Gugong bowuyuan yuankan*, no. 3 (1990): 54–61.

Loehr, Max. "Chinese Paintings with Sung Dated Inscriptions." *Ars Orientalis* 4 (1961): 219–84.

———. "The Question of Individualism in Chinese Art." *Journal of the History of Ideas* 22, no. 2 (April–June 1961): 147–58.

———. "Some Fundamental Issues in the History of Chinese Painting." *Journal of Asian Studies* 23, no. 2 (February 1964): 185–93.

Lovell, Hin-cheung. *An Annotated Bibliography of Chinese Painting Catalogues and Related Texts*. Michigan Papers in Chinese Studies 16. Ann Arbor: Center for Chinese Studies, University of Michigan, 1973.

Lu Xinyuan 陸心源 (1834–1894), *Rangliguan guoyan xulu* 穰梨館過眼續錄, published together with *Rangliguan guoyan lu* 穰梨館過眼錄 (Wuxing: Yigutang, 1891), *juan* 3: 13a–29a.

Lu Yü (733–804). *The Classic of Tea*. Trans. Francis Ross Carpenter. Boston: Little, Brown, 1974.

Maeda, Robert. "The Chao Ta-nien Tradition." *Ars Orientalis* 8 (1970): 243–53.

Mair, Victor H., ed. *The Shorter Columbia Anthology of Traditional Chinese Literature*. New York: Columbia University Press, 2000.

Mingren zhuanji ziliao suoyin 明人傳記資料索引 (Index to Biographies of Ming Figures). 2 vols. Taipei: Guoli zhongyang tushuguan, 1965.

Mote, F. W. "The Arts and the 'Theorizing Mode' of the Civilization." In *Artists and Traditions: Uses of the Past in Chinese Culture*, ed. Christian F. Murck, 3–8. Princeton: The Art Museum, Princeton University, 1976.

———. "Confucian Eremitism in the Yuan Period." In *The Confucian Persuasion*, ed. Arthur F. Wright, 202–40. Stanford: Stanford University Press, 1960.

———. "A Millennium of Chinese Urban History: Form, Time, and Space Concepts in Soochow." *Rice University Studies* 59, no. 4 (Fall 1973): 35–65.

———. *The Poet Kao Ch'i, 1336–1374*. Princeton: Princeton University Press, 1962.

Murase, Miyeko. "Farewell Paintings of China: Chinese Gifts to Japanese Visitors." *Artibus Asiae* 32, nos. 2/3 (1970): 211–36.

Murck, Christian F., ed. *Artists and Traditions: Uses of the Past in Chinese Culture.* Princeton: The Art Museum, Princeton University, 1976.

Murray, Julia K. "A Southern Sung Painting Regains Its Memory: *Welcoming the Imperial Carriage* (*Ying-luan t'u*) and Its Colophon." *Journal of Sung and Yuan Studies* 22 (1992): 109–24.

———. "Ts'ao Hsün and Two Southern Sung History Scrolls." *Ars Orientalis* 15 (1985): 1–29.

Nivison, David. "Aspects of Traditional Chinese Biography." *Journal of Asian Studies* 21, no. 4 (August 1962): 457–63.

Owen, Stephen, ed. and trans. *An Anthology of Chinese Literature: Beginnings to 1911.* New York: W. W. Norton, 1996.

———. *The Poetry of the Early T'ang.* New Haven: Yale University Press, 1977.

Pang Yuanji 龐元濟 (1864–1949). *Xuzhai minghua lu* 虛齋名畫錄 (Catalogue of Paintings in the Author's Collection). 16 *juan.* Yishu shangjian xuanzhen sanji 藝術賞鑑選珍三輯 series. Preface dated 1909; repr., Taipei: Hanhua wenhua shiye gufen youxian gongsi, 1971.

Rogers, Howard, and Sherman E. Lee. *Masterworks of Ming and Ch'ing Painting from the Forbidden City.* Lansdale, PA: International Arts Council, 1988.

Rogers, Mary Ann. "Visions of Grandeur: The Life and Art of Dai Jin." In Richard M. Barnhart et al., *Painters of the Great Ming: The Imperial Court and the Zhe School,* 127–94. Exhib. cat. Dallas: Dallas Museum of Art, 1993.

Sensabaugh, David. "Guests at Jade Mountain: Aspects of Patronage in Fourteenth-Century K'un-shan." In *Artists and Patrons: Some Social and Economic Aspects of Chinese Painting,* ed. Chu-tsing Li, James Cahill, and Wai-kam Ho, 93–100. Lawrence, KS: Kress Foundation Department of Art History, University of Kansas; Kansas City: Nelson-Atkins Museum of Art in association with University of Washington Press, 1989.

———. "Life at Jade Mountain: Notes on the Life of the Man of Letters in Fourteenth-Century Wu Society." In *Chūgoku kaigashi ronshū: Suzuki Kei Sensei kanreki kinen* 中國繪畫史論集: 鈴木敬先生還曆記念 (Essays on the History of Chinese Painting: Festschrift for Professor Suzuki Kei), 45–69. Tokyo: Yoshikawa Kōbunkan, 1981.

Shih Shou-chien 石守謙. "'Yuyu chunshu' yu Mingdai zhongqi Suzhouzhi Songbietu" 雨餘春樹與明代中期蘇州之送別圖 ("*Spring Trees after Rain* and Ming Dynasty Departure Paintings in Suzhou"). In *Fengge yu shibian: Zhongguo huihua shi lunji* 風格與世變：中國繪畫史論 (Stylistic Change: Essays on Chinese Painting), 226–55. Meishu kaogu congkan 4. Taipei: Yunchen wenhua, 1996.

Shiming biehao suoyin 室名別號索引 (Index to Studio and Alternate Names). Comp. Chen Naiqian 陳乃乾. Beijing: Zhonghua shuju, 1982.

Shiqu baoji 石渠寶笈 (Treasured Boxes of the Stone Moat [Pavilion]). Comp. Zhang Zhao et al. 1745; facsimile repr. in *Bidian zhulin Shiqu baoji hebian.* 2 vols. Taipei: Guoli gugong bowuyuan, 1971.

Shiqu baoji sanbian 石渠寶笈三編 (Treasured Boxes of the Stone Moat [Pavilion], 3rd series). Comp. Hu Jing et al. 1817; facsimile repr. in *Bidian zhulin Shiqu baoji hebian.* 10 vols. and index. Taipei: Guoli gugong bowuyuan, 1969.

Shiqu baoji xubian 石渠寶笈續編 (Treasured Boxes of the Stone Moat [Pavilion], sequel). Comp. Wang Jie et al. 1793; facsimile repr. in *Bidian zhulin Shiqu baoji hebian.* 7 vols. Taipei: Guoli gugong bowuyuan, 1971.

Sickman, Laurence, ed. *Chinese Calligraphy and Painting in the Collection of John M. Crawford, Jr.* Exhib. cat. New York: Pierpont Morgan Library, 1962.

Siggstedt, Mette. "Zhou Chen: The Life and Paintings of a Ming Professional Artist." *Bulletin of the Museum of Far Eastern Antiquities* 54 (1982): 1–239.

Sirén, Osvald. *Chinese Painting: Leading Masters and Principles.* 7 vols. New York: Ronald Press, 1956–58.

Sō Gen Min Shin meiga taikan 宋元明清名畫大觀 (Collection of Famous Paintings of the Song, Yuan, Ming, and Qing Dynasties). 2 vols. Tokyo: Otsuka Kōgeisha, 1931.

Song Liao Jin huajia shiliao 宋遼金畫家史料 (Documentary Materials on Painters of the Song, Liao, and Jin Dynasties). Comp. Chen Gaohua 陳高華. Beijing: Wenwu chubanshe, 1984.

Soper, Alexander C., trans. and annot. *Kuo Jo-Hsü's Experiences in Painting (T'u-hua chien-wên chih): An Eleventh-Century History of Chinese Painting, together with the Chinese Text in Facsimile.* Washington, D.C.: American Council of Learned Societies, 1951.

Spiro, Audrey G. *Contemplating the Ancients: Aesthetic and Social Issues in Early Chinese Portraiture.* Berkeley: University of California Press, 1990.

Strassberg, Richard E. *Inscribed Landscapes: Travel Writing from Imperial China.* Berkeley: University of California Press, 1994.

Suzuki Kei 鈴木敬, comp. *Chūgoku kaiga sōgō zuroku* 中國繪画總合図錄 (Comprehensive Illustrated Catalogue of Chinese Painting). 5 vols. Tokyo: Tōkyō Daigaku Shuppankai, 1982–83.

Tang shi jianshang cidian 唐詩鑒賞辭典 (Anthology of Tang Poetry). Comp. Xiao Difei 蕭滌非 et al. Shanghai: Shanghai cishu chubanshe, 1983.

Tō Sō Gen Min meiga taikan 唐宋元明名畫大觀 (Famous Paintings of the Tang, Song, Yuan, and Ming Dynasties). 4 vols. Tokyo: Ōtsuka Kōgeisha, 1929.

Tuhui baojian 圖繪寶鑑 (Precious Mirror of Painting). Comp Xia Wenyan 夏文彥. Preface dated 1365. In *Huashi congshu* 畫史叢書, ed. Yu Anlan 于安瀾, vol. 2. Shanghai: Shanghai renmin meishu chubanshe, 1963; repr., Taipei: Wenshizhe chubanshe, 1974.

Twitchett, D.C. "Chinese Biographical Writing." In *Historians of China and Japan*, ed. W.G. Beasley and E.G. Pulleyblank, 93–114. London: Oxford University Press, 1961; repr., Taipei, n.d.

———. "Problems of Chinese Biography." In *Confucian Personalities*, ed. Arthur F. Wright and Denis Twitchett, 24–39. Stanford: Stanford University Press, 1962.

Vinograd, Richard. "Family Properties: Personal Context and Cultural Pattern in Wang Meng's *Pien Mountains* of 1366." *Ars Orientalis* 13 (1982): 1–29.

———. "Wang Meng's 'Pien Mountains': The Landscape of Eremitism in Later Fourteenth Century Chinese Painting." PhD dissertation, University of California, Berkeley, 1979.

Wang Keyu 汪砢玉 (b. 1587). *Shanhu wang hualu* 珊瑚網畫錄 (The Shanhu wang Record of Paintings). Preface dated 1643. Guoxue jiben congshu 國學基本叢書 series. Shanghai: Shangwu yinshuguan, 1936.

Watt, James C.Y. "The *Qin* and the Chinese Literati." *Orientations* 12, no. 11 (November 1981): 38–49.

Wen Zhaotong 温肇桐. *Mingdai si da huajia* 明代四大畫家 (The Four Great Masters of the Ming Dynasty). Hong Kong: Xianggang Xingfu chubanshe, 1960.

Wen Zhengming 文徵明 (1470–1559). *Wen Zhengming huigao* 文徵明彙稿 (Collected Material on Wen Zhengming). Shanghai: Shenzhou guoguangshe, 1929.

Wilkinson, Endymion. *Chinese History: A Manual.* 2nd ed. Cambridge, MA: Harvard University Asia Center in association with Harvard University Press, 2000.

Wilson, Marc F., and Kwan S. Wong. *Friends of Wen Cheng-ming: A View from The Crawford Collection.* New York: China House Gallery, China Institute in America, 1974.

Wright, Arthur F., ed. *The Confucian Persuasion.* Stanford: Stanford University Press, 1960.

Wright, Arthur F., and Denis Twitchett, eds. *Confucian Personalities.* Stanford: Stanford University Press, 1962.

Wu Rongguang 吳榮光 (1773–1843). *Xinchou xiaoxia ji* 辛丑消夏記 (Record of Calligraphies and Paintings), 1841. 5 *juan.* Yishu shangjian xuanzhen ji 藝術賞鑑選珍續輯 series.Taipei: Han-hua wenhua shiye gufen youxian gongsi, 1971.

Wu Sheng 吳升 (18th century). *Daguan lu* 大觀錄 (Record of Calligraphy and Painting). 20 *juan.* Preface dated 1712. Yishu shang ian xuanzhen 藝術賞鑑選珍 series. Taipei: Guoli zhongyang tushuguan, 1970.

Wuxi shi bowuguan 無錫市博物館 (Wuxi City Museum), ed. *Tao Xinhua juanxian shuhua jingpin ji* 陶心華捐獻書畫精品集 (Masterpieces of Calligraphy and Painting Presented to the Wuxi City Museum by Tao Xinhua). Exhib. cat. Wuxi: Wuxi shi bowuguan, 2001.

Xie Zhiliu 謝稚柳 (1910–1997). *Tang Wudai Song Yuan mingji* 唐五代宋元名迹 (Paintings of the Tang, Five Dynasties, Song, and Yuan Dynasties). Shanghai: Gudian wenxue chubanshe, 1957.

Yang Xin 楊新, ed. *Gugong bowuyuan cang Ming Qing huihua* 故宮博物院藏明清繪畫 (Painting of the Ming and Qing Dynasties). Beijing: Zijincheng chubanshe, 1994.

Yuandai huajia shiliao 元代畫家史料 (Historical Source Materials on Yuan Dynasty Painters). Comp. Chen Gaohua 陳高華. Shanghai: Shanghai renmin meishu, 1980.

Yuanren zhuanji ziliao suoyin 元人傳記資料索引 (Index to Biographical Material on Yuan Figures). 5 vols. Ed. Wang Deyi 王德毅 et al. Beijing: Zhonghua shuju, 1987.

Yuhas, Louise. "The Landscape Paintings of Lu Chih, Part I." *National Palace Museum Bulletin* 20, nos. 5–6 (November–December 1985, January–February 1986): 1–23.

———. "The Landscape Paintings of Lu Chih, Part II." *National Palace Museum Bulletin* 21, nos. 1–2 (March–April 1986, May–June 1986): 1–25.

Zeitlin, Judith T. "The Petrified Heart: Obsession in Chinese Literature, Art, and Medicine." *Late Imperial China* 12, no. 1 (June 1991): 1–26.

Zhang Chou 張丑 (1577–1643). *Qinghe shuhua fang* 清河書畫舫 (Catalogue of Calligraphy and Painting Seen by the Author). Preface dated 1616; repr., Taipei: Xuehai shuju, 1975.

Zhongguo gudai shuhua tumu 中國古代書畫图目 (Illustrated Catalogue of Selected Works of Ancient Chinese Painting and Calligraphy), ed. Zhongguo gudai shuhua jianding zu. 23 vols. Beijing: Wenwu chubanshe, 1986–2001.

Zhongguo gujin diming dacidian 中國古今地名大辭典 (Dictionary of Chinese Place-Names in Ancient and Modern Times). Hong Kong: Shangwu yinshuguan, 1931.

Zhongguo huajia renming dacidian 中國畫家人名大辭典 (Biographical Dictionary of Chinese Painters), comp. Sun Ta 孫䲭. Beijing: Zhongguo shudian, 1982.

Zhongguo huihua quanji 中國繪畫全集 (Compendium of Chinese Painting), ed. Zhongguo gudai shuhua jianding zu. 30 vols. Beijing: Wenwu chubanshe, 1997–2001.

Zhongguo lidai shuhua zhuanke jia zihao suoyin 中國歷代書畫篆刻家字號索引 (Index to Alternate Names of Chinese Calligraphers, Painters, and Seal Carvers). Beijing: Renmin meishu chubanshe, 1960.

Zhongguo renming dacidian 中國人名大辭典 (Chinese Biographical Dictionary). Hong Kong: Taixing shuju yinxing, 1931.

Zhongguo wenxue jia dacidian 中國文學家大辭典 (Biographical Dictionary of Chinese Scholars). Taipei: Shijie shuju, 1974.

Zhou Daozhen 周道振 and Zhang Yuezun 張月尊. *Wen Zhengming nianpu* 文徵明年譜 (Annual Record of Wen Zhengming's Works). Shanghai: Baijia chubanshe, 1998.

Zhou Mi 周密 (1232–1308) et al. *Qidong yeyu* 齊東野語 (Back-Country Stories). Annot. Li Deqing. Preface dated 1291. Shanghai: Huadong shifan daxue chubanshe, 1987.

Glossary of Chinese Names and Terms

A Xian 阿戎
Unidentified

Bai Juyi 白居易 (772–846)
The son of a scholar's family in Henan, Bai took the *juren* degree in 800 and served the Tang government in several official positions. He won his chief fame in poetry, in which he included critical works on social issues.

ben zhuan 本傳
Official biography

Bian Mountains 弁山
A range of mountains in Wuxing, about thirty-three miles long, six miles south of Lake Tai.

bie zhuan 別傳
Private or family biography

biehao 別號
Literally, other name, pen name, literary name. In traditional China a man might adopt as many as he liked to recognize a variety of occasions or circumstances.

biji 筆記
Record

Binghe 冰壑

Cai Jing 蔡京 (1046–1126)
Jinshi 1070, Huizong's grand councilor in 1102, he led the reform party seeking to establish his New Policies in opposition to the Yuanyou conservatives. He alternated three times between serving and banishment.

Cao Xun 曹勛 (1098–1174)
Jinshi 1124, official and emissary to Jin court from Southern Sung court. Promoted to grand marshal about 1169. Retired to Mount Tientai.

Chen Ruyan 陳汝言
(ca. 1331–1371)
Chen began to paint in the early 1350s, favoring topographical subjects. He served first in Zhang Shicheng's government and then, after the fall of the Yuan dynasty, in the Ming government in Shandong. Accused of treason and executed in 1371.

Chen Shiming 陳事茗
Friend and Suzhou neighbor of Tang Yin who practiced the art of brewing and serving tea. Otherwise unknown.

Chen Yongzhi 陳用志
A native of Yancheng in Henan, he served in the Northern Song Painting Academy for an unknown period of time between 1023 and 1032, afterward returning to his home town. An able painter of Buddhist and Daoist subjects, he was praised for his detail.

Cui Yanhui 崔彥暉
(early 14th century–after 1381)
Cui was the great-grandson of Zhao Mengfu and one of the few real recluses of his time. He took refuge in the Bian Mountains, where he made a living as a druggist apothecary.

Dai Jin 戴進 (ca. 1388–1462)
Born in Hangzhou, Dai Jin was recognized as the leader of the Zhe school of professional painters. He sought,

but failed, to win an appointment at court, but as a brilliant technician and master of several ancient and modern styles he was extremely successful in the southeast provinces.

Dark Dragons 蒼虬
Tea leaves expanding and coiling in hot water.

Dong Yuan 董源
Painter active 930s–960s at the Southern Tang court in Nanjing, where he held a sinecure. Famous for large tranquil landscapes impressionistically rendered. In the Ming dynasty he was declared the founder and fountainhead of the Southern School of landscape painting.

Du Qiong 杜瓊 (1397–1474)
An able Suzhou painter who played a role in the founding of the Wu school as friend and teacher of Wu Kuan and Shen Zhou.

Duan Muzhi 端木智
(ca. 1347–after 1407)
A high-ranking government official in Nanjing, capital of the Ming dynasty until 1422. He was a Hanlin compiler and an officer of the Board of War, and was much esteemed as a calligrapher.

Fan Kuan 范寬 (ca. 960–ca. 1030)
Leading Northern Song master of classical landscape and member of the court painting academy.

fu 賦
Prose poem

Gao Kegong 高克恭 (1248–1310)
Descended from a Turkic family living in Datong, Gao held a series of appointments at the Mongol court, where he rose to be president of the Board of Justice. In landscape painting he followed the Mi family painters as well as Zhao Mengfu.

Gao Qi 高啟 (1336–1374)
Leading poet and man of letters of the Yuan dynasty, Gao was the center of a Suzhou circle of writers, artists, and ambitious young men. He lived as a recluse until 1369, when he briefly served the first Ming emperor. In 1374 he was executed for treason on trumped-up charges.

Gefeng tai 歌風臺
Famous site in Zhejiang where Liu Bang in the third century BCE mobilized an army before entering the pass to attack Qin Shihuangdi.

Gu Dehui 顧德輝 (1310–1369)

Gu, Master
An as yet unidentified recipient of a painting by Shi Rui.

Han Yu 韓愈 (768–824)
Litterateur par excellence, he was a good poet and great essayist, who also served at court. A critic of Buddhism, he led a movement in favor of an earlier form of Confucianism and a simpler, more expressive prose style. I have not found anything on the *ding* used in his tea service.

He Xuanming 郝玄明
Northern Sung emissary to the Qin court. Otherwise unidentified.

Hu Shunchen 胡舜臣
(active early 12th century)
From Zhejiang. Classified as a follower of Guo Xi.

Hu Yuan 胡瑗 (993–1059)
From Anding. A much admired professor of classical literature and a specialist in ceremonial music, teaching in Wu.

Huang Quan 黃筌 (903–968)
Served in the court academy of the later Shu Sichuan, specializing in the bird-and-flower genre; also did figures and Buddhist and Daoist subjects.

Huang Yiqing 黃一清 (1263–1337)
By his own choice he remained a recluse all his life. He is now best known as a writer and longtime friend of Li Meng.

Huishan 慧山
A mountain north of Lake Tai and west of Wuxi, famous for a pure and limpid stream much esteemed by tea masters as far back as the court of Song Huizong.

Jade River 玉河
River flowing eastward from Chinese Turkistan into northwest China. A source of fine jade, which is harvested when the river dries up in autumn.

Jie Valley 嶰谷
The northernmost valley in the Kunlun Mountains of Tibet. There, according to legend, grew a stand of finest bamboo, and to that grove Huangdi (the Yellow Emperor) sent his court musician, Ling Lun, who cut a two-node length of the local bamboo, and from it fashioned a flute. Thus, at the behest of the Yellow Emperor, Ling Lun (also legendary) discovered the laws of harmony.

Jiehua 界畫
A technique used in painting architecture, using fine ruled lines.

Jingxi 荊溪
A town on the northern shore of Lake Tai.

Lake Tai 太湖
A large lake west of Suzhou with one arm reaching almost to the city. It was surrounded by the country houses and farms of the local gentry.

(Lao) Shao 老韶
Unidentified

Li Anzhong 李安忠
(active ca. 1117–1140)
Member of the first Northern Song Painting Academy, after 1127 of Southern Song Academy, specializing in bird-and-flower subjects and landscapes in a distinctive style.

Li Gonglin 李公麟 (ca. 1041–1106), *hao* Longmian 龍眠, *zi* Boshi 伯時
Li served in several middle-rank positions in the Song government. He was also one of the most admired literati painters of his time, specializing in antiquarian styles in both landscape and figures.

Li Jie 李結 (ca. 1124–after 1191)

Li Meng 李孟 (1255–1321)
Served twenty-four years at the Mongol court as lecturer, grand councilor, officer of the Secretariat and the Hanlin.

Li Si 李斯 (d. 257 BCE)
First minister and historiographer of Qin who promulgated laws for the state and ordered the "burning of the books." He developed small seal script out of the large seal script inherited from the Zhou dynasty.

Li Tang 李唐 (ca. 1070s–ca. 1150s)
Served as *daizhao* in Northern Song Court Academy and, after 1127, in Southern Song Academy. Best known for a distinctive analytical style of landscape, often revived in later years.

Li Yangbing 李陽冰 (721/22–785)
Skilled at small seal script which was said to be the equal of Li Si's.

Li Yingzhen 李應禎 (1431–1493)
Li took the *juren* degree in 1453 and served in several government positions, but, being outspoken in his opinions, he was demoted to the Nanjing branch and soon retired to Suzhou. He moved in upper literati circles, where he practiced and taught calligraphy, notably to Zhu Yunming and Wen Zhengming.

Liu Bang 劉邦 (256–195 BCE)
A peasant leader who conquered the Qin in the Wei River region in the third century BCE, established the Han Dynasty, and became its first emperor.

Lu Can 陸粲 (1494–1551)
A promising scholar who took the *jinshi* degree in 1526, ran into political trouble, was exiled to the provinces, but later restored to the civil service as a district magistrate. He belonged to the group of writers of honorific biographical essays in Suzhou.

Lu Hong 盧鴻 (active ca. 713–742)
Teacher, poet, painter in Luoyang; afterward withdrew to Mt. Song, where he painted the *Ten Views from a Thatched Cottage*.

Lü Min 吕敏 (later 14th century)
One of the Ten Friends of the North Wall.

Lu Tong 盧仝 (ca. 775–835), *hao* Yuchuan (zi) 玉川(子)

Lu Yu 陸羽 (733–804), zi 鸿渐; *hao*, including 竟陵子, 桑苎翁, 东冈子, 茶山御史

Lu Zhi 陸治 (1496–1576)
In straitened circumstances most of his life, Lu Zhi lived until 1557 on a scholar's stipend, painting in the intervals between provincial examinations. His painting style is notably independent of his contemporaries, revealing a preference for Ni Zan's art and for mild fantasy.

Ma Xun 馬尋
Unidentified prefect of Wuxing in 1046.

Ni Zan 倪瓚 (1301–1374)
Wealthy resident of Wuxi, who created in his lifetime a fine, idiosyncratic style of landscape that made a deep impression on his fellow artists and on every generation after him. During the 1350s and later, he lived an itinerant style of life.

Paoan 匏庵
Wu Kuan's *ci*

Peixian 沛縣
The town of Peixian in present-day Jiangsu Province was founded in the Qin dynasty.

penjing 盆景
Miniature gardens grown in containers, i.e., *bonsai*.

Qian Dejun 錢德鈞 (late 13th century–after 1324), *zi* Zhongding
Qian retired from government service at the fall of Song and became director of a village school. When he retired a second time in 1314 he took up residence on the shore of Lake Fen.

Qiu Ying 仇英 (ca. 1495–1552)

Qu Ding 屈鼎
(active ca. 1023–ca. 1056)

Ruan Ji 阮籍 (210–263)
One of the Seven Sages of the Bamboo Grove, skilled in prose and poetry and of a philosophical bent. His character was admirable but his manners and temperament erratic.

Sanhai Shrine 三害祠

Shao 韶 music
The music of the mythical Emperor Shun, pronounced by Confucius to be perfect in beauty and virtue.

Shen Zhou 沈周 (1427–1509)
Traditionally named the founder of the Wu school, Shen Zhou was the predominant figure in fifteenth-century Suzhou artistic circles, both as a practicing painter and as the informal teacher of younger men.

shengyuan 生員
Lowest rank of student-scholar receiving a regular stipend from the government.

Shi Rui 石鋭 (active ca. 1426)
An early Ming court painter who specialized in the blue-green style derived from Li Sixun and Li Zhaodao. Best known for exquisitely elegant landscapes and architectural subjects.

Sima Xiangru 司馬相如 (active second half of 2nd century BCE; d. ca. 117)
Courtier, scholar, musician, and poet at the court of Emperor Wu of Han. Later in his life he was appointed supervisor of an imperial tomb in a park outside Chang'an ("the Han Garden"), probably in consequence of ill health. He suffered from a disease similar to diabetes that kept him in constant thirst for tea.

Song Ke 宋克 (1327–1387)
One of the Ten Friends of the North Wall. Song had a taste for the military life, which he found little opportunity to satisfy. He served in office briefly during the Ming, but in his private life was an able poet, calligrapher, and painter of bamboo.

Songs of Chu 楚辭
The third-century BCE poems of Chu Yuan and his followers.

Su Che 蘇轍 (1039–1112),
zi Xinyou 子由

Su Shi 蘇軾 (1037–1101),
zi Zizhan 子瞻

Sun Jue 孫覺 (1028–1090)
Jinshi. Studied with Hu Yuan in his youth. A moderate conservative who served with Wang Anshi for a short time but disapproved of his fiscal policy. Was sent to a prefectural post in Wu, where he wrote a preface for Zhang Xian in 1072.

Tan Stream 貪泉
The Stream of Avarice, in Shimen (Stone Gate) in Guangdong Province, Nanhai District. It was said that whoever drank its water would become corrupt and self-serving.

Tang Yin 唐寅 (1470–1524)

Tiao River 苕水
In Wuxing

Wang Ao 王鏊 (1450–1524)
Wang Ao, from a peasant family on Lake Tai, took the *jinshi* degree in 1475, was appointed to the Hanlin, and over the next thirty-four years occupied a series of high posts at court. In his few years of freedom in Suzhou, he was the center of a group of writers and painters whom he befriended and patronized.

Wang Huan 王渙 (active ca. 1030)
Served as vice president of the Board of Ceremonies under the Song, a post from which he retired at age ninety.

Wang Laibin = Wang Yutian
王玉田 (1509–after 1550)
A medical doctor in Suzhou who preferred to be recompensed with paintings rather than with cash. He either commissioned or was given, possibly by a grateful patient, Lu Zhi's *The Jade Field.*

Wang Meng 王蒙 (ca. 1308–1385)
The grandson of Zhao Mengfu and youngest of "the Four Great Masters of the Yuan," Wang Meng combined his art with government service, first to Zhang Shicheng, after 1368 to the Ming dynasty.

Wang Wei 王維
(701–761; alt. 699–759)
A Tang master who was the first painter to think of representing his own estate. He executed the painting called *Wangchuan tu* (Picture of the Wang River Estate) on the wall of a house on the estate, thus initiating

one of the longest continuous iconographical traditions in Chinese art.

Wang Yu 王裕
Unidentified friend of Cui Yanhui.

Wang Yuntong 王允同
(active mid-14th century)
He was a son of the Wang family of Jingxi, who commissioned Chen Ruyan to paint his family estate.

Wei Yousong 魏友松
"Friend of Pines," the brother-in-law of Du Qiong. Otherwise unknown.

Wen Boren 文伯仁 (1502–1575)
Wen Zhengming's nephew, Boren was trained by his uncle and followed in his path, becoming the second generation of Wen painters.

Wen Yanbo 文彥博 (1006–1097)
Jinshi. From a Shanxi family, Wen was a senior member of the Yuanyou conservative faction opposing Wang Anshi; he served at court off and on for fifty years. He was enfeoffed Duke of Lu, retired in the early 1070s, and became the host of the Luoyang Septuagenarian Society.

Wen Zhengming 文徵明 (1470–1559)
The son of a civil-service family, Wen undertook a career in government, withdrew after a few years, and returned to Suzhou. There he turned his attention permanently to the fine arts and over a period of thirty years became the leading master of sixteenth-century Ming painting.

Wu Kuan 吳寬 (1436–1504)
Wu Kuan was a younger son of a family successful in the textile business. He won the *jinshi* degree in 1472 and entered the Hanlin Academy. Thereafter he held a series of high appointments at court. He was a prolific composer of commemorative works for a wide circle of friends in Suzhou.

Wu school 吳派
A school of painters active in Suzhou in the fifteenth and sixteenth centuries, sometimes taken to be literati, sometimes to be all the best who worked there. A major historical line which brought Chinese painting to a pitch of excellence in the middle Ming.

Xi Kang 嵇康 (223–262)
One of the Seven Sages of the Bamboo Grove: a dedicated recluse, poet, writer, seeker after immortality. A player and historian of *qin* music. He was executed for "political intrigue."

Xiao and Xiang Rivers 瀟湘
The confluence of the Xiao and Xiang Rivers lies in Hunan Province south of Lake Dongting, in a humid marshy area famous for its luxuriant scenery.

xingzhuang 行狀
An account of a person's conduct giving biographical information.

xu 序 (preface)
Preface explaining a work of art, often inscribed on it.

Xu Ben 徐賁 (1335–1380)
One of the Ten Friends of the North Wall, Xu Ben was a fine painter in the tradition of Wang Meng and a highly regarded poet. In 1374 he joined the Ming government.

Xu Yikui 徐一夔
(1318–1399/1402)
A southern scholar, widely read, considered a fine writer. He held office under the Yuan and Ming.

Yan Wengui 燕文貴
(active ca. 970–ca. 1030)

Yang Weizhen 楊維禎 (1296–1370)

Yongmen Zhou 雍門周
Famous *qin* player of the Warring States period whose performance could move men to tears and bring cities down in ruins.

Yuan An 袁安 (d. 92 CE)
Active under the Eastern Han government and instrumental in curbing the power of the feudal families opposing the throne.

Yuan Bao 袁褒 (1499–1576)
One of the six Yuan cousins of Suzhou, a bibliophile, art collector, and recipient of two paintings by Wen Zhengming.

Yuan Yi 袁易 (1262–1306)
A Yuan scholar-recluse and poet for whom Zhao Mengfu painted a version of *Yuan An woxue.*

Zhang Chou 張丑 (1577–1643)
Ming critic, cataloguer of Chinese painting, and author of *Chinghe shuhua fang.* A knowledgeable collector of paintings from a famous family of collectors.

Zhang Gong's Grotto 張公洞
A cave with spectacular stalactites in Yixing on the west shore of Lake Tai, a natural wonder visited by tourists and painted by several artists. Legend

associates the cave with the Daoist Immortal Zhang Gong.

Zhang Shicheng 張士誠 (1321–1367)
An erstwhile salt smuggler, Zhang Shicheng gathered most of the Yangtze delta towns under his military control in the early 1350s, conquered Suzhou in 1356, and established himself as Grand Commandant of Wu. Thereafter he defended himself against Zhu Yuanzhang's attacks until Suzhou fell in 1367 and he died a prisoner.

Zhang Xian 張先 (990–1078)

Zhang Yu 張羽 (1333–1385)
One of the Ten Friends of the North Wall. A poet and painter. He served the Hongwu emperor after 1373 until his death.

Zhao Fu 趙黻 (active 1131–1162)

Zhao Mengfu 趙孟頫 (1254–1322)
One of the most active and liberal minds of the Yuan dynasty, Zhao served the Yuan court and accompanied government service with a second career in calligraphy and painting that lasted his lifetime.

Zhe school 浙派
Fifteenth- and sixteenth-century school of professional painters active at the Beijing and Nanjing courts and at several centers in the south.

Zhou, Mme 周
Known only as the recipient of an honorary scroll presented by the citizens of Suzhou.

Zhou Chen 周臣 (ca. 1455–ca. 1535)

Zhou Chu 周處
A third-century hero of Jingxi who saved the people from a water monster. The Sanhai Shrine was built to honor him.

Zhou Fang 周昉
Zhou Fang, from Danxi, is not mentioned in the biographical dictionaries. His second colophon, dated 1381, on Cui Yanhui's *Small Retreat of Master Cloudy Woods* identifies him as a Confucian scholar who made a living tutoring in Hangzhou. In 1379 he was appointed to a government position probably in the same field.

Zhou Zimei 周子美
Unidentified

Zhu Yuanzhang 朱元璋 (1328–1398)
Born to a poor farming family, Zhu grew up in real deprivation. He joined a rebel army, gathered troops of his own which he turned against several warlords in succession, eventually driving the Mongols out of China. After establishing the Ming dynasty, he ruled with absolute power on Legalist principles.

Zhu Yunming 祝允明 (1461–1527)
From an old and distinguished family, Zhu was the foremost calligrapher in Suzhou in the middle Ming period. He progressed as far as the *juren* degree, but his official career was brief, and in his later years he evidently depended on honorific writing for a living.

Index

Tang Center Lecture Series

2003
Three Lectures on Chinese Art History
WEN C. FONG

2007
Commemorative Landscape Painting in China
ANNE DE COURSEY CLAPP
Published in 2012

2007
Body Talk, in Two Chinese Films by Director Jiang Wen
JEROME SILBERGELD
Published in 2008 as *Body in Question: Image and Illusion in Two Chinese Films by Director Jiang Wen*

2008
Icons, Rituals, and Paths to Salvation: Three Lectures on the History of Japanese Buddhist Sculpture
JOHN M. ROSENFIELD
Publication forthcoming

2012
Empire and Artistic Practice in the Era of Manchu Rule
CLAUDIA BROWN